AF745569

Advances in Japanese Business and Economics

Volume 14

Editor in Chief
RYUZO SATO
C.V. Starr Professor Emeritus of Economics, Stern School of Business, New York University

Senior Editor
KAZUO MINO
Professor, Kyoto University

Managing Editors
HAJIME HORI
Professor Emeritus, Tohoku University

HIROSHI YOSHIKAWA
Professor, The University of Tokyo

KUNIO ITO
Professor, Hitotsubashi University

Editorial Board Members
TAKAHIRO FUJIMOTO
Professor, The University of Tokyo

YUZO HONDA
Professor Emeritus, Osaka University; Professor, Kansai University

TOSHIHIRO IHORI
Professor, The University of Tokyo

TAKENORI INOKI
Professor Emeritus, Osaka University
Special University Professor, Aoyama Gakuin University

JOTA ISHIKAWA
Professor, Hitotsubashi University

KATSUHITO IWAI
Professor Emeritus, The University of Tokyo
Visiting Professor, International Christian University

MASAHIRO MATSUSHITA
Professor Emeritus, Aoyama Gakuin University

TAKASHI NEGISHI
Professor Emeritus, The University of Tokyo; The Japan Academy

KIYOHIKO NISHIMURA
Professor, The University of Tokyo

TETSUJI OKAZAKI
Professor, The University of Tokyo

YOSHIYASU ONO
Professor, Osaka University

JUNJIRO SHINTAKU
Professor, The University of Tokyo

KOTARO SUZUMURA
Professor Emeritus, Hitotsubashi University; The Japan Academy

Advances in Japanese Business and Economics showcases the research of Japanese scholars. Published in English, the series highlights for a global readership the unique perspectives of Japan's most distinguished and emerging scholars of business and economics. It covers research of either theoretical or empirical nature, in both authored and edited volumes, regardless of the sub-discipline or geographical coverage, including, but not limited to, such topics as macroeconomics, microeconomics, industrial relations, innovation, regional development, entrepreneurship, international trade, globalization, financial markets, technology management, and business strategy. At the same time, as a series of volumes written by Japanese scholars, it includes research on the issues of the Japanese economy, industry, management practice and policy, such as the economic policies and business innovations before and after the Japanese "bubble" burst in the 1990s.

Overseen by a panel of renowned scholars led by Editor-in-Chief Professor Ryuzo Sato, the series endeavors to overcome a historical deficit in the dissemination of Japanese economic theory, research methodology, and analysis. The volumes in the series contribute not only to a deeper understanding of Japanese business and economics but to revealing underlying universal principles.

More information about this series at http://www.springer.com/series/11682

Michihiro Ohyama

Macroeconomics, Trade, and Social Welfare

Springer

Michihiro Ohyama
Professor Emeritus
Keio University
Tokyo, Japan

ISSN 2197-8859 ISSN 2197-8867 (electronic)
Advances in Japanese Business and Economics
ISBN 978-4-431-55805-7 ISBN 978-4-431-55807-1 (eBook)
DOI 10.1007/978-4-431-55807-1

Library of Congress Control Number: 2016942887

© Springer Japan 2016
This work is subject to copyright. All rights are reserved by the Publisher, whether the whole or part of the material is concerned, specifically the rights of translation, reprinting, reuse of illustrations, recitation, broadcasting, reproduction on microfilms or in any other physical way, and transmission or information storage and retrieval, electronic adaptation, computer software, or by similar or dissimilar methodology now known or hereafter developed.
The use of general descriptive names, registered names, trademarks, service marks, etc. in this publication does not imply, even in the absence of a specific statement, that such names are exempt from the relevant protective laws and regulations and therefore free for general use.
The publisher, the authors and the editors are safe to assume that the advice and information in this book are believed to be true and accurate at the date of publication. Neither the publisher nor the authors or the editors give a warranty, express or implied, with respect to the material contained herein or for any errors or omissions that may have been made.

Printed on acid-free paper

This Springer imprint is published by Springer Nature
The registered company is Springer Japan KK

Preface

This book develops new elementary methods of welfare comparison and comparative dynamics between distinct and discretely positioned (rather than continuously related) socio-economic situations. They are not only realistic but also uniquely relevant to important problems of economic policy. Using these methods, I comprised the book to shed a new light to the theoretical analysis of Keynesian economics, international trade and social welfare.

Three chapters in Part I illustrate the merits of these methods applying them to the reconstruction of Keynesian economics, an important task in the current scene of political economy. Chapter 1 reexamines the Keynesian multiplier theory focusing on the concept of "public goods" as the object of government fiscal policy. The distinction between public goods and private goods is blurred in the standard multiplier theory spoiling its applicability considerably. In contrast, the government is here supposed to dictate the provision of public goods democratically or dictatorially while the amount of private goods (including labor services required for production of public goods) is determined by the adjustment of income in the market. Using the real general equilibrium model I show that the government is capable of achieving full employment even when the public good is intrinsically useless. It will, *a fortiori*, increase national economic welfare if the public good is useful in some sense or another. Furthermore, I demonstrate by the use of "expansion path" how the government can increase employment and welfare over time depicting the dynamic adjustment path under rational expectatons. The ultimate destination of the path is *not* the neoclassical synthesis suggested by Samuelson (1954), but close to the neo-Keynesian synthesis advanced in General Theory (1936). With fixed production technology and static resource endowment, however, the steady state would degenerate to the long-run stagnation in the absence of government intervention, or its growth strategy.

Chapter 3 extends the real general equilibrium model of Chap. 2 taking account of firm-union transactions scheme introduced in Chap. 2. It develops the whole story of Keynesian Economics in light of liquidity trap and $IS - LM$ equilibrium originated by Hicks (1936). I explicitly consider the optimizing behavior of households, firms and the government to delineate the monetary transactions between them and examine the effects of monetary policy in the short and long runs in the name of the general theory of money, income and distribution, The traditional monetary policy is well designed to realize the short-run effects on employment, but not necessarily appropriate as the means of attaining the long-run desirable effects on welfare and economic growth. In order to achieve such long-run effects, we may have to invoke the inflation-targeting. The final goal of Chap. 3 is to formulate inflation targeting rigorously and show how to switch from the traditional monetary policy to inflation targeting on the path leading to the long run steady state in some details.

I employed similar comparative methods in chapters in Part II to reexamine the modern trade policy issues such as gains from trade, the theory of tariffs, free trade agreements and the role of WTO. In Chap. 9, for instance, I reconsidered the role of WTO in the face of propagating regional free trade agreements and argue that it is high time to alleviate the restrictive stipulation of GATT Article 24 with a view to promoting global welfare even beyond the Kemp-Wang theorem. Chapter 10 modifies the general equilibrium model of Chap. 4 to incorporate elements of imperfect competition and variable returns to scale covering a related wide range of topics on trade and welfare.

In Part III, I applied our elementary methods of welfare comparison to dissolve modern controversies over welfare and efficiency in various socio-economic situations. In Chap. 11, we challenged the popular view that the pursuit of efficiency damages the realization of social values such as safety, health, environment, fairness and what not. I considered several examples that suggest the seeming existence of trade-offs between value and efficiency and reveal that trade-offs exist between different values but not between values and efficiency. The common fallacy stems from the neglect of cost required to realize value. The purpose of Chap. 12 is to comprehend a number of problems of mixed economies such as public goods, environments, peak load problems in a unified framework to deal with externalities, elucidating the structure of socially optimal tax-subsidy policies.

I wish to express my gratitude to the board of editors, Professors Ryuzo Sato, Hajime Hori, Kazuo Mino and Mariko Fujii for giving me the opportunity to publish this book in the Springer series of Advances in Japanese Business and Economics. Moreover, they freely gave me many searching comments which led to substantial improvements of the draft.

I would also like to thank my teachers, Professor Ronald Jones, late Professors Lionel McKenzie, Walter Oi at the University of Rochester, Professor Masao Fukuoka, late Professor Noboru Yamamoto at Keio University, late Professor Hirofumi Uzawa at the University of Tokyo, and Professor Murray Kemp at the University of New South Wales for continued interest in my works and encouragement. I am grateful to late Professors Kiyoshi Kojima, Miyohei Shinohara, Akira Takayama and Akihiro Amano for their inspiring instructions. I thank Ryutaro Komiya, Nobuo Minabe, Takashi Negishi, Koichi Hamada, Keimei Kaizuka, Hideyuki Adachi, Wilfred Ethier, Elhanan Helpman, Yasuhiro Sakai, Masayoshi Hirota, Walter Diewert, Makoto Ikema, Alok Ray, Anjan Mukherji, Shiro

Yabushita, Alan Woodland, Kotaro Suzumura, Kazuo Nishimura, Takahiko Muto, Ryuhei Okumura, Masao Satake, Masahiro Matsushita, Akiyoshi Horiuchi, Masahiro Okuno, Katsuhito Iwai, Miyako Suda, Motoshige Ito, Toshihiro Ihori, Hiroshi Yoshikawa, Nobuhiro Nakagawa, Toshihiro Ichida, and Hiroyuki Mizuta for their instructive and constructive comments.

Moreover, I am indebted to my colleagues and former students at Keio University for their helpful comments and advices on part of the papers collected in this book. They are Kunio Kawamata, Hiroaki Osana, Kunikazu Karaki, Yoko Wake, Keiichi Umada, Ryuhei Wakasugi, Miki Seko, Toru Maruyama, Kazuhito Ikeo, Eiji Hosoda, Shuhei Shiozawa, Yasuhiro Nakagami, Atsuko Matsumura, Fukunari Kimura, Sahoko Kaji, Yuri Okina, Shinichi Suda, Hiroshi Amari, Koji Ishibashi, Yoshihiko Fukushima, Yoshimasa Shirai and Ichiroh Daitoh. Masatoshi Tsumagari carefully read the draft of original chapters and cooperated for their improvement at the last stage of its compilation.

Last but not least, I would like to thank the editorial staff at Springer Japan KK for considerate and efficient preparation for this project in Springer's Advances in Japanese Business and Economics book series.

Tokyo, Japan
February 24, 2016

Michihiro Ohyama

Contents

About the Author

Michihiro Ohyama is a professor emeritus of Keio University, Tokyo, Japan. He is the former president of the Japanese Economic Association and the Japan Society of International Economics. His major publications include "On the Stability of Generalized Metzlerian Systems," *Review of Economic Studies*, Vol. 39 (1972); "Trade and Welfare in General Equilibrium," *Keio Economic Studies*, Vol. 9 (1972); and "Market, Trade and General Equilibrium," *Japanese Economic Review*, Vol. 50 (1999).

Professor Ohyama conducted research at the University of New South Wales, Tel Aviv University, and the University of Minnesota. His research has ranged from general equilibrium theory to welfare economics, macroeconomics, and international economics. References to his works are found in *Keio Economic Studies* 42(1–2), 2005, a special issue in his honor.

Part I
Welfare and Macroeconomics

Chapter 1
Multiplier Theory and Public Goods: Macroeconomics of the Mixed System

1.1 Introduction

Since the collapse of the Bubble in the early 1990s, the expenditures of the government of Japan have continued to expand for more than 20 years, but have failed to improve business conditions, leaving the national rate of unemployment at high levels. In the meantime, the government deficit increased and consequently the balance of the government bond accumulated enormously. This experience cast doubt on the effectiveness of fiscal policy[1] intended to increase the aggregate income and employment in Japan. The Keynesian multiplier theory that originated in the midst of the great depression of the 1930s has served as the cornerstone of fiscal policy in the standard textbooks for a long time. It emphasized multiplier effects of government deficit expenditure on national income and employment, symbolizing the Keynesian revolution in the history of macroeconomic policy. The recent experience of the stagnation of Japan and other countries, however, has revealed that the multiplier effect was not so large as believed in the past. Moreover, frequent use of fiscal policy undermined government fiscal discipline, giving rise to inefficient resource allocation in Japan as well as in many other countries.

The multiplier theory typically abstracts from the coexistence of public and private goods regarding the aggregate output as a composite product. Keynes considered public works as an important element of fiscal policy, but he somehow

The draft of this chapter was first presented at the workshop presided by Ryuzo Sato on November 29, 2014. I benefited from instructive comments by Sato on the contributions by Richard Musgrave regarding the concept of public goods, together with constructive discussions from other attendants of the workshop. The paper was subsequently published in *Keio Economic Studies*, Vol. 51, 2015. I am indebted to Masatoshi Tsumagari and an anonymous referee of *Keio Economic Studies* for their helpful comments.

[1] Fiscal policy is here defined as a macroeconomic policy designed to stabilize national income and aggregate employment by controlling government revenue and expenditure. It should be distinguished from public finance in the narrow sense limited to the provision of public goods.

© Springer Japan 2016

M. Ohyama, *Macroeconomics, Trade, and Social Welfare*, Advances in Japanese Business and Economics 14, DOI 10.1007/978-4-431-55807-1_1

glossed over the distinction of private and public goods when he spoke of the national product as if it were one good tradeable in the market. At the time of the General Theory, the concept of public goods introduced by Musgrave (1959) and Samuelson (1954, 1955a, b) was not yet known. In their interpretation, public goods differ from private goods in that they are provided by the dictation of the government whereas private goods are provided through demand and supply in the market. This distinction is not really understood even now, after more than half a century.

Another problem with the multiplier theory is its disregard of welfare economics. It tends to undervalue the welfare effect of public goods while overestimating the income and employment effects arising from public works. In fact, the use of unemployed workers for the production of public goods may yield an increase in social welfare surpassing its direct income and employment effects. In terms of the simple Keynesian theory, however, an expansion of government deficit expenditure brings about far more increase in welfare through its multiplier effects than its direct meager effects through the accompanying provision of public goods. A well-known illustration given by Keynes himself is the employment of workers for burying old bottles in disused coal mines and digging them up again. It would increase the real income of the community through its multiplier effect even though there is no sense in such a project in terms of social welfare.

One of the most controversial problems with the multiplier theory was whether the public expenditure financed by the government deficit would really create much more national income than its face value. To finance the project, the government must issue the corresponding value of bonds, which it has to repay later by taxation in the future. The real burden of the project to taxpayers is, therefore, equivalent, regardless of whether it is financed by deficit or by taxation. This recognition, attributed to Ricardo and Barro, is now well known as the equivalence theorem.[2] The simple multiplier theory ignores the message of this theorem completely. In fact, many public work projects put into practice in Japan by deficit financing during the "lost two decades" since the collapse of the Bubble failed to revive the slumped economy. Moreover, they created a number of public facilities such as dams and buildings that were detrimental to both the environment and social welfare. During the decades, the government deficit increased and its resulting debt continued to increase at unprecedented pace. In the twenty-first century, the sovereign risks attributable to government debt financing began to threaten business prospects of many countries all over the world.

In what follows, we reconsider the effects of fiscal policy using a simple real model of macroeconomics. In the absence of innovations and new frontiers, the effective demand of the economy may become insufficient to ensure full employment even when the interest rates decline to zero, as in the "liquidity trap" envisioned by Hicks (1937).[3]

[2] Ricardo's idea is recorded in his "Essays in the Funding System," in McCulloch (1888). Barro (1974, 1979) formalized his idea clearly in the words of modern economics.

[3] Ohyama (2004, 2007) developed a version of the *IS-LM* model with a microeconomic foundation to characterize the "liquidity trap" as its special case.

In Sect. 1.2, we consider the simple real economy without public goods, in which only private goods are traded in the market. Money and government are assumed away. This basic model is useful for the purpose of illuminating the deep depression economy envisioned by Hicks (1937) as a "liquidity trap" where monetary policy becomes ineffective and fiscal policy does not exist. The fundamental cause of such a depression is deficiency of effective private demand. To remedy such a situation, it is necessary to introduce government fiscal policy conjugating private and public goods.

In Sect. 1.3, we modify the preceding setup and assume that the government intervenes in the economy providing public goods and transfer payment by means of taxation. It abides by a balanced budget in the sense that its payment for public goods and transfer is fully financed by taxation.

The amount of public goods is determined by the government democratically or dictatorially, whereas the amount of private goods (including labor services required for production of public goods) is determined by the adjustment of income in the market. It will be shown that the national disposable income expressed in terms of private goods becomes constant independently of the level of the government taxation. One unit of government expenditure generates one unit of private goods and associated labor services, meaning that the multiplier of government expenditure is exactly unity.

In Sect. 1.4, we develop a two-goods model in which public as well as private goods are considered explicitly and distinctly. When the economy is underemployed, an increase in the government expenditure increases employment and the output of the public good, but does not affect the national disposable income. If the public good is defined to be useful by a given social utility function, however, it clearly increases social welfare. Furthermore, if the public good is so designed to stimulate the demand for private goods, the fiscal multiplier will be strengthened. Once full employment is realized, a further increase in government expenditure, that is, a further increase in the provision of public goods, gives rise to "crowding out," or a corresponding decrease in the supply of private goods. This development means that the opportunity cost of public goods is positive rather than zero.

In Sect. 1.5, we explore the effects of macroeconomic policy under full employment. In this phase, an increase in public expenditure may not be justified in view of the given social utility function even though the public good is useful in its own. In other words, it may be desirable to decrease government expenditure. The optimal provision of the public good is illustrated by looking at how the social indifference curve intersects with the production frontier of public and private goods. The purpose of public finance in this phase is to optimize the supply of the public good rather than just to preserve full employment. At a first glance, this idea may seem to resemble the neoclassical synthesis introduced by Samuelson (1954). But as we argue in Sect. 1.5, the government must realize full employment and optimize the supply of the public good at the same time. Thus, it should be named the neo-Keynesian (or mixed system) synthesis of employment and public finance.

1.2 The Principle of Effective Demand

Let us begin by considering a simplest model in which there is only one good. It is supposed to be a private good used for production and investment, as well as for consumption, and tradeable in the market. For simplicity, it may be named "rice," the most popular Japanese staple. A unit of rice is supposed be produced using a unit of homogeneous labor. The representative worker is bestowed a given amount of leisure and chooses to work for h hours per day for the wage rate, w^C, determined by labor contract on the basis of the social convention. Figure 1.1 depicts the representative worker's indifference curves between wage rate and leisure and the determination of contract wage on the vertical line showing the given labor hours. Contract wage is supposed to be negotiated at a value between reservation wage, w, which the worker requires as least, and unity, which the employers can pay at most, or $w \leq w^C \leq 1$. See McDonald and Solow (1981) and Ohyama (1987) for models of wage bargaining under unemployment.

The total number of workers in the economy is denoted $\overline{N}$. Let us denote by N^S the number of workers who are willing to be employed, or the supply of workers, and by N^D the number of workers demanded by the economy. When contract wage satisfies the foregoing inequality, the economy is in the state of full employment, or $N^S = \overline{N}$. Figure 1.2 shows how the supply of workers may not be equilibrated to the demand for workers, or $\overline{N} > N^D$. We assume here that the demand of workers falls short of the supply of workers, giving rise to the emergence of involuntary unemployment. Such a situation occurs when the demand for national product at full employment is insufficient to absorb the supply of national product at full employment, as in the case of the Great Depression in the United States (U.S.) and the "lost two decades" after the Bubble in Japan.

What then are the determinants of social demand for the national product? In the present setup abstracting from the government, social private demand for the national product consists of private consumption C and investment demand I. Private consumption demand depends on contract wage rate w^C, real rate of interest r, national income Y, and capital stock K, which may be written as an aggregate consumption function:

$$C = c(w^c, r, Y, K), \tag{1.1}$$

assuming

$$c_w = c_{w^c} \geq 0,\ 0 \leq c_Y = \frac{\partial c}{\partial Y} \leq 1,\ c_r = \frac{\partial c}{\partial r} \leq 0,\ c_K = \frac{\partial c}{\partial K} \geq 0.$$

For simplicity, investment demand I is supposed to be given exogenously depending on the firm's long-term expectation, among other factors.

The market equilibrium condition under unemployment is

$$Y = c\left(w^C, Y, K\right) + I \tag{1.2}$$

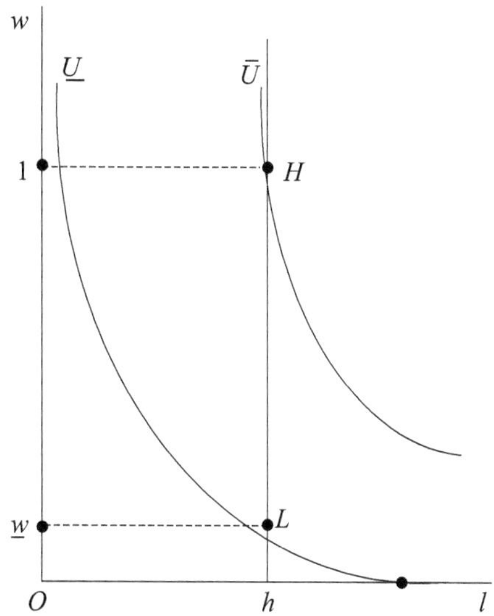

Fig. 1.1 Standard labor hour and reservation wage

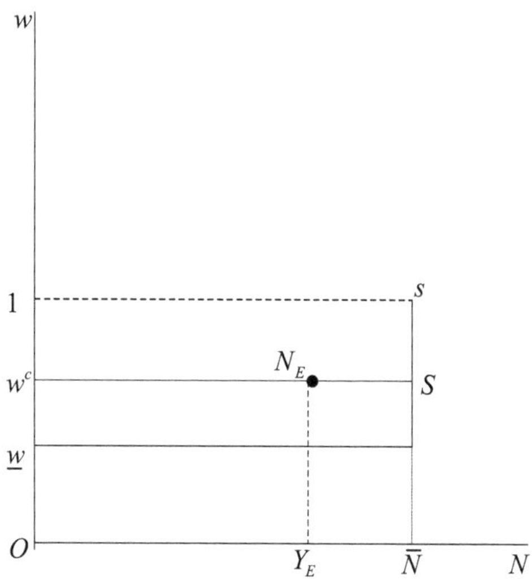

Fig. 1.2 Supply curve of labor

where Y works as an adjustment factor to equilibrate the demand and supply of private goods given w^C, K, and I. Figure 1.3 shows the equilibrium national income Y_E at the intersection E of aggregate demand curve Dd and a 45° line, whereas Fig. 1.4 illustrates the determination of national disposable income. Figure 1.5 shows the equilibrium F_B or E_{UG} supported by the government expenditure G_B.[4] In the absence of government intervention, the market mechanism fails to realize

[4] Keynes (1936), p. 25. "The point of intersection of the aggregate demand function and the aggregate supply function will be called *the effective demand*."

full employment in this situation. The market equilibrium income falls short of full employment income, Y_F, by "deflationary gap" FG in the case of Fig. 1.3, or by $G_A G_B$ in the case of Fig. 1.5, implying the existence of corresponding unemployment. Reverting to Fig. 1.2, we observe that the deflationary gap coincides with unemployment equal to segment $N_E S$. Figure 1.3 is essentially identical to the familiar illustration of the "Keynesian Cross," whereas Fig. 1.5 is invoked to take full advantage of the newly introduced general equilibrium model covering private and public goods.[5]

1.3 Government and Fiscal Policy (Two-Good General Equilibrium)

Let us now introduce government and consider the multiplier effects of changes in government expenditure and other exogenous variables on national income and related endogenous variables. Suppose that proportion α of national tax revenue, T, is to be spent on government expenditure, G, on public goods and proportion $(1-\alpha)$ on transfer payments:

$$T = G + R, \tag{1.3}$$

$$G = \alpha T, \tag{1.4}$$

$$R = (1-\alpha)T, \tag{1.5}$$

$$Z = Y - T + R = Y - \alpha T. \tag{1.6}$$

With the introduction of the government, private consumption function is modified as

$$C = c(w^c, Y - \alpha T, K). \tag{1.7}$$

Given the reservation wage w^C, tax T, private investment I, and consumption function, the new market equilibrium condition is written as

$$Y - \alpha T = c(w^c, Y - \alpha T, K) + I \tag{1.8}$$

which determines equilibrium income Y_E and equilibrium disposable income $Z_E = Y_E - \alpha T$.

[5] The private goods used in the production of public goods may be subject to decreasing returns to proportion, given the stock of private capital. In such a case, the production frontier of private and public goods becomes convex to the origin and the aggregate supply function depends positively on the relative price of public goods.

This modification is not necessary, however, for our conclusions but is agreeable to the Keynesian concepts of aggregate supply functions.

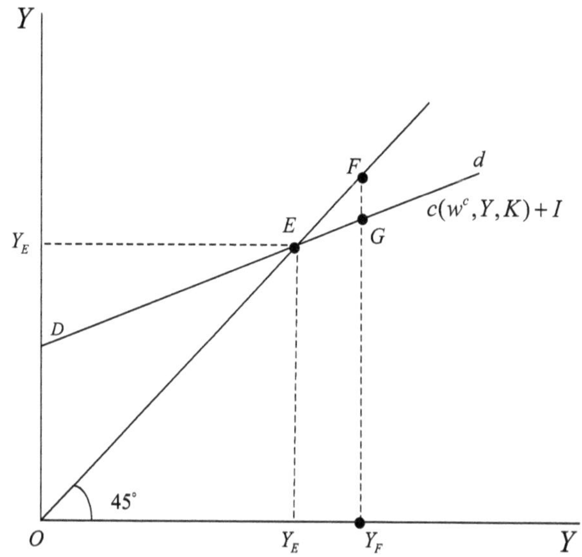

Fig. 1.3 The principle of effective demand

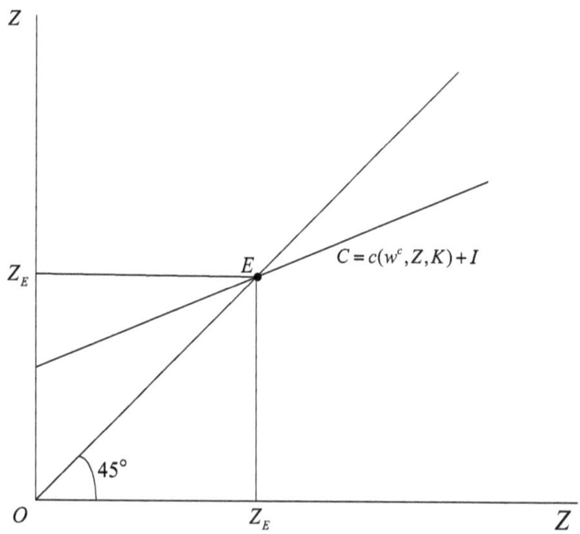

Fig. 1.4 Equilibrium disposable income

The effect of an increase in autonomous investment on equilibrium income and equilibrium disposable income is shown by

$$\frac{\partial Y_E}{\partial I} = \frac{\partial Z_E}{\partial I} = \frac{1}{1 - c_Z} \tag{1.9}$$

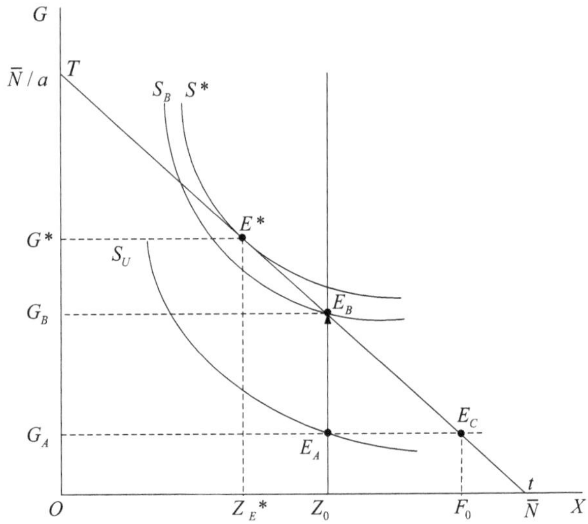

Fig. 1.5 Expansion path of mixed economy. The supply of public goods to be increased beyond the point of full employment

The marginal propensity to spend out of disposable income, c_Z, is assumed to be positive and smaller than 1, which implies that the investment multiplier is positive and could be much greater than 1. This conclusion is nothing more than the familiar investment multiplier. The effect of a rise in contract wage, w^C, is not quite clear but is usually supposed to be positive as workers spend more than capitalists on private goods more often than not.

How about the effect of government expenditure? First suppose that the government spends its tax revenue on useless goods. This is exactly the case of the Keynesian parable of burying old bottles in disused coal mines and digging them up again. The effect of an increase in government expenditure under a balanced budget is

$$\frac{\partial Y_E}{\partial T} = \alpha. \tag{1.10}$$

To be sure, the balanced budget multiplier is equal to unity, or

$$\frac{\partial Y_E}{\partial G} = 1. \tag{1.11}$$

Needless to say, the multiplier effect on the equilibrium disposable income becomes

$$\frac{\partial Z_E}{\partial G}\left(=\frac{\partial Z_E}{\partial T}\right)=0. \tag{1.12}$$

Proposition 1.1: Balanced Budget Multiplier *Suppose that unemployment prevails under the balanced budget. Given the proportion of government transfer payment at* $(1-\alpha)$ *of tax revenue, a unit increase of tax increases the equilibrium in national income by* α *but leaves the equilibrium of disposable income unaffected.*

A standard textbook of macroeconomics tells us that the balanced budget multiplier is just unity. Here, we say that if the proportion of government transfer is set at $1-\alpha$ of tax revenue, the tax-based multiplier becomes equal to α or smaller than 1. If $\alpha = 1$, the standard balanced budget multiplier of unity obtains. The larger the value of α, the smaller becomes the multiplier.

These conclusions are the results of our implicit assumption that the *net* effect of transfer payments on aggregate demand is zero. In fact, however, transfer payments are often related to social security benefits, which distribute income from rich to poor people, thereby increasing aggregate consumption expenditure. This is one of the most controversial problems regarding the simultaneous reform of tax and social security systems recently discussed in Japan. In this chapter, we assume that consumers are homogeneous and therefore transfer payments tend to decrease government expenditure on private goods used in the production of public goods.

It should also be noted that a tax-financed government expenditure does not affect the disposable national income; this obtains because an increase in T brings about an equal increase in Y_E/α under a balanced budget. The increase in government expenditure financed by tax increases government expenditure on its supply of public goods and therefore its labor employment, but it does not affect the income and employment in the private sector. Caesar's money used for the provision of the public goods is returned to Caesar through taxation, as it were. Although the aggregate employment increases, per capita income of employed workers decreases in the face of constant aggregate income. Thus, the increase in government expenditure amounts to work (income) sharing among potential workers.

Proposition 1.2: Work and Income-Sharing Effect of Government Expenditure *An increase in government expenditure on public goods increases aggregate employment and realizes work and income sharing among workers.*

The government is supposed to provide public goods and public investment in addition to transfer payment. Here, the public good is as a flow good, distinguished from public capital stock (or social common capital, in the words of Uzawa 1974).[6] It is specified as a labor service used in the production of public goods in collaboration with public capital. Public investment is investment in public capital stock such as roads, harbors, parks, embankments, or national defense forces that are

[6] Also see Musgrave (1959), pp. 13–14. The merit wants considered there are related to flow of public goods.

publicly owned. We consider the economic significance of public investment and public capital stock in more detail in the next section.

For simplicity, 1 unit of public goods is supposed to be produced using a unit of private goods. The total number of workers, N, employed in national production is the sum of workers employed in the government and private sectors:

$$N = X + aG, \tag{1.13}$$

where X denotes the output of the private good. Note that G is equal to the amount of labor employed in the production of the public good. Figure 1.5 shows the equilibrium of the mixed economy where the government undertakes to provide the public good and the private sector supplies private goods through the market. The vertical axis measures the government expenditure G and the horizontal axis that of the private goods. The equilibrium employment N_E involves unemployed workers when

$$N_E = X_E +^E aG < \overline{N}. \tag{1.14}$$

The curve Tt depicts a straight-line production frontier between G and X on the simplifying assumption that the labor coefficient a is given and fixed. The curves Ss are the social indifference curves between G and X on the assumption that the marginal utility of the public goods decreases given the aggregate consumption of the private goods.

The curve $S_O s_O$ is the social indifference curve where the government expenditure on public goods is given at G_O and the consumption of the private goods X_O is correspondingly determined on $S_O s_O$. As already pointed out, an increase in government expenditure increases the aggregate income and employment in the same proportion, but what can we say about its welfare effects? An increase in the aggregate income and employment would increase the expected utility of the potential workers by increasing the probability of their employment. Moreover, the associated increase in the provision of public goods would increase the welfare (social utility) by itself. To make this point clear, let us define the social utility function (the graphical representation of which is the social indifference curve) as

$$W = u(X, G),\ u_X > 0,\ u_G > 0. \tag{1.15}$$

Proposition 1.3: Expansion Path in the Presence of Unemployment *The expansion of tax-financed government expenditure shifts the equilibrium point under unemployment to increase social welfare along the expansion path* $\overrightarrow{E_A E_B}$.

According to the old Keynesian view, a bond-financed government expenditure brings about a multiplied increase in national income, whereas a tax-financed increase in government expenditure results in an equal increase in national income. As already argued, this view is untenable in that it overlooks the future tax burden of the expenditure increase. Furthermore, it focuses only on the income effects of the expenditure increase, neglecting its welfare effects. In light of Eq. (1.15), an increase in tax-financed government expenditure creates extra income and employment without incurring opportunity costs under unemployment. It is bound to increase social welfare.

There are some public goods that complement and promote private consumption and investment. For example, the provision of care and nursing services by the government may increase consumption by creating leisure time for housekeepers. The maintenance of public roads and port facilities may be important for business opportunities and investments in general. Under such circumstances, consumption function may be rewritten as a function of government expenditure as well as on the real interest rate r, national income, and on capital stock:

$$C = c(w^c, r, Y - T, K, \alpha T), \tag{1.16}$$

and investment function may be similarly.modified as

$$I = i(r, \alpha T, K), \tag{1.17}$$

where $c_r < 0$, $i_r < 0$.

Proposition 1.4: Government Expenditure Complementing Private Expenditure *The balanced budget multiplier of a government expenditure that complements private expenditure has a multiplier greater than* α *under unemployment.*[7]

After all, the prevalence of unemployment stems from deficiency of effective demand, that is, the result of unwillingness on the part of people to consume or invest. It may reflect the shortage of public goods in the broad sense including those that complement private expenditure.

1.4 Fiscal Policy Under Full Employment

In the presence of unemployment, it is possible to carry out the production of the public goods by using labor from the pool of unemployed workers without reducing the output of private goods, that is, incurring no opportunity costs. Once full employment is achieved and maintained, however, this is no longer the case. In Fig. 1.5, indifference curve $S_B s_B$ passing though E_B cut production frontier Tt from

[7] Aside from the demand-increasing effects from the introduction of public goods considered here, it is also worth taking note of the supply-increasing effects from the public goods. In the present model, however, the supply shocks of this kind do not affect the short-run adjustment process under unemployment. We shall explore the long-run effects of public investment (increase in the stock of public capital) later in the next section.

lower left to upper right, which means that the supply of the public good is insufficient and there is room for improving social welfare by increasing its supply. The socially optimal equilibrium is shown by E^* where indifference curve S^*s^* touches Tt. Under full employment, however, an increase in the supply of the public good is achievable only if the supply of the private good is correspondingly decreased along Tt. Throughout the process, labor moves from the private sector to the public sector and the equilibrium point from E_B to F^*, and social welfare increases along the expansion path (or adjustment path) E_BF^*. To induce workers to move out of the private sector to the public sector, the wage rate in the public sector must be kept at a level higher than the contract wage in the private sector.

Figure 1.6 depicts the case where the output of public goods at the socially optimal point F^* is smaller than that of E_B. It is desirable to decrease the production of public goods and increase that of private goods along the expansion path (or adjustment path) E_BF^*. To induce workers to move out of the public sector to the private sector, the wage rate in the public sector must be kept at a level lower than the contract wage in the private sector.

Proposition 1.5: Expansion Path Under Full Employment *When the government expenditure that ensures full employment differs from its socially optimal level, a further adjustment has to be pursued along the expansion path (or adjustment path) E_BF^* of the production frontier. To be more precise, if $G^* > G_B$, the government must increase its expenditure and the supply of public goods. In contrast, if $G^* < G_B$, the government must decrease its expenditure and the supply of public goods. Social welfare increases in the process of the adjustment process along E_BF^*.*

1.5 Neo-Keynesian Synthesis

Early in the 1950s, Samuelson put forward the idea that once the government succeeds in maintaining full employment, labor embodied in the employed workers will be optimally allocated through the market mechanism, and named it the "neo-classical synthesis."[8] If full employment is maintained by the government's fiscal policy, the resource allocation of private goods will be achieved by the market mechanism optimally to maximize social welfare. Within the simple model devoid of public goods, the fundamental theorem of welfare economics is established that general equilibrium becomes Pareto optimal under the condition of perfect competition and in the absence of externalities.

In the present model the shortage of social public goods in the short run and social capital stock in the long run may depress consumption and investment, bringing about short-run unemployment and long-run stagnation, as mentioned

[8] See Samuelson (1955a, b), p. 212.

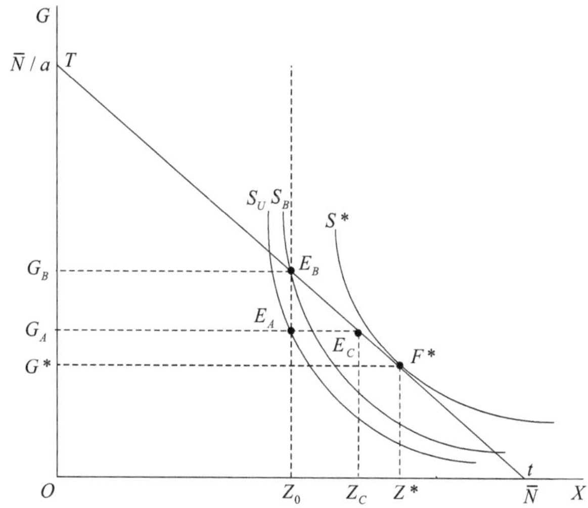

Fig. 1.6 Expansion path of mixed economy equilibrium. The supply of public goods to be decreased beyond the point of full employment

earlier. Thus, the government provision of social public goods in the short run and social capital stock in the long run may exert positive externalities in the sense that it promotes private consumption and investment, easing short-run unemployment and long-run stagnation. Figures 1.5 and 1.6 illustrate how the optimal allocation of national resources may be achieved by the government intervention along with the market mechanism starting from the unemployment equilibrium, E_A, through full employment equilibrium, E_B, culminating in the optimal equilibrium, E^*.

Proposition 1.6: Neo-Keynesian or Mixed-Economy Synthesis *Suppose that given resource endowment, production technology, and consumers preference, a static stationary state prevails where net investment and saving become zero and real interest rate stabilizes at the natural level. Also suppose that perfect competition prevails in the market for private goods with no technological externalities. The government is assumed to anticipate the short-run as well as the long-run effects of public investment with perfect foresight. The government should then be able to use fiscal and labor policy appropriately to increase employment in the short run and maintain full employment and achieve the optimal provision of public goods in the long run. This design of economic policy may be named the neo-Keynesian (or the mixed-economy) synthesis.*[9]

So far we have abstracted from the dynamic effects of investment on production technology and formation of resources. It is the essence of investment either private or public, however, that it improves the quality of technology and resources. We have to reconsider the present model taking explicit account of these dynamic

[9] For simplicity, we have assumed away the externalities of any kind. It would be easy to extend this proposition introducing the government tax-cum-subsidy scheme to internalize externalities.

effects of investment. Let us divide government expenditure, G, into government consumption, G_C, and government investment, G_I. The former is supposed to produce public services and the latter to improve the quality and efficiency of public capital stock, K_G. Similarly, private investment I is supposed to improve the quality and efficiency of private capital stock, K. Considering these relationship, we may rewrite here the employment constraint 1.14 as

$$N(K, K_G) = X + a(K_G)G \tag{1.18}$$

where $a(K_G)$ is supposed to be a decreasing function of K_G because government investment certainly increases future government capital stock, thereby improving labor productivity in the production of public goods (or lowering labor coefficient a), and $N(K, K_G)$ shows the national supply of labor in efficiency units as an increasing function of K, K_G because private and government capital stock serve as the basis of labor supply in efficiency units.

Figure 1.7 illustrates the effects of public and private investment on the position and shape of the production frontier. The present frontier is shown by Tt. An increase in private and public investment improving labor productivity in projects such as environment, roads, harbor facilities, and education may increase the supply of labor measured in efficiency units, bringing about a parallel upward shift of production frontier expected in the future to $T't'$. Given the social indifference curves as before, the present and future optimal equilibria are shown by F^*, $F^{*\prime}$, or the points of contact with $T't'$. Barring inferior goods, social consumption of the present and future goods will increase in that event. Similarly, Fig. 1.8 depicts how the production frontier shifts as a result of an increase in public investment because of its expansive effects on future public capital stock. It will decrease the labor coefficient a of the public goods and expand the production frontier asymmetrically from Tt to $T't'$. The relative cost of future public goods will decrease and the optimal production point will change from F^* to $F^{*\prime}$. As a result, the future output of the public goods will normally increase, but the future output of the private goods may decrease.

Proposition 1.7: Growth Strategy *Investment in general, both public and private, increases income and employment in the short run and works as the engine of economic growth by accumulating public and private capital stock in the long run.*[10]

Investment is capable of generating positive economic effects beyond consumption in both the short run and the long run. As witnessed by the current difficulties in public finance in Japan and many other advanced countries, however, misguided public investment can lead to serious government indebtedness and tremendous

[10] The third arrow of "Abenomics" in the Japanese Economic policy calls for the growth strategy of useful public investment and deregulatory measures to improve the opportunities of private investment.

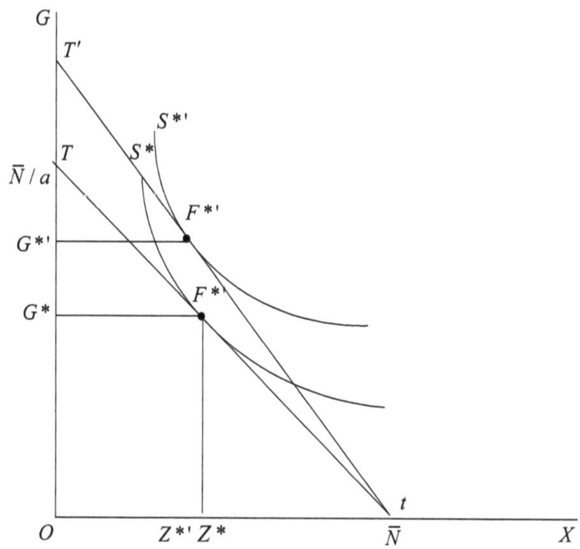

Fig. 1.7 Productivity improvement in public goods production

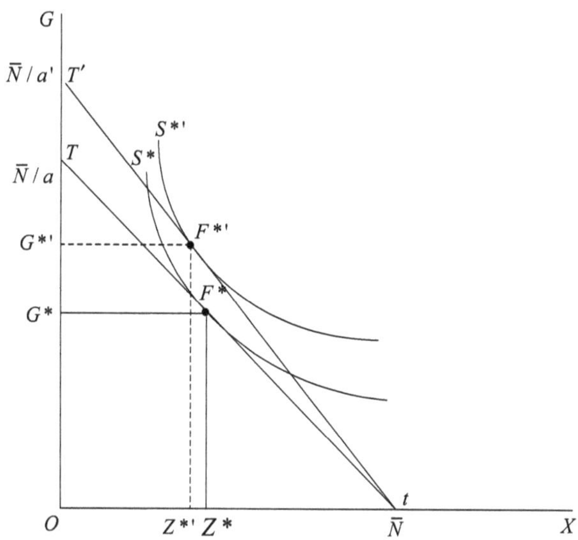

Fig. 1.8 Innovation in the public sector

misallocation of resources. Useless and untimely public investments destroy the natural environment and educational facilities, resulting in the loss of aggregate labor supply in efficiency units and contraction of the production frontier. Therefore, it is vitally important to take into full account the welfare implications of public expenditure and investment in particular.

1.6 Concluding Remarks

In this chapter, we attempted to reconsider and extend the economic theory of deep depression initiated by Keynes (1936) taking explicit account of the concept of public goods largely blurred in his general theory and after. To contrive the model of secular stagnation where the interest rate falls to zero and monetary policy is restricted by the zero bound, we concentrate on a real economy featuring the theory of public finance. In so doing, we synthesize the traditional theory of public finance and the Keynesian fiscal theory and cast new light on their welfare significance.

1. As the basic setting, we assume the Schumpeterian stationary state in which there are no market-originated private innovations and investments and the interest rate has fallen to zero. Using a simple macroscopic general equilibrium model, we show that Keynesian involuntary unemployment equilibrium can arise there from deficient Keynesian effective demand. This underemployment equilibrium is realized through the adjustment of national income, not through the adjustment of interest rate nor through the adjustment of commodity prices. To reduce or remove unemployment in the equilibrium, it is necessary for the government to intervene by producing public goods or carrying out public investment. Conversely, government intervention in this fashion is justified only under the present setup.
2. In line with the Ricardo–Barro equivalence theorem, the government is supposed to abide by the balanced budget discipline. Even so, the government should be able to increase labor employment (private goods) in the government sector, keeping the national disposable income at a constant level. This may be called the work (income)-sharing effects of government expenditure (Propositions 1.1 and 1.2).
3. If the government expenditure is sufficiently large, it will realize full employment theoretically in no time. In reality, however, it may take some time to accomplish full employment. The process of adjustment toward full employment may be divided into discrete periods during which the government increases expenditure on goods and services continuously. It may be visualized as an expansion path of unemployment equilibrium as in $\overset{\frown}{E_A E_B E^*}$ in Fig. 1.1. If the public goods are useful, national welfare will increase along the path of Proposition 1.3.
4. The public good is supposed to be desirable in itself in the sense that it directly enhances social welfare, but it is often designed to increase the propensity to consume or invest thereby adding to effective demand. In such a case, the multiplier of the government expenditure will be greater than 1 even under a balanced budget (Proposition 1.4).
5. The production of the public good, whether it is useful or not, incurs opportunity cost except in the presence of involuntary unemployment. Starting from the initial unemployment equilibrium, an increase in the government expenditure will initially increase the production of the public goods and employment

without decreasing that of the private goods, but as soon as full employment is maintained, there arises trade-off between the public good and the private good so that a further increase in the supply of the public good may not warrant improvement of national welfare. It may become necessary to decrease the supply of the public good on the way. The optimal supply of the public good must be determined in view of some welfare criterion and its opportunity cost in terms of the private good. Figure 1.6 illustrates this point using the social indifference curve and the production frontier (Proposition 1.5).

6. Samuelson (1954) proposed the so-called neo-classical synthesis to the effect that once full employment is established by the government, the market will accomplish the Pareto optimum of the rest of resource allocation. As shown earlier, however, the government's role goes beyond the achievement of full employment. It extends to the optimization of social welfare through appropriate provision of the public goods. The neo-Keynesian (or the mixed-economy) synthesis that requires optimization of public good provision as well as full employment of labor is appropriate (Proposition 1.6).
7. The foregoing analysis is applicable only to the "short-run" setting where the production technology and labor resources of the economy and therefore the production frontier are given and fixed. Investment, public as well as private, is not only conducive to short-run recovery but also to the "long-run" growth of the economy through its dynamic effects on the production frontier. In fact, it extends the future production frontier by means of the accumulation of public and private capital stock (Proposition 1.7). As argued by the advocators of "Abenomics," public investment and active deregulation should serve as the growth strategy of the Japanese economy stagnant during the 20 years since early 1990.

References

Barro, R. L. (1974). Are government bonds net wealth? *Journal of Political Economy, 82*(6), 1095–1117.

Barro, R. L. (1979). On the determination of the public debt. *Journal of Political Economy, 87*(5), 940–971.

Hicks, J. R. (1937). Mr. Keynes and classics: A suggested interpretation. *Econometrica, 5*(2), 147–159.

Keynes, J. M. (1936). *The general theory of employment interest and money*. London: Macmillan.

McCulloch, J. R. (1888). *The works of David Ricardo. With a notice of the life and writings of the author*. London: John Murray.

McDonald, I. M., & Solow, R. M. (1981). Wage bargaining and employment. *American Economic Review, 71*(5), 896–908.

Musgrave, R. A. (1959). *The theory of public finance: a study in public economy*. New York: McGraw-Hill.

Ohyama, M. (1987). Unemployment and inflation: Natural wage rate hypothesis. *Keio Economic Studies, 24*, 11–26.

Ohyama, M. (2004). Effective demand and national income. *Keio Economic Studies, 41*(2), 1–23.

Ohyama, M. (2007). The Mundell–Fleming model revisited: A microeconomics. *Keio Economic Studies, 45*, 1–18.
Samuelson, P. A. (1954). The pure theory of public expenditure. *Review of Economics and Statistics, 36*, 387–389.
Samuelson, P. A. (1955a). Diagrammatic exposition of a theory of public expenditures. *Review of Economics and Statistics, 32*, 350–356.
Samuelson, P. A. (1955b). *Economics* (3rd ed., p. 21). New York: McGraw-Hill.
Uzawa, H. (1974). Sur la theorie du capital collecvtif social. *Cahier du Econometrie et economique, 15*, 101–122.

Chapter 2
Unemployment and Inflation: The Natural Wage Rate Hypothesis

2.1 Introduction

We have witnessed at least two distinct types of economic depression in the current century, aptly named "stagnation" and "stagflation," respectively. Stagnation refers to the situation in which the general price level (or the rate of inflation) declines together with the quantitative indices of aggregate economic activities such as output and employment. Needless to say, a most important example of stagnation is the Great Depression, which began in 1929 and extended into the 1930s. In contrast, an economy is said to suffer from stagflation when the general price level (or the rate of inflation) rises in the face of falling output and employment. This form of depression was observed most typically in industrialized countries from the late 1960s and through the 1970s when they were exposed to wage explosions, oil price hikes, and other cost-increasing pressures.

The Keynesian theory of unemployment was developed to explain stagnation in general and in the Great Depression in particular. According to this theory, stagnation is caused by a deficiency in the aggregate demand of the private sector (i.e., consumption and investment) for output and, therefore, the remedy for stagnation is to be found either in a compensating increase in the government expenditure or in an expansion of the money supply designed to stimulate the private sector aggregate demand. It served as a theoretical underpinning for macroeconomic policies for many years. With the advent of stagflation, however, the general validity of this theory began to be questioned, because it apparently failed to explain the phenomenon and to prescribe for effective countermeasures. The monetarists led by Milton Friedman, who were particularly harsh and effective in their indictment of the Keynesian economics, put forward an alternative theory to explain stagflation on

This chapter is adapted from my original article, entitled "Unemployment and Inflation: Natural Wage Rate Hypothesis," *Keio Economic Studies*, Vol. 24, 1987, 11–26.

© Springer Japan 2016

M. Ohyama, *Macroeconomics, Trade, and Social Welfare*, Advances in Japanese Business and Economics 14, DOI 10.1007/978-4-431-55807-1_2

the basis of the celebrated natural rate hypothesis.[1] There is no doubt that their theory made an important contribution to the understanding of unemployment and inflation, but they swung the pendulum to the opposite extreme by presuming that there is virtually no involuntary unemployment, at least in the long run.[2] This presumption is based on nothing but their belief in the advantages of the market mechanism.

In this chapter, we attempt to rationalize an eclectic point of view in the context of a simple macroeconomic model, which is Keynesian in the short run but becomes classical in the long run.[3] The money wage rate, fixed in the short run, is assumed to be adjusted over time to realize a certain real wage rate to be determined by the economic and social conditions of the society, which we refer to as the "natural wage rate" in analogy with the classical natural price of labor. The natural wage rate may be interpreted in some special cases to coincide with the real wage rate, which supports the Friedmanian natural rate of unemployment, but it is generally compatible with the existence of involuntary unemployment.[4]

We organize the chapter as follows. In Sect. 2.2, we describe the model and define its short-run and long-run equilibria. The concept of the natural wage rate is introduced as a key element in the definition of the long-run equilibrium. In Sect. 2.3, we formulate a dynamic adjustment process of the money wage rate on the basis of the natural wage rate hypothesis and investigate its stability under alternative hypotheses of price expectations. The Phillips curves are shown to depict the adjustment paths of the economy when expectations are stationary or rational. Finally, Sect. 2.4 is devoted to the discussion of stagnation and stagflation within the framework of the present model. Stagnation is shown to arise from a decrease in the aggregate demand for output and stagflation from an increase in the natural wage rate relative to labor productivity under all hypotheses of price expectations. It is then argued that Keynesian policies, monetary or fiscal, are effective in combating stagnation but powerless if employed against stagflation, and that the remedy for stagflation is to be found among the measures that affect directly the magnitude of the natural wage rate relative to labor productivity.

---

[1] See, for instance, Friedman (1977).

[2] In their view, the observed employment fluctuations merely reflect adjustments in voluntary labor supply caused primarily by changing expectations about future price levels. See, for instance, Friedman (1968) and Lucas (1973).

[3] See Dornbusch and Fischer (1981) for an alternative model with similar motivations.

[4] The rate of unemployment associated with the natural wage rate is more in line with the noninflationary rate of unemployment discussed by Modigliani and Papademos (1975) than with the natural rate of unemployment.

2.2 The Model: Short- and Long-Run Equilibria

In this section we develop a simple macroeconomic model capable of explaining both stagnation and stagflation. The behavior of the wage rate is important in distinguishing the short- and long-run equilibria in this model. In the short run, the money wage rate is assumed to be fixed so that the resulting equilibrium of the economy is of a Keynesian nature in many ways. The money wage rate is, however, adjusted over time so as to achieve a certain real wage rate (or the "natural" wage rate), which depends on the economic and social conditions of the society. Involuntary unemployment may exist in both the short run and the long run.

2.2.1 *The Labor Market and the Short-Run Equilibrium*

For simplicity, let us assume that all potential workers are alike, not only in their ability to work but also in their preferences for leisure and income. If hired, each person is supposed to work for a given, standard length of time (8 h per day, say). If unemployed, he or she is supposed to survive on his or her past savings, unemployment insurance payments, and economic assistance from friends and relatives. It then follows that all potential workers desire to be employed if and only if the prevailing wage rate exceeds a certain positive level, which may be called the reservation rate of labor. The aggregate supply schedule of labor may thus be illustrated by $O\omega Ss$ in Fig. 2.1. The supply of labor is equal to the total labor force $\overline{N}$, or zero according as the existing real wage rate, ω, is greater than or less than the reservation rate of labor, ω. It becomes indeterminate between $\overline{N}$ and zero if ω is just equal to ω.

The demand for labor is derived from the profit maximization of firms. The gross national product, Y, of the economy is assumed to be a function of the aggregate employment of labor, N, such that

$$Y = F(N), F'(N) > 0, F''(N) < 0 \tag{2.1}$$

where the stock of capital is fixed and suppressed. The profit maximization of competitive firms implies that the marginal productivity of labor be equal to the wage rate:

$$F'(N) = \omega \tag{2.2}$$

where the real wage rate, ω, is defined as the ratio of the money wage rate, w, to the price level, p, and given by

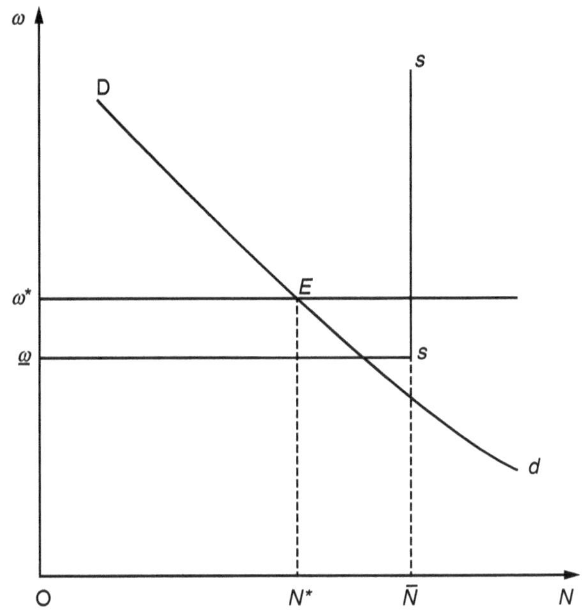

Fig. 2.1 Demand and supply in the labor market

$$\omega = w/p.$$

The aggregate demand schedule of labor is implicitly defined by Eq. (2.2). We may draw its graph as the downward-sloping curve, Dd, in Fig. 2.1. We assume that the money wage rate is fixed in the short run.[5]

Let us turn to the commodity and money markets. The expenditure of the private sector is assumed to be a function of the real rate of interest, r, the real disposable income, $Y - T$, and the real cash balance, R, and is written as

$$D = D(r, Y - T, R), D_r \leq 0, D_R > 0, 0 < D_Y < 1 \tag{2.3}$$

where T denotes the government tax revenue, and D_r, D_R, and D_Y indicate the partial derivatives of $D(\cdot)$ with respect to r, R, and $Y - T$, respectively. The real rate of interest, r, is defined as the difference between the nominal rate of interest, i, and the expected rate of inflation, π, and the real cash balance, R, as the ratio of the nominal cash balance, M, to the price level, p,:

$$r = i - \pi, \; R = M/p.$$

[5] The justification of this assumption is an important task that lies outside the scope of the present study. See, for instance, Tobin (1972) and Solow (1980) for the discussion of possibilities that may account for the short-run rigidity of the money wage rate.

The total expenditure of the economy is the sum of the private sector expenditure, D, and the government expenditure, G. Therefore, the equilibrium condition for the commodity market runs as

$$Y = D\left(i - \pi, Y - T, \frac{M}{p}\right) + G. \tag{2.4}$$

Finally, the equilibrium condition for the money market is given by

$$L(i, Y) = \frac{M}{p}, \; L_i < 0, \; L_Y > 0 \tag{2.5}$$

where $L(\cdot)$ is the standard Keynesian liquidity preference function, and L_i and L_Y denote the partial derivatives of $L(\cdot)$ with respect to i and Y, respectively.

Suppose that the money wage rate w, the nominal cash balance M, government expenditure G, tax revenue T, and the expected rate of inflation π are given exogenously in the short run. The short-run equilibrium of the economy is then defined as the state in which the marginal productivity condition, Eq. (2.2), and the equilibrium conditions for the commodity and money markets, Eqs. (2.4) and (2.5), are satisfied. The equilibrium values of the gross national product Y, the nominal rate of interest i, the employment of labor N, and the price level p are determined by these four equations: Eqs. (2.1), (2.2), (2.4), and (2.5). This concept of the short-run equilibrium is analogous to the unemployment equilibrium of the standard Keynesian model. There is little need to expound it further. Clearly, it is suitable to the analysis of economic depression arising from deficient aggregate demand and rigid money wage rates. Expansionary fiscal and monetary policies are indeed capable of alleviating this kind of depression in the sense that they lead to recoveries in output and employment, at least in the short run.

2.2.2 *The Natural Wage Rate and the Long-Run Equilibrium*

The money wage rate, fixed in the short run, is assumed to be adjusted over time to attain a certain real wage rate in the long run, given the underlying structure of the economy. This long-run real wage rate is labeled the natural wage rate, a modern-day version of the natural price of labor discussed by the classical economists.[6] The rate is determined in each society depending on a wide range of economic and social conditions such as production technologies, environmental factors, the level

[6] For instance, Ricardo (1951) defines it as that price of labor "which is necessary to enable the laborers, one with another, to subsist and to perpetuate their race, without either increase or diminution," (p. 93). He also notes that "it varies at different times in the same country, and very materially differs in different countries," essentially depending on "the habits and the customs of the people." (pp. 96–97).

and composition of capital stock, the size and distribution of national wealth, labor employment practices, the bargaining power of labor unions, and the level and duration of unemployment insurance payments.

In some special cases, the natural wage rate may be regarded as the real wage rate, which is consistent with the natural rate of unemployment defined by Friedman (1968). Generally, it does not coincide with the rate that clears the labor market. The real wage rate may be expected to converge in the long run to such a level as to make workers clearly better off than non-workers. The reasons are as follows. First, if workers are not paid enough, they will lose the incentive to keep their job. Thus, firms may find it advantageous to set the wage rate somewhat above the reservation (or subsistence) rate of labor. Second, the labor-side participants in wage bargaining often represent the interests of those who are already employed rather than the needs of those who are unemployed. At any rate, if there are non-workers who are worse off than workers, they are involuntarily unemployed.[7] See Fig. 2.1 illustrating the natural wage rate ω^* relative to the reservation wage rate $\underline{\omega}$.

We may simplify the determination of the natural wage rate by focusing on the special case where it is a linear function of the reservation rate of labor $\underline{\omega}$, that is,[8]

$$\omega^* = \alpha \underline{\omega}, \alpha \geq 1. \tag{2.6}$$

On the one hand, $\underline{\omega}$ is affected by those factors that determine the utility level of a worker when he or she is unemployed. For instance, an increase in his or her wealth or a gain in the unemployment insurance payment raises his or her utility in the state of unemployment, thereby increasing $\underline{\omega}$. On the other hand, α depends on those factors that affect wage bargaining. An increase in labor productivity, or an improvement in the bargaining power of labor unions, is thus expected to raise α. It is also conceivable that α is influenced by the rate of unemployment. For simplicity, however, we assume this possibility is not included in what follows.

In the long-run equilibrium of the economy, the real wage rate equals the natural wage rate and the expected rate of inflation coincides with the exogenously given growth rate of money supply:

$$\omega = \omega^*, \tag{2.7}$$

[7] The natural wage rate seems conceptually identical to the "goal of wage policy" as defined by Pigou (1933), a great classical economist of the twentieth century. He writes that "the goal at which wage policy aims is sometimes, in some centers of production at all events, a wage rate substantially higher than the rate which, if adopted everywhere, would yield nil unemployment." (p. 253). He bases this conclusion on "several considerations" regarding the bargaining position of wage-earners and public opinion in a modern civilized state about a reasonable living wage.

[8] This special case indeed arises under some simplifying assumptions.

$$\pi = \mu \tag{2.8}$$

where μ denotes the growth rate of the money supply. The long-run equilibrium values of labor employment and gross national product, denoted by N^* and Y^*, respectively, are determined by Eqs. (2.1), (2.2), and (2.7). Substituting these values into Eqs. (2.4) and (2.5), and assuming a balanced budget for the government, $(T = G)$, we obtain

$$Y^* = b(i - \mu, Y^* - G, R) + G, \tag{2.9}$$

$$R = L(i, Y^*). \tag{2.10}$$

Given μ and G, these equations determine the equilibrium values of the real balance R, the nominal interest rate i, and the real interest rate $r\,(= i - \mu)$.

The position of the long-run equilibrium just defined is clearly dependent on natural wage rate, production function, government expenditure, and also on the growth rate of the money supply. To begin with, let us consider the effects of an increase in the natural wage rate on the long-run equilibrium of the economy. In Fig. 2.1, the equilibrium value of labor employment N^* is shown as the abscissa of the point E where the Dd curve (depicting the marginal productivity of labor) has the height of the natural wage rate ω^*. It should be clear that an increase in the natural wage rate brings about a reduction in labor employment and, therefore, a decrease in gross national product in the long run. Similarly, a decrease in the productivity of labor can be shown to exert depressive effects because it shifts the Dd curve downward.

To obtain the effects of a decrease in gross national product on the real cash balance and the rate of interest, differentiate Eqs. (2.9) and (2.10) with respect to Y^*. The result is

$$\frac{\partial R}{\partial Y^*} = -\frac{1}{\Delta}[D_r L_Y + (1 - D_Y)L_i],$$

$$\frac{\partial i}{\partial Y^*} = \frac{1}{\Delta}[D_R L_Y - (1 - D_Y)]$$

where $\Delta = -(D_r + D_R L_i) > 0$. Given the supply of money, a decrease in gross national product induces a rise in the price level and leads to a reduction in the real cash balance. Its effect on the rate of interest is ambiguous.

Similarly, we can work out the effects of fiscal and monetary policies on the long-run values of these variables. An increase in government expenditure drives the interest rate upward and reduces the real balance. Notice that it also diminishes the real disposable income of the private sector so long as it leaves intact the natural wage rate and the production function of the economy. Naturally enough, a sustained increase in the government budget cannot be justified from the private sector point of view unless it is accompanied with a compensating increase in the provision of public services.

A rise in the growth rate of money supply raises the nominal interest rate but lowers the real interest rate. It also brings about a decline in the real balance, which means a loss in national welfare by itself; this suggests that the cost of inflation is not zero even if the future course of the price level is perfectly foreseen by the public. In this sense, money is not a veil even in the long run.

2.3 The Wage Dynamics and the Phillips Curve

In the preceding section, we distinguished between the "Keynesian" short-run equilibrium and the "classical" long-run equilibrium. The money wage rate is fixed in the short run, whereas the real wage rate is equalized to the natural wage rate in the long run, which is determined by the social as well as the economic conditions of the society. The task of this section is to formulate the adjustment process of the money wage rate and study its implications.

2.3.1 *Adjustment of the Money Wage Rate*

We assume that the money wage rate, w, is adjusted over time so as to (1) diminish the gap between the natural wage rate, ω^*, and the existing real wage rate, ω, on the one hand, and (2) keep the existing real wage rate intact in view of the expected rate of inflation, π, on the other hand. This process of adjustment may be described by the differential equation

$$\frac{\dot{w}}{w} = \phi\left(\omega^* - \omega\right) + \pi,\ \phi(0) = 0,\ \phi'(0) \geq 0 \tag{2.11}$$

where the dot $(\cdot)$ signifies the time derivative of the variable. This formulation is based on the presumption that in general the natural wage rate is not realized instantaneously. The money wage rate is determined by the bargaining between firms and workers, but they may not be perfectly convinced of the appropriateness of the natural wage rate before it comes into force. Thus, the realization of the natural wage rate may be resisted by workers (respective to firms) if it requires a large decrease (respective to increase) in the money wage rate.

Given the total number of potential workers, $\overline{N}$, let us normalize the unit of labor such that $\overline{N} = 1$. We may then rewrite Eq. (2.2) as

$$\omega = F'(1 - U), \tag{2.12}$$

where U is the rate of unemployment. In view of Eqs. (2.11) and (2.12),

$$\frac{\partial \phi}{\partial U} = \phi' F'' \leq 0$$

which means that the rate of change in the money wage rate defined by the dynamic equation, Eq. (2.11), is a nonincreasing function of the rate of unemployment. Therefore, Eq. (2.11) may be interpreted to represent the Phillips curve augmented by expectations (its wage rate version). The rate of unemployment, U^*, consistent with the natural wage rate, ω^*, is implicitly defined by

$$\omega^* = F^*\left(1 - U^*\right). \tag{2.13}$$

So long as the natural wage rate exceeds the reservation rate of labor, U^* stands for the share of those involuntarily unemployed in the total labor force. In general, it differs from the Friedmanian natural rate of unemployment.[9]

It should be noted here that the wage adjustment process just defined contains two important special cases. The one is the Keynesian case where there is no expectation of inflation $(\pi = 0)$ and the money wage rate becomes downwardly rigid for the real wage rates higher than the natural rate ($\phi = 0$ for $\omega \geq \omega^*$). In this case, the same rate of unemployment persists over time when $U \geq U^*$. The other is the rationalist case where firms and workers are shrewd enough to realize the natural wage rate instantaneously $\left(\omega = \omega^*\right)$.[10] The dynamic equation (Eq. 2.11) then becomes $\dot{w}/w = \pi = \mu$ and, for a given value of $\pi\left(= \mu\right)$, the Phillips curve degenerates to a point on the vertical line corresponding to U^*. In what follows, however, we shall consider the broad class of economies intermediate between these extreme cases.

2.3.2 *The Phillips Curve as the Dynamic Path of the Economy*

Suppose that the exogenous variables of long-run equilibrium such as natural wage rate, technology of production, government expenditure, and growth rate of money supply are given and invariable. As the money wage rate is adjusted, the short-run equilibrium of the economy changes in position over time. The dynamic behavior of the economy is affected by the way the public forms its expectation about the rate of inflation. To compare the dynamic paths of the economy under alternative hypothesis of price expectations, we simplify the model of the preceding section

---

[9] U^* may be said to coincide with the natural rate of unemployment only in the case where the natural wage rate happens to equal the reservation rate of labor.

[10] See, for instance, Sargent and Wallace (1975).

by assuming that the private sector expenditure is independent of the real rate of interest.[11]

1. Stationary Expectations

First, let us consider the case where the public always expects the price level to rise at the given growth rate of money supply. In this case, we have $\pi = \mu$, so that Eq. (2.11) is written as

$$\frac{\dot{w}}{w} = \phi\left(\omega^* - \omega\right) + \mu. \tag{2.14}$$

By the definition of $\omega\,(= W/p)$ and $R\,(= M/p)$,

$$\frac{\dot{\omega}}{\omega} = \frac{\dot{W}}{W} - \frac{\dot{p}}{p}, \frac{\dot{R}}{R} = \mu - \frac{\dot{p}}{p}$$

Thus, Eq. (2.14) is further transformed to

$$\frac{\dot{\omega}}{\omega} = \phi\left(\omega^* - \omega\right) + \frac{\dot{R}}{R}. \tag{2.15}$$

Differentiating Eqs. (2.1), (2.2), (2.3), and (2.4) totally, and assuming $D_r = 0$ and $dG = 0$, we obtain

$$\frac{\dot{R}}{R} = -\beta\frac{\dot{\omega}}{\omega}, \tag{2.16}$$

where

$$\beta = -\frac{(1 - D_Y)\omega F'}{D_R R F''} > 0.$$

Substituting Eq. (2.16) into Eq. (2.15) yields

$$\frac{\dot{\omega}}{\omega} = \frac{1}{1+\beta}\phi\left(\omega^* - \omega\right), \tag{2.17}$$

$$\frac{d\dot{\omega}}{d\omega} = -\frac{\omega}{1+\beta}\phi' < 0$$

where $\omega = \omega^*$.; this implies that the long-run equilibrium of the economy is globally stable. In view of Eq. (2.2), the rate of unemployment U is an increasing function of ω. Thus, we may conclude that if ω converges to ω^*, U converges to U^*.

[11] This assumption can be relaxed easily without significantly affecting our conclusions.

Making use of Eq. (2.16), we can express the actual rate of inflation as a weighted average of the growth rate of money supply and that of the money wage rate, or

$$\frac{\dot{p}}{p} = \frac{1}{1+\beta}\mu + \frac{\beta}{1+\beta}\frac{\dot{w}}{w}. \tag{2.18}$$

Substituting Eq. (2.14) into Eq. (2.18), we obtain

$$\frac{\dot{p}}{p} = \frac{\beta}{1+\beta}\phi(\omega^* - \omega) + \mu. \tag{2.19}$$

As already mentioned, ω is an increasing function of U so that Eq. (2.19) expresses the relationship between the rate of inflation and the rate of unemployment, or the Phillips curve (its price-level version) as the dynamic path of the economy. The schedule *aa* in Fig. 2.2 illustrates this relationship. Starting from any point on this curve, the rates of inflation and unemployment rate vary along the curve in the direction indicated by arrows and converge to their long-run equilibrium values, μ and U^*, as time tends to infinity.

2. Rational Expectations

Next, we turn to the case in which the public is perfectly informed of the structure of the economy and forms rational expectations about the rate of inflation. Set $\pi = \dot{p}/p$ in Eq. (2.11) to get

$$\frac{\dot{w}}{w} = \phi(\omega^* - \omega) + \frac{\dot{p}}{p}, \tag{2.20}$$

or

$$\frac{\dot{\omega}}{\omega} = \phi(\omega^* - \omega), \tag{2.21}$$

From this, it is clear that the long-run equilibrium is also globally stable in this case. Substituting Eq. (2.18) into Eq. (2.20) gives

$$\frac{\dot{p}}{p} = \beta\phi(\omega^* - \omega) + \mu, \tag{2.22}$$

which defines the Phillips curve relationship under the hypothesis of rational expectations. The schedule *bb* in Fig. 2.2 depicts this relationship graphically. Comparison of Eq. (2.19) and Eq. (2.22) reveals that given the rate of unemployment, the speed of price adjustment is greater when the public forms its expectations rationally than when it adheres to stationary expectations, reflecting the difference in the speed of wage adjustment under rational and stationary

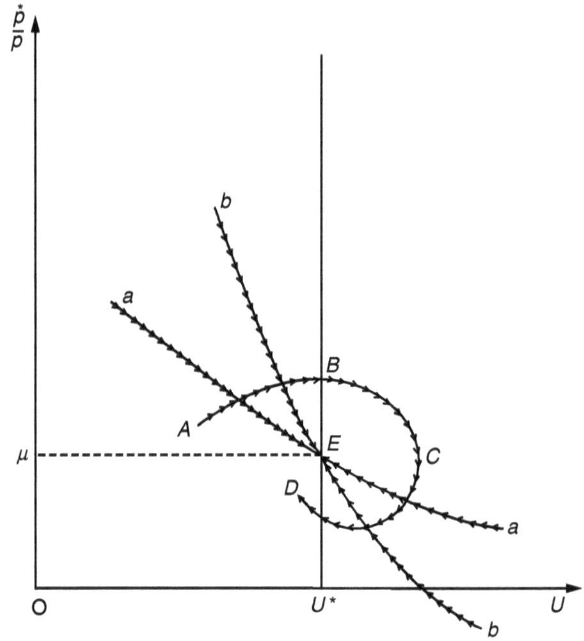

Fig. 2.2 Phillips curves under adaptive expectations

expectations. In fact, from Eq. (2.20) and Eq. (2.22), we may express the rate of money wage variation under rational expectations as

$$\frac{\dot{w}}{w} = (1+\beta)\phi\left(\omega^{*} - \omega\right) + \mu. \tag{2.23}$$

It should be clear that the money wage rate is adjusted more rapidly under rational expectations than under stationary expectations in response to a given difference between ω and ω^{*} (and therefore a given difference between U and U^{*}).

3. Adaptive Expectations

Finally, let us consider briefly the case where the public modifies its price expectation sluggishly in an adaptive manner. In addition to the wage adjustment equation, Eq. (2.11), we have to introduce a dynamic equation describing the adjustment of price expectations:

$$\dot{\pi} = \gamma\left(\frac{\dot{p}}{p} - \pi\right), \gamma > 0 \tag{2.24}$$

Making use of Eq. (2.19), we may rewrite Eqs. (2.11) and (2.24) as

$$\frac{\dot{\omega}}{\omega} = \frac{1}{1+\beta}\phi(\omega^* - \omega) + \pi - \mu, \tag{2.25}$$

$$\dot{\pi} = \gamma\left[\frac{\beta}{1+\beta}\phi(\omega^* - \omega) - \pi + \mu\right]. \tag{2.26}$$

Proposition 2.1: The Stability of Long-Run Equilibrium *The long-run equilibrium of the economy is locally stable and the real wage rate, together with the expected rate of inflation, oscillate around their equilibrium values, ω* and μ, under alternative hypotheses of expectations in the dynamic process of adjustment.*

By virtue of Eq. (2.18), the rate of inflation must satisfy the relationship

$$\frac{\dot{p}}{p} = \beta\frac{\dot{\omega}}{\omega} + \mu, \tag{2.27}$$

which suggests that the rate of inflation also oscillates around its equilibrium value μ. In Fig. 2.2, the dynamic behavior of the rates of inflation and unemployment is illustrated by the path $ABCD\cdots$, approaching the equilibrium point E while oscillating around it clockwise.

2.4 Stagnation, Stagflation, and Policy Implications

The macroeconomic model described here is designed as a simplest possible framework for the theoretical analysis of unemployment and inflation. It may be interpreted to embrace the Keynesian model of involuntary unemployment and the monetarist model of natural unemployment as its special cases. The Keynesian case may be characterized by the downward rigidity of the money wage rate, which allows involuntary unemployment to persist over time, and the monetarist case by the flexibility of the money wage rate in both directions, which works to wipe out involuntary unemployment, at least in the long run. In this section, concerning ourselves with the more "realistic" intermediate cases, we clarify how the present model is capable of explaining both stagnation and stagflation consistently and consider its implications for stabilization policies.

2.4.1 Stagnation

Let us define stagnation broadly as the phenomenon wherein the rate of unemployment rises above its conventional level while the rate of inflation falls below its conventional level. The present model may be used to demonstrate that stagnation arises from an unanticipated decline in the aggregate expenditure of the economy

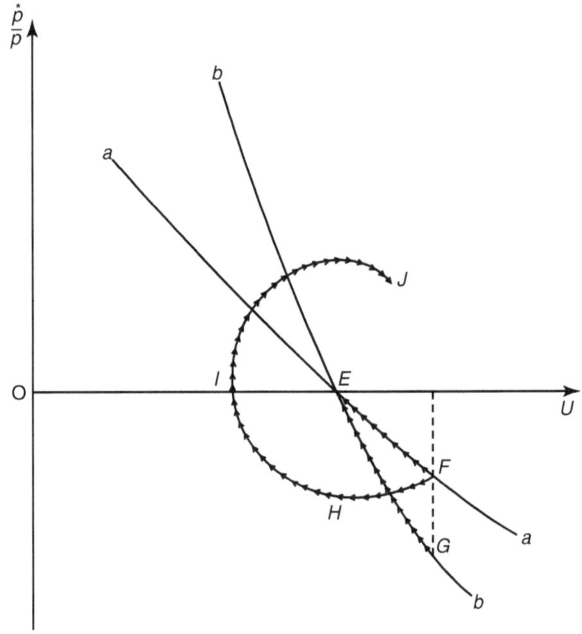

Fig. 2.3 Wage explosion and its aftereffect under alternative expectations

under all hypotheses of price expectations. For simplicity, suppose that the economy is initially in the long-run equilibrium indicated by the intersection *E* of the Phillips curves, *aa* and *bb*, with the horizontal axis in Fig. 2.3. (Note that the rate of inflation is initially zero.) A sudden decline in the propensity to consume, say, will shift the position of the economy from *E* to *F* on the Phillips curve *aa* under stationary or adaptive expectations and to *G* on the Phillips curve *bb* under rational expectations. Clearly, the impact effect of this change is to increase unemployment and lower the rate of inflation, bringing the economy down into stagnation regardless of the manner in which the public forms their price expectations.

This is, however, not the end of the story. Because the real wage rate rises above the natural wage rate in parallel with the increase in the rate of unemployment, the money wage rate begins to be adjusted downward. As time elapses, the position of the economy moves along the Phillips curve *aa* (respectively, *bb*) back to the original equilibrium *E* under stationary (rational) expectations. In the meantime, the unemployment rate falls and the inflation rate rises monotonically to their conventional levels. It should be noted here that this return to the initial position proceeds more rapidly under rational expectations than under stationary expectations. In contrast, the dynamic response of the economy is not monotonic and proceeds along an oscillatory path such as $FHIJ\cdots$ to converge to *E* under adaptive expectations. The economy suffers from stagnation in phase *FH* immediately after the disturbance but evolves out of it afterward.

Proposition 2.2: Stagnation *An unanticipated decline in the propensity to consume, or the propensity to invest, say, increases unemployment and lowers the rate of inflation, bringing the economy down into stagnation in the short run.*

As time elapses, however, the money wage rate begins to be adjusted downward, bringing the economy back to the original equilibrium. The adjustment path toward the original equilibrium differs depending on the mode of price expectations.

In any case, the economy is expected to recover automatically from the incipient stagnation. The speed of the recovery is, however, another question that cannot be neglected in practice. Because the recovery from stagnation is fueled by the continuous reduction of the real wage rate, realized presumably against the resistance of workers, it may take a long time for the adjustment process to become terminated. Thus, the policy authority may be justified to speed up the recovery by employing expansionary macroeconomic policies, fiscal or monetary, when it is clear that the economy is in the state of stagnation.

2.4.2 Stagflation

Stagflation may be defined broadly as the phenomenon wherein the rates of unemployment and inflation rise above their conventional levels simultaneously. Within the framework of the present model, we can show that stagflation is the outcome of a rise in the natural wage rate relative to labor productivity (a "wage explosion," so to speak) under all hypotheses of price expectations. Let us suppose as before that the economy is initially in the long-run equilibrium with stable prices, as indicated by point E in Fig. 2.4. An exogenous rise in the natural wage rate (or a fall in labor productivity) increases the difference between the natural wage rate and the marginal productivity of labor at a given rate of unemployment and shifts the Phillips curves accordingly. If the supply of money remains constant, the new long-run equilibrium after this disturbance may be illustrated by the intersection E' of the new Phillips curves, $a'a'$ and $b'b'$, with the horizontal axis. As a result of this change, the long-run equilibrium rate of unemployment is shown to increase from U^* to $U^{*\prime}$.

A rise in the natural wage rate does not affect the rate of unemployment in the short run but brings about an increase in the rate of inflation immediately. The position of the economy will jump from E to F under stationary and adaptive expectations, and further to G under rational expectations, in response to the upward adjustment of the money wage rate that is to take place immediately. As the real wage rate begins to rise, the rate of unemployment starts to increase as well. As time elapses, the position of the economy moves along the Phillips curve $a'a'$ (respectively, $b'b'$) under stationary (respectively, rational) expectations to converge to the new equilibrium E'. The economy may be said to suffer from stagflation, especially in the early stage of this process, because the rate of inflation remains high and the unemployment rate rises over time. Under adaptive expectations, the adjustment

Fig. 2.4 A wage hike and stagflation under alternative expectations

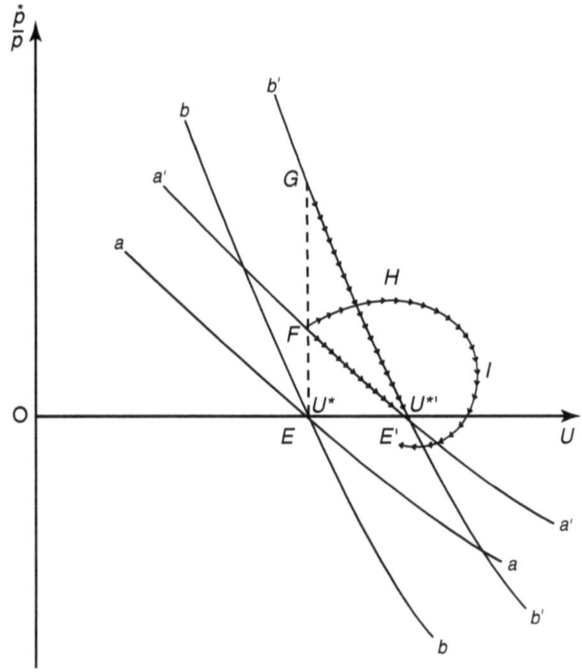

process becomes oscillatory, as illustrated by the path *FHIJ*. In this case, the emergence of stagflation is even more conspicuous because the unemployment rate and the inflation rate rise simultaneously in the beginning (i.e., in phase *GH*). In a similar fashion, it can be shown that a fall in labor productivity causes the economy to suffer from stagflation in the subsequent adjustment process.[12]

Proposition 2.3: Stagflation *A rise in the natural wage rate gives rise to upward adjustment of the money wage rate and an associated rise in the rate of inflation immediately. As the real wage rate begins to rise, the rate of unemployment starts to increase as well. The economy may be said to suffer from stagflation, especially in the early stage of this process.*

The consequent adjustment process of the economy depends on the mode of price expectations, as illustrated in Fig. 2.4.

The question may now be raised as to whether and how the policy authority should intervene when the economy is in the state of stagflation. Needless to say, the answer to this question depends on one's judgment about the desirability of the

[12] Some argue that stagflation results from an unanticipated increase (caused by an increase in the money supply, say) in the aggregate expenditure. See, for instance, Dornbusch and Fischer (1981, Chap. 13). This view of stagflation differs from ours in that it allows the rate of unemployment to be below its conventional level. Note also that it is valid only if the public forms its price expectations adaptively.

current wage rate and the associated rate of unemployment under the given state of technologies. If it is judged socially desirable, the authority may be justified to promote its realization by means of contractionary macroeconomic policies. As already noted, however, the natural wage rate is generally compatible with the existence of involuntary unemployment. Therefore, the long-run equilibrium under the current natural wage rate may not be socially desirable. Suppose that the economy is afflicted with stagflation and that the current rate of unemployment is already higher than the socially acceptable level. Then, what are the appropriate measures which the authorities should pursue to reduce the rate of unemployment?

In view of the present model, it would be impractical and even harmful to try to suppress unemployment below the level associated with the natural wage rate for a long time. If the central bank adheres to an expansionary monetary policy to maintain "full employment," it is bound to accelerate the rate of inflation. An increase in the growth rate of money decreases the rate of unemployment in the short run but does not affect it in the long run.[13] Similarly, if the government increases its expenditure for the same purpose, it has to continue increasing its share in the gross national product indefinitely. Obviously, these are not outcomes acceptable to any society. This conclusion is not to deny, however, the possibility of lowering the rate of unemployment associated with the natural wage rate. First, the government may be able to help improve labor productivity by tax cuts and subsidies designed to promote work efforts as well as investments in research and development. Second, the natural wage rate itself is by no means unchangeable. The government may be able to affect it through income policies in the broad sense of the word, ranging from revising the unemployment insurance system to setting guideposts for wage adjustment, or to interfering in wage bargaining, for example.[14]

References

Dornbusch, R., & Fischer, S. S. (1981). *Macroeconomics* (2nd ed.). New York: McGraw-Hill.

Friedman, M. (1968). The role of monetary policy. *American Economic Review, 58*, 1–17.

Friedman, M. (1977). Nobel lecture: Inflation and unemployment. *Journal of Political Economy, 85*, 451–472.

Lucas, R. E., Jr. (1973). Some international evidence on output–inflation tradeoffs. *American Economic Review, 63*, 141–163.

Modigliani, F., & Papademos, L. (1975). Targets for monetary policy in the coming year. *Brookings Papers on Economic Activity, 1*, 141–163.

Pigou, A. C. (1933). *The theory of unemployment.* London: Macmillan.

Ricardo, D. (1951) *The principles of political economy and taxation.* London, 1817, Sraffa edition. London: Cambridge University Press.

[13] As is well known, this point is emphasized by Friedman (1968).

[14] Tobin (1972) also recommends these policies, although "not with great confidence or optimism."

Sargent, T. J., & Wallace, N. (1975). Rational expectations, the optimal monetary instrument and the optimal money supply rule. *Journal of Political Economy, 4*, 103–124.
Solow, R. M. (1980). On theories on unemployment. *American Economic Review, 70*, 1–11.
Tobin, J. (1972). Inflation and unemployment. *American Economic Review, 62*, 1–18.

Chapter 3
A Macroeconomic Theory of Money, Income, and Distribution

3.1 Introduction

In fall 2008, the world economy plunged into a severe recession and the relevance of macroeconomics was questioned once again. Economists were wondering about the cause of the sharp drop in production and employment triggered by the fall of celebrated financial companies such as Lehman Brothers.

The best known economic model of deep depression was initiated by John Maynard Keynes in the 1930s. He repudiated the famous Say's law that supply creates demand and instead advocated the principle of effective demand, stating that the shortage of demand suppresses supply. See Keynes (1936). Demand and supply of goods are somehow equilibrated through the adjustment of income rather than the adjustment of prices. The labor market remains, however, out of equilibrium, at least in the short term. In contrast, the counter-Keynesian revolution began in the 1960s with the message that the price mechanism works effectively to clear the good *and* labor markets after all. Starting from Milton Friedman's "natural rate of unemployment" hypothesis, his radical followers advanced the "rational expectations revolution" in the 1970s, culminating in the "real business cycle theory" in the 1980s propagating the belief in market perfectionism. On the other hand, Neo-Keynesian revived the message of old Keynesian beliefs supporting the government intervention in market equilibrium models saddled with monopolies and externalities. The needs of macroeconomic policy were generally recognized after all, but the antagonism between the Keynesian disequilibrium theory and the anti-Keynesian equilibrium belief has remained deep and unresolved until now.

This chapter attempts to reconsider the Keynesian theory of multipliers in the framework of monetary economy. The most popular, but much criticized, analysis of monetary economy is provided by the *IS-LM* model of John Hicks in the wake of the Keynesian theory of deep depression. The severe recession in 2008 and afterward provided a last and foremost chance to reconsider not only the academic significance of the model but also its usefulness in university textbooks. In this

© Springer Japan 2016

M. Ohyama, *Macroeconomics, Trade, and Social Welfare*, Advances in Japanese Business and Economics 14, DOI 10.1007/978-4-431-55807-1_3

chapter, we challenge this task by reexamining its microeconomic foundation and applying the method of dynamic period analysis developed in Chap. 1 of this book.

3.2 The Structure of the Model

We consider a recurrent two-period model in which households, firms, and the government plan their activities in periods t and $t+1$ (or indefinitely after period t) and repeat them each period. Firms produce a homogeneous good using labor and real capital supplied by households, who receive wages, dividends, and interest from firms and use them for consumption, investment, and tax payment. The government expends tax revenue to purchase goods and services for public purposes. The purchase and sales of goods and services between these agents are performed in the form of monetary transactions.

The behavior of households is described by the representative consumer with the utility function

$$u_t = C_t^{\gamma} F_t^{1-\gamma}, 1 > \gamma > 0 \tag{3.1}$$

where C_t is its consumption in period t and F_t is the real purchasing power reserved for consumption in period $t+1$ and after. The consumer's rate of time preference is shown by $\gamma/1-\gamma$.

The government is supposed to abide by the balanced budget constraint on the assumption of Ricard-Barro's (1974) equivalence theorem. Denoting government expenditure, tax revenue, and transfer payments in period t by G_t, T_t, and F_t, respectively, its budget constraint is given by

$$T_t = G_t + F_t \tag{3.2}$$

In money terms, the government collects p_tT_t as tax receipts from households at the beginning of period t and pays its expenditures p_tG_t and transfer payments p_tF_t at the end of period t where p_t signifies the money price of goods and services in period t. The central bank can affect the money holdings of households through monetary policy. For simplicity, we assume that homogeneous, fixed-price bonds are used by all agents for investment purposes with a uniform interest serving as an adjustment factor to clear the bond market.

At the beginning of period t, firms pay wages, dividends, and interest to households from the proceeds in period $t-1$ [payment lag introduced by Dennis Robertson (1936), who originated the period analysis of monetary economies]. Nominal cash balance M_t, possessed by households at the beginning of period t, consists of *non-interest* nominal receipts from firms (wages and dividends), interest receipts from bond holding at the end of period $t-1$, and net increase in money supply, ΔM_t, newly created by the monetary policy of the government (here integrated with the central bank for simplicity) at the beginning of period t.

Denoting the household holding of bonds at the end of period s by $A_s (s = t - 1, t)$, we may write

$$L_t = p_{t-1} H_{t-1} + i_{t-1} A_{t-1} + \Delta M_t \tag{3.3}$$

where L_t denotes the household demand for cash balances, p_{t-1} stands for the price level, H_{t-1} is thc non-interest real receipt from firms, i_{t-1} is the nominal interest rate in period $t - 1$, and $i_{t-1} A_{t-1}$ is the interest received from firms at the beginning of period $t - 1$, respectively. In the case where money supply is increased by open market operations, the holding of bonds by households must be decreased by the same amount, so that

$$\Delta M_t + \Delta B_t = 0 \tag{3.4}$$

Denoting by B_t the household holding of bonds at the beginning of period t, we have

$$B_t = A_{t-1} + \Delta B_t \tag{3.5}$$

From Eqs. (3.3), (3.4), and (3.5), we obtain

$$M_t = p_{t-1} H_{t-1} + (1 + i_{t-1}) A_{t-1}{}^{t-1t-1} \tag{3.6}$$

where the value of financial assets, $L_t + B_t$, held by households in period $t - 1$, is equalized to the supply of money M_t in money market equilibrium. We assume here that the transaction of financial assets (Istock) is carried out much more speedily tha that of goods and sevices (flow). M_t is predetermined in period $t - 1$ and is unaffected by the open market operation.

$$M_t = p_{t-1} H_{t-1} + (1 + i_{t-1}) A_{t-1} + \Delta M_t$$

3.2.1 Household Behavior

In this section, we analyze the behavior of representative households on the basis of intertemporal utility maximization and derive its macroeconomic consequences (see Chap. 13 for the concept of representative agents and its welfare economic implications in general equilibrium models).

In period t, households receive money income from firms and the government and use the money for consumption C_t, to pay their tax T_t, and to prepare for future consumption F_t. Its budget constraint for period t is written as

$$p_t(C_t + T_t) + A_t - A_{t-1} = p_{t-1}H_{t-1} + i_{t-1}A_{t-1} + \Delta M_t + \Delta B_t \tag{3.7}$$

where ΔM_t is the additional injection of money that the government supplies newly to households and ΔB_t is the value of the bonds it buys from households at the beginning of period t. On the other hand, the real purchasing power R_t that households intend to set aside for period $t+1$ and after is defined as

$$F_t = H_t + J_{t+1} + \frac{A_t}{p_t}. \tag{3.8}$$

where H_t is the real basic income (wage and dividend) contracted in period t to be paid in period $t+1$ and J_{t+1} is the expected real value of the basic income in period $t+1$ and after (assumed to be a finite value).

Eliminating A_t from Eq. (3.7) and using Eq. (3.6), we obtain

$$C_t + \frac{1}{1+i_t}F_t = \frac{M_t}{p_t} - T_t + \frac{1}{1+i_t}(H_t + J_{t+1}) \tag{3.9}$$

where i_t is the nominal rate of interest in period t. As already noted, households determine C_t and F_t so as to maximize utility function (Eq. (3.2)). The first-order conditions for utility maximization solve for the optimal solutions:

$$C_t = \gamma\left[\frac{M_t}{p_t} - T_t + \frac{1}{1+i_t}(H_t + J_{t+1})\right] \tag{3.10}$$

$$F_t = (1-\gamma)\left[(1+i_t)\left(\frac{M_t}{p_t} - T_t\right) + H_t + J_{t+1}\right] \tag{3.11}$$

In line with Chap. 1 of this book, we assume the effective demand of the economy is insufficient to ensure full employment even when the nominal interest rate declines to zero or is on the verge of the "liquidity trap" envisioned by Hicks (1937).[1] The real value of demand for bonds, $\frac{A_t{}^t}{p_t}$, may be taken as "capital" that households wish to hold in period t. It may be interpreted as their right to a claim to the real capital that firms have accumulated with the funds they have borrowed from households. From Eqs. (3.8) and (3.11), it can be calculated that

[1] Ohyama (2004, 2007) developed an alternative version of the $IS - LM$ model with a microeconomic foundation to characterize the "liquidity trap" as its special case.

$$\frac{A_t}{p_t} = (1-\gamma)(1+i_t)\left(\frac{M_t}{p_t} - T_t\right) - \gamma(H_t + J_{t+1}) \tag{3.12}$$

If the amount households wish to set aside from their current income exceeds the future expenditures they plan to make, they are in the position to hold a positive amount of "capital."

To simplify matters, let as posit that i_t is set equal to zero in the long-run stationary state of the economy with given technology and factor endowment. Equations (3.10), (3.11), and (3.12) are then modified to

$$C_t = \gamma\left[\frac{M_t}{p_t} - T_t + (H_t + J_{t+1})\right] \tag{3.10$'$}$$

$$F_t = (1-\gamma)\left(\frac{M_{t\,t}}{p_t}{}^{t} - T_t + H_t + J_{t+1}\right) \tag{3.11$'$}$$

$$\frac{A_t}{p_t} = (1-\gamma)\left(\frac{M_t}{p_t} - T_t\right) - \gamma(H_t + J_{t+1}) \tag{3.12$'$}$$

respectively. To apply these relationships to the analysis of market equilibrium in the next section, it is convenient to express consumption and real capital, etc., as functions of national income, Y_t, rather than the pedantic concept of real basic income, H_t. National income in period t happens to be equivalent to basic income in the same period if i_t is set equal to zero, or $Y_t = H_t + \frac{M_t}{p_t}$. Substituting this into Eqs. (3.10′), (3.11′), and (3.12′), we obtain

$$C_t = \gamma(Y_t - T_t + J_{t+1}) \tag{3.13}$$

$$F_t = (1-\gamma)(Y_t - T_t + J_{t+1}) \tag{3.15$'$}$$

$$\frac{A_t}{p_t} = \frac{M_t}{p_t} - \gamma(Y_t - T_t + J_{t+1}) \tag{3.16$'$}$$

3.2.2 Consumption Function

Consumption in period t and in period $t+1$ and after are linear functions of current disposable income and current value of disposable income anticipated for all future periods, as is shown by Eqs. (3.14) and (3.15). For instance, a tax increase will generally depress consumption in all periods. If the rate of time preference is positive and smaller than 1, the marginal propensity to consume becomes also positive and smaller than 1. Keynes attached importance to this property of consumption function as the stability condition of Keynesian equilibrium, naming it the "fundamental psychological law." Consumption is positively affected by a fall in the nominal and real rates of interest through "intertemporal substitution effects." If the nominal rate of interest is greater than zero, it can be used to control effective demand given the real interest rate, as explained in the standard textbook of macroeconomics.

3.2.3 Capital Function

In the present model, firms obtain money capital by borrowing from households. The household demand for bonds becomes positive if and only if the current balance of their financial assets exceed the amount of money they want to use for future consumption, as is shown by Eq. (3.16). It is the condition indispensable to the maintenance of the capitalist regime as households must keep holding "capital" as the right of claim to the productive equipment of firms. The holding of capital increases in the current real financial asset but decreases in response to an increase in disposable income anticipated in future decreases. It is also positively affected by an increase in nominal interest rate and negatively affected by an increase in the expected rate of inflation and an increase in future income uncertainty.

3.3 *IS* – *LM* Equilibrium

In this section, we formulate a macroeconomic equilibrium covering markets for products and money. As for markets for products, we follow the basic lines adopted in Chap. 1. For simplicity, however, we minimize the role of public goods here, simply disregarding their intrinsic usefulness. We assume the Keynesian equilibrium condition given by

$$C_t + I_t + G_t = {}^t Y_t \tag{3.14}$$

where

$$C_t = \gamma(Y_t - T_t + J_{t+1})$$

is the consumption function introduced in Eq. (3.14) above and I_t is autonomous private investment and G_t is government expenditure. Equation (3.14) stipulates the "Keynesian law," that demand for national products gives rise to its own supply under unemployment through adjustment of national income in the market. It is equivalent to the balance of saving and investment, so that it is usually referred to as "*IS*" equilibrium. In Keynes' words, the demand for national products that matches "*IS*" equilibrium is "effective demand."

Up to this point, demand for money is motivated solely by the transactions motive with liquidity preference assumed as out of the picture. Money is prepared at the beginning of period t for the purchases of consumption, investment, and government expenditure in the same period. It is now necessary to take into explicit account the Keynesian speculative motive of holding money, which depends negatively on nominal interest rate i_t and is signified by $L_t(i_t)$. The equilibrium condition for money is written as

$$L_1(C_t + I_t + G_t) + L_2(i_t) = \frac{M_t}{p_t}, L_t^{'}(i_t) < 0 \tag{3.15}$$

Equation (3.15) is usually referred to as "*LM*" equilibrium. Substituting Eq. (3.14) into Eq. (3.15), we obtain

$$\frac{M_t}{p_t} = L_1(Y_t) + L_2(i_t) \tag{3.16}$$

Equations (3.14) and (3.16) constitute the *IS* − *LM* equilibrium system of the present economy. Although often criticized for lack of micro-foundation, the present formulation of the *IS* − *LM* model is based on the optimizing behavior of households and takes account of the explicit time structure of monetary transactions. The exogenous variables of this system are γ, p_t, I_t, G_t, and J_{t+1}. There are four candidates for endogenous variables: i_t, p_t, Y_t, M_t. In the classical system, full employment is attained through flexible adjustment of wages in the labor market and national income is induced to reach full employment level, Y_{Ft}. On this assumption, p_t and i_t are determined in money and commodity markets in their equilibrium. In the typical Keynesian system, however, the labor market stays out of equilibrium because of money wage rigidity, and national income is employed as a workhorse to equilibrate the commodity market. Following common and well-understood explanations adopted in macroeconomic textbooks, we assume here that money supply is determined by the central bank, and interest rate i_t is determined to clear the money market.[2] Together with this convention for short- or intermediate-term analysis, we also consider a unique scheme of long-run stationary state as envisaged in Chap. 1, the advent of which the government anticipates with perfect foresight and sets the nominal interest rate to zero consistently with resource endowment, technology, and real and financial capital being given and fixed in period t and after.

---

[2] In recent years, an alternative interpretation has become popular regarding interest rate as a short-term target of the central bank and money supply as the endogenous variable in the money market. For instance, see Romer (2000) and Woodford (2003).

3.3.1 *IS* – *LM* Analysis and the Law of Change

Let us consider *IS* – *LM* equilibrium under the condition of unemployment. As in Chap. 1, the government is assumed to use proportion α of tax revenue T_t for its expenditure and proportion $1 - \alpha$ for transfer payment. Rewriting Eq. (3.14) in view of these assumptions and combining with Eq. (3.16), we obtain

$$Y_t = \alpha T_t + \left(1 - \frac{\gamma}{1 + (1 - \gamma)i_t}\right)\left(I_t + J_{t+1} + \frac{M_t}{p_t}\right), \tag{3.17}$$

and

$$\frac{M_t}{p_t} = Y_t + L_t(i_t) \tag{3.18}$$

The system of equations explains national income Y_t and nominal rate i_t, given T_t, and $\frac{M_t}{p_t}$. Figure 3.1 shows this Keynesian equilibrium using *IS* – *LM* analysis. Measuring interest rate on the vertical axis and national income on the horizontal axis, respectively, the graph of *IS* depicts the locus of (i_t, Y_t) that satisfies Eq. (3.20), a downward sloping curve, whereas the graph of *LM* depicts the locus of (i_t, Y_t) that satisfies Eq. (3.19), also a downward sloping curve. The intersection E_t shows the *IS* – *LM* equilibrium.[3] We can apply the method of comparative statics or dynamics to the *IS* – *LM* equilibrium as just defined to elucidate the effects of macroeconomic policy and other structural changes. This exercise, named "law of changes" by Hicks (1937), includes the effects not only on the short-run equilibrium in period t but also those on the intermediate or long-run equilibrium in period $t + 1$ and after. For instance, investment in period t may increase the capital stock in period $t + 1$ and after and improve labor productivity in the long run. Let us take up here just a simple exercise using this equilibrium to see the effects of monetary expansion. An increase in money supply M_t gives rise to a rightward shift of the *LM* curve to $L'M'$ and a corresponding movement of equilibrium from E_t to E_t'. The equilibrium interest rate falls from i_{tE} to i_{tE}' and income increases from Y_{tE} to Y_{tE}': this is only a partial equilibrium analysis in that disequilibrium or unemployment is left unexplained. From here, we must proceed to a general equilibrium analysis beyond the well-known *IS* – *LM* equilibrium exercises.

[3] Tobin (1958) rationalized this Keynesian concept of speculative demand for money on the basis of optimizing behavior under risk, which we legitimately smuggle into the present riskless model.

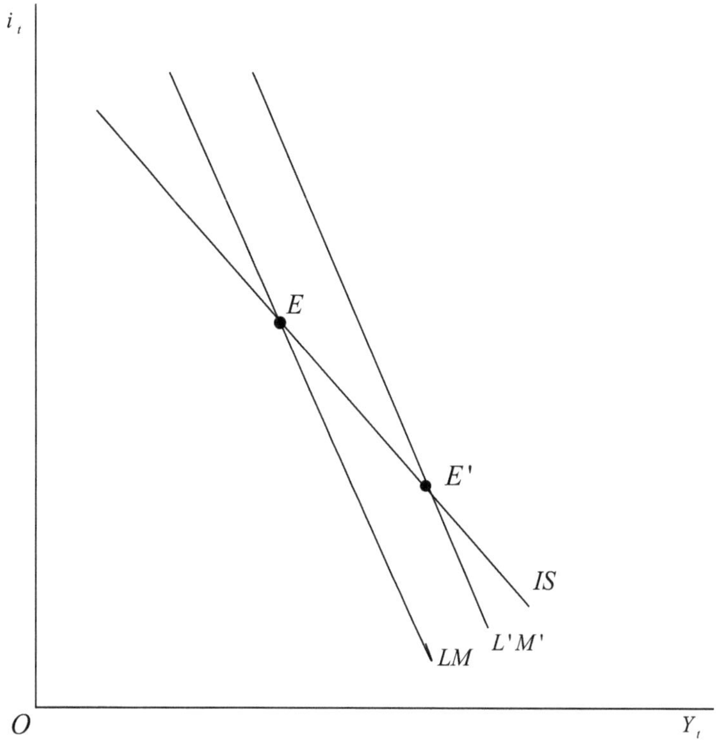

Fig. 3.1 IS-LM equilibrium

3.4 Comparative Analysis of Macroeconomic Policies

With the results of the $IS - LM$ analysis in mind, we now consider a more general model covering the markets for national product, labor service, and money on the road paved in Chap. 1 in a simplified model without public goods: 1 unit of good 2 is produced using a units of good 1. The total number of employed workers N is written as

$$N = X_1 + aX_2 \tag{3.19}$$

where X_1 denotes the output of good 1 (we may interpret it as labor service) and X_2, that of good 2. Figure 3.1 shows the equilibrium of the economy where the government undertakes to purchase good 1 by way of fiscal policy and to adjust money supply to ease unemployment. The vertical axis measures the government expenditure G and the horizontal axis the private purchase of good 2. The equilibrium employment N_E contains unemployed workers when

$$N_E = G + aX_{2_E} < \overline{N} \tag{3.20}$$

The curve Tt depicts a straight-line production frontier between G and X on the simplifying assumption that labor coefficient a is given and fixed. The curves $S's$ are the social indifference curves between G and X_2 on the assumption that the marginal utility of good 1 (labor service) decreases given the consumption of good 2.

The curve S_U is the social indifference curve where the government expenditure on good 1 is given at G_A and the consumption of good 2, Z_A, is correspondingly determined on S_U. As already shown, an increase in money supply increases national income from Z_A to Z_E*. To determine its welfare effects, however, we need to introduce the social welfare function (the graphical representation of which is the social indifference curve) as

$$W = u(G, X), u_G, u_X > 0 \tag{3.21}$$

where u_G and u_{X_2} signify the marginal social utility of employment and public goods, respectively. Thus, an increase in money supply increases social welfare by shifting the equilibrium point along the expansion path E_AE_BF*.

Proposition 3.1: Conventional Monetary Policy *Under unemployment, an expansion of money supply increases employment and national income (concomitantly with the output of good 2).*

Under the condition of unemployment when prices p_t are given and p_{t+1} are statically expected, monetary expansion is a standard short- and intermediate-run policy instrument to ease unemployment. It is generally supposed to be quicker and more flexible than fiscal policy as a means of macroeconomic stabilization.[4] The government may fail to achieve full employment, however, even if it sets the nominal interest rate equal to zero, when the effective demand is extremely weak. What can the government do under such circumstances?

It is able to invoke as the next step the so-called inflation targeting recently advocated by Krugman (1998) as a policy to increase the expected rate of inflation with a view to lowering the real interest rate. The real interest rate r_t in period t is defined by the Fisher (1977) equation:

$$1 + r_t = \frac{1 + i_t}{1 + \mu} \tag{3.22}$$

where μ_t is the expected rate of inflation such that

[4] Cf. Adachi et al. (2015) for an alternative concept of intermediate-run macroeconomics.[1]

$$\mu = \frac{p_{t+\tau}{}^{e} - p_{t+\tau}}{p_{t+\tau}}, (\tau = 0, 1, 2, \ldots).$$

Using Eq. (3.24), we can compute

$$J_{t+1} = \frac{1-\mu}{\mu + r_t}\left(\frac{1}{1+i_t}H_t - T_t\right).$$

Thus, $J_{t+1}{}^{t+1t+1}$ is considered to be an increasing function of the expected disposable income in period t (or an increasing function of the expected rate of inflation given a nominal interest rate).

Proposition 3.2: Inflation Targeting *Suppose that the government anticipates with perfect foresight and sets the nominal interest rate to zero to maximize employment consistently with resource endowment and technology, real and financial capital being given and fixed in period t and after. If it also adopts the inflation targeting policy manipulating the expected rate of inflation appropriately, it may be able to achieve full employment.*

Figure 3.2 depicts an expansion path reaching the long-run stationary state starting from an initial situation with unemployment, made possible by inflation targeting policy together with traditional monetary policy. The traditional monetary policy increasing money supply to lower the nominal interest rate may end up in an intermediate point on $\overrightarrow{E_A E_B}$ short of full employment, even with a zero interest rate. In such a case, the switch to the inflation targeting policy capable of achieving the full employment equilibrium E_B is appropriate.

The full employment equilibrium E_B may not be optimal, as illustrated in Fig. 3.2. The optimal point $F*$ is located at northwest of E_B with a greater amount of government expenditure on employment. This observation implies the need for expenditure policy in addition to monetary policy. In view of the social welfare function, the optimal solution implies the maximization of consumption in the stationary state, that is, the golden rule of economic growth in the steady state with zero rate of growth, $r_t = g$. In light of the Fisher (1977) equation (3.23) with a zero nominal interest rate, it can be approximated to

$$\mu = -r_t + g \tag{3.23}$$

In words, the rate of inflation must be set equal to the growth rate of the economy minus the real interest rate.

Proposition 3.3: Golden Rule Rate of Inflation *Suppose that the government switches to the inflation targeting policy from the traditional regime of monetary policy with nominal interest rate set equal to zero to maximize employment. To achieve the optimal allocation of resources with full employment, it must adopt the "golden rule" rate of inflation, that is, $\mu = -r_t + g$, in anticipation of a long-run steady state with a given growth rate g of the economy.*

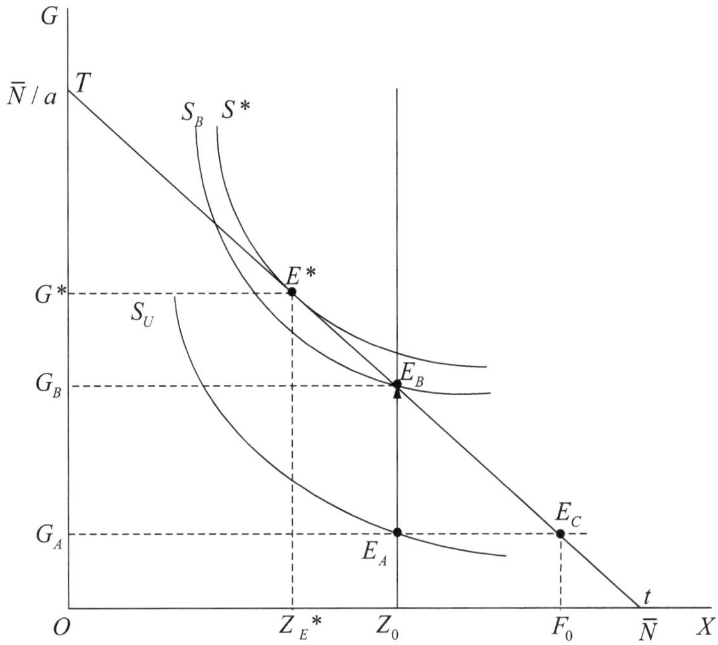

Fig. 3.2 Expansion path of the mixed economy equilibrium supply of the public good to be increased beyond the point of full employment

This rule reduces to $\mu = -r_t$ if the government anticipates the stationary state with $g = 0$, as we have so far assumed. This structure implies that the concomitant rate of targeting can be determined independent of growth rate. If g increases for any reason, the government can increase μ by increasing r_t and i_t conformably. This change dampens the effect of targeting on aggregate demand, postponing the advent of secular stagnation. There is no guarantee, however, that inflation targeting with the golden rule realizes the optimal solution in itself. As argued in Chap. 1, government expenditure and wage policies may be necessary to implement the optimal solution along the path E_BF^*. Moreover, an expenditure policy with useful public goods should introduced to achieve innovations, shifting the production frontier outward to better the situation.

3.5 Concluding Remarks

We introduced the money and monetary policy model of the depressed economy with serious unemployment such as the Great Depression in the 1930s and the financial panic triggered by the Lehman crisis in 2008. We already considered the real economy version of the model in Chap. 1, in which we focused on the role of government expenditure on useful public goods. In this chapter, we extended the

$IS - LM$ model of Hicks (1937) to highlight the relevance of the liquidity trap and secular stagnation of the economy, searching for the monetary steps to cope with the situation.

1. We considered a two-period model wherein households, firms, and the

government plan their activities in the periods t and $t+1$, repeating them each period afterward. The purchase and sales of goods and services between these agents are performed in the form of monetary transactions. At the beginning of period t, firms pay wages, dividends, and interest to households from the proceeds in period $t-1$. The nominal cash balance M_t possessed by households at the beginning of period t is equalized to their demand L_t for cash balances, bringing about the LM equilibrium. On the other hand, we obtain IS equilibrium as the balance of real aggregate demand for and supply of goods and services. Given p_t, we can show that the $IS - LM$ equilibrium determine the nominal rate of interest i_t and real national income Y_t.

2. Under unemployment, monetary expansion increases employment

and national income; this is the well-known conclusion of conventional monetary policy (Proposition 3.1). The government may fail to achieve full employment, however, even when it sets the nominal interest rate equal to zero, if the aggregate demand is extremely weak. In such a case, the government is advised to switch to inflation targeting as a next step. As advocated strongly by Krugman (1998), it is a new monetary policy designed to increase the expected rate of inflation with a view to lowering the real rate of interest (Proposition 3.2). It may not be powerful enough, however, to achieve full employment, implying the need for an expenditure policy in addition to the monetary policy.

3. Even if inflation targeting succeeds in achieving full employment, it may

not be optimal in that it fails to maximize per capita consumption in the steady state. The golden rule of economic growth, so named by Phelps (1961) as the condition for optimal steady state, is approximated here to $\rho_t = -r_t + g$, meaning that the rate of inflation be set equal to the growth rate of the economy minus the real interest rate (Proposition 3.3). The golden rule inflation targeting can be maintained at a given value $\widetilde{\mu}$ irrespective of the economy growth rate if r_t is adjusted to keep $r_t = g + \widetilde{\mu}$. In other words, an increase in g can be accommodated by the corresponding increase in r_t. It dampens the effect of monetary policy, postponing the advent of secular stagnation. The employment of expenditure policy may be needed to complement monetary policy to increase the potential growth rate of the economy.

References

Adachi, H., Nakamura, T., & Osumi, Y. (Eds.). (2015). *Studies in medium-run macroeconomics: growth, fluctuations, unemployment, inequality and policies*. London: World Scientific Publishing.

Barro, R. L. (1974). Are government bonds net wealth? *The Journal of Political Economy, 82*(6), 1095–1117.

Fisher I (1977) [1930] *The theory of interest*. Philadelphia: Porcupine Press

Hicks, J. R. (1937). Mr. Keynes and classics: A suggested interpretation. *Econometrica, 5*(2), 147–159.

Keynes, J. M. (1936). *The general theory of employment interest and money*. London: Macmillan.

Krugman, P. (1998). It's baaack! Japan's slump and the return of the liquidity trap. *Brookings Papers on Economic Activity, 2*, 137–187.

Ohyama, M. (1987). Unemployment and inflation: Natural wage rate hypothesis. *Keio Economic Studies, 24*, 11–26.

Ohyama, M. (2004). Effective demand and national income. *Keio Economic Studies, 41*(2), 1–23.

Ohyama, M. (2007). Effective demand and national income: A microeconomics of the IS-LM analysis and its application to the stagnation of the Japanese economy. *Keio Economic Studies, 41*, 1–24.

Phelps, E. S. (1961). The golden rule of accumulation: A fable for growthmen. *The American Economic Review, 51*, 638–643.

Romer, D. (2000). Keynesian macroeconomics without the LM curve. *Journal of Economic Perspective, 14*, 149–169.

Tobin, J. (1958). Liquidity preference as behavior towards risk. *The Review of Economic Studies, 25*(1), 65–86.

Part II
Welfare and Trade

Chapter 4
Trade and Welfare in General Equilibrium

4.1 Introduction

In his 1939 article, Samuelson initiated the modern discussion of the gains from trade. Concerning himself with a small price-taking country and basing his cases on the compensation principle and the axiom of revealed preference, he established that the introduction of external trade could make all citizens better off. His approach received a considerable amount of notice, but no further result came of it for some time. It was not until two decades later that Kemp (1962), along with Samuelson (1962), revived the subject by showing, under a more general condition, that the consumption possibility frontier of the post-trade situation lies uniformly outside that of the pre-trade situation.[1] Their findings, however, seem to call for further generalization.

Meanwhile, trade theorists have propagated the use of the "social indifference" map with the same properties as those of the "individual indifference" map. To substitute for the old tool of numerical example, Leontief (1933) provided a classic employment of this technique in his analysis of trade equilibrium. Scitovsky (1942) and Meade (1952), through their efforts to demonstrate the welfare implications of trade policies, made further contributions to the methodology, and thus stimulated a surge of similar analysis. In the face of this development, Samuelson (1956) reexamined the conditions required to justify the fundamental concept of social indifference. Today, many analysts are more critical than ever of this concept, but its use is still prevalent in the literature on trade and welfare.

This chapter is adapted from "Trade and Welfare in General Equilibrium," *Keio Economic Studies*, Vol. 9, No.2, 37–73, 1972

[1] Kemp is concerned with the welfare properties of tariff-restricted trade equilibria (including as a limiting case free trade equilibria), providing a proof of the proposition for a general n-commodity case. In a separate companion paper, Samuelson illustrates the same point by the help of the famous "Baldwin" envelope (see Baldwin 1952) for a special two-commodity case.

© Springer Japan 2016
M. Ohyama, *Macroeconomics, Trade, and Social Welfare*, Advances in Japanese Business and Economics 14, DOI 10.1007/978-4-431-55807-1_4

Most of the theorists, while employing a social indifference map, assumed no allegiance to any *particular* map as a matter of course, and thus were, in reality, puristic in their conclusions. The more policy-oriented economists, notably Meade (1955a, b), often eschewed this nonchalant approach by invoking a specific social utility function. Needless to say, the latter restrictive convention, although objectionable in many respects, makes it possible to evaluate the welfare of all situations without glossing over the underlying social value premises. For instance, per capita real income as a measure of national welfare may be justified on the basis of a very special class of social utility functions.[2]

This chapter is devoted to the study of trade and welfare in general equilibrium in which trade in intermediate goods and factor services, as well as the presence of non-tradeable commodities, is not excluded.[3] For this purpose, we propose to employ a methodological device that captures the results of different approaches in one procedure. In the following section the stage will be set for our analysis by considering a static competitive economy from a single country's point of view. We shall define the basic concepts of this chapter, such as an economic situation, distribution, and competitive equilibrium. In Sect. 4.3 will be the introduction of a welfare criterion, which, with an appropriate reinterpretation, will imply each of the aforementioned prototypes. In Sect. 4.4, a general theorem of welfare comparison is presented in the form of a simple formula derived from the definition of the country's excess demand, the aggregate budget constraint, and the welfare criterion. We shall then make extensive use of this theorem to analyze a number of important issues in trade and welfare. Toward the end of the chapter, we also show that our single country's point of view is applicable to a group of countries and the world as a whole under appropriate assumptions. Thus, this approach will enable us to generalize familiar theses, and, at the same time, simplify their derivations. It should be noted that, at several points, we put forward somewhat novel propositions.

[2] We refer here to the crude usage of this measure disregarding the problem of income distribution. We shall have occasion to discuss it again in Footnote 14.

[3] Most of the existing literature in this field still remains within the confines of the views of "trade-as-exchange-of consumer goods." In a famous survey of trade literature Bhagwati (1964, p. 42) warns that a vast range of interesting problems applicable to economies using intermediate and produced goods cannot get within the range of analysis until the theorists get away from the traditional picture of primary factors and integrated process of production. As he carefully notes, however, it does not follow that the present stock of knowledge will not survive the required change in the formulation of the models. On the contrary, we should make it clear in advance that our investigation will confirm all the traditional welfare propositions in the presence of trade in non-consumer commodities.

4.2 A Trading Economy: The Model

Let us assume that there are n commodities in the world, some of which are primary factors and intermediate goods. Imagine the competitive economy of a single country engaging in trade with the rest of the world. There are three distinct classes of economic agents, namely, producers, consumers, and the government. A producer is supposed to carry out a production plan that is a specification of the quantities of his inputs and outputs. Formally, let Y^j be the production set of the jth producer, which is closed in the n-dimensional commodity space and contains the origin. We assume that it is possible for all producers together to dispose of all commodities. A consumer is supposed to carry out a consumption plan that is a specification of his consumption of commodities. A consumption plan is made subject to the constraint of the consumer's income, composed of the value of his endowment of commodities, his share in producers' profits, and his net transfer receipt. Let X^k be the kth consumer's consumption set, which is closed, convex, and bounded below in the nonnegative orthant of the n-dimensional commodity space. The set X^k is assumed to be completely pre-ordered by the kth consumer's preference relationship (denoted by $\succ^k$). No consumer is satiated in all commodities. We abstract from transportation costs and static external economies and diseconomies.

The role of the government, the third class of our economic agent, is manifold. First, it is assumed to tax and/or subsidize various economic activities, that is, production, consumption, and external trade. Second, it distributes income among consumers in a lump-sum fashion by changing the structure of individual shares in all income sources. For this purpose, the government is able to impose personal tax subsidy schemes on incomes derived from the ownership of commodity endowment, the share in profits, and the net *private* transfer receipt. The government's net revenue (or cost) from all the taxes and subsidies is assumed to be disposed of by lump-sum transfers to consumers to help achieve the purpose of income redistribution.[4] Third, the government carries out the production and consumption of commodities on its own. In this capacity, it is assumed to belong to the first two classes of economic agents, the producers and consumers. Together with the absence of externalities, this simplifies the problem of public production and consumption. We discuss this point briefly at the end of the chapter.[5]

Let us now turn our eyes to the aggregate picture of our trading economy. We use the following basic notation:

[4] The government's lump-sum taxes and subsidies are exempt from the distortion of price system because they effectuate nothing but the direct redistribution of income sources such as commodity endowment, profits, and transfer receipt among individual consumers.

[5] For an alternative treatment of public production and consumption, see Diamond and Mirrlees (1971a, b).

x	A nonnegative n vector of aggregate consumption.
y	An n vector of aggregate production; a positive (respectively negative) component denotes output (respectively input).
a	A nonnegative n vector of aggregate endowment exogenously available to the country.
$e = x - y - a$	An n vector of aggregate excess demand.
q	A nonnegative n vector of world price.
p	A nonnegative n vector of domestic price.
p_c	A nonnegative n vector of domestic consumer price.
p_r	A nonnegative n vector of domestic producer price.[6]
b	A scalar denoting net aggregate transfer from abroad to consumers.
	$Y = \sum_j Y^j$, the set of all possible y.
T	An $n \times n$ diagonal matrix of ad valorem rates of tariffs (i.e., taxes or subsidies on imports and exports).
C	An $n \times n$ diagonal matrix of ad valorem rates of taxes or subsidies on consumption.
R	An $n \times n$ diagonal matrix of ad valorem rates of taxes or subsidies on production.

The model allows for the existence of non-tradeable commodities resulting from international difference of tastes. If commodity i happens to be non-tradeable, then the ith component of vector e is identically zero. Similarly, if commodity i is *not* consumed at home, the ith component of x is identically zero, and if commodity i is not produced at home, the ith component of y is nonpositive. Note also that we take into account the consumers' use of primary factors, especially in the form of leisure.[7]

It is important to understand the relationships between the four different price vectors q, p, p_c, and p_r pertaining to the economy under trade with the rest of the world. Needless to say, this difference arises in the presence of governmental intervention in private transactions via taxes and subsidies.[8] Let us denote by t_i the ith diagonal element of tariff matrix T, and by q_i and p_i the ith components of q and p, respectively. We have then the arbitrage relationship:

$$p_i = q_i(1 + t_i)$$

[6] We will consider x, y, a, and e as column vectors, and p and q as row vectors in what follows.

[7] Thus, this model includes as a special case the classical setup in which primary factors, especially labor, are not tradeable.

[8] We assume that the unit of domestic currency is adjusted such that the exchange rate is always unity.

If t_i is positive, it represents an import tax or an export subsidy, depending on whether the commodity i is imported or exported. If $t_i$is negative, it represents an export tax or an import subsidy. We can rewrite this relationship in matrix form as

$$p = q(I + T) \tag{4.1}$$

where I is an identity matrix. Similarly, we have

$$p_c = p(I + C) \tag{4.2}$$

$$p_r = p(I + R) \tag{4.3}$$

which implicitly define the ith diagonal element c_i of matrix C and ith diagonal element of matrix R, respectively. If c_i is positive (respectively negative), it indicates an tax (respectively a subsidy) on the consumption of commodity i. On the other hand, if i is positive (respectively negative), it represents a subsidy (respectively tax) on the production, or a tax (respectively subsidy) on the use in production, of commodity i, depending on whether commodity i is an output or an input in the aggregate production process.

To delineate the posture of the economy completely, it is also necessary to take account of the external conditions with which the economy is faced. The net aggregate income transfer b stands for the country's net receipt of purchasing power from abroad available in the form of reparation, aid, personal remittance, and the like. In addition to this, we need to introduce here the concept of the "foreign environment" as a catchall terminology representing the state of technologies, tastes, commodity endowments, and governmental policies in the rest of the world. In a limiting case in which the country is too small to affect the world market significantly, the foreign environment can be approximated by the prevailing world price of *tradeable* commodities. We refer to this special case as the state of a price-taking country without any monopoly power in world trade. In another limiting case in which the country keeps to itself in autarky, the specification of the foreign environment is still possible, but evidently irrelevant.

Definition (economic situation). An economic situation (or simply situation) S is a specification of the following.

1. The set of producers: Y^J for all j;
2. The set of consumers: $\left(X^k, \succ^k\right)$ for all k;
3. The government's taxes and subsidies: (T, C, R);
4. The aggregate endowment and net income transfer: (a, b);
5. The foreign environment.

Definition: distribution. A distribution V is a specification of the percentage share of individual consumers in all income sources.[9]

[9] Thus, if prices are given, a distribution V is a specification of the percentage share of individual consumers in the aggregate expenditure, and it can be represented by an interior point of the standard simplex.

Given an economic situation S and a distribution V, we assume the existence of a (usual) competitive equilibrium such that, under the prevailing prices, (a) each producer maximizes his profits over his production set; (b) each consumer maximizes his satisfaction over his budget set; and (c) all markets are cleared.[10] To write out these conditions of an equilibrium, let a bar on top of a vector indicate its equilibrium value. First, we write the equilibrium condition for producers as

$$\overline{p}_r\overline{y}^j \geq \overline{p}_r y^j \quad \text{for all} \quad y^j \in Y^j$$

where y^j is the jth producer's production vector; this implies the aggregate profit maximization condition

$$\overline{p}_r\overline{y} \geq \overline{p}_r y \quad \text{for all} \quad y \in Y \tag{4.4}$$

Second, the equilibrium condition for consumers runs as

$$\overline{x}^k \succsim^k x^k \text{ for all } x^k \in X^k \text{ such that } \overline{p}_c\overline{x}^k \geq \overline{p}_c x_k \tag{4.5}$$

where x^k is the kth consumer's consumption vector. Finally, in an autarkic situation, we have

$$\overline{e} \leq 0; \overline{p}\overline{e} = 0; \tag{4.6}$$

for any distribution. In an open-economy situation, we simply have

$$\overline{q}\overline{e} = b \tag{4.6$'$}$$

for any distribution. As a result of free disposability and non-satiation, we may take all equilibrium vectors to be semi-positive. Condition (4.6) shows the market clearance in an autarkic situation. Some components of $\bar{e}$ in Eq. (4.6) may be negative as some commodities may be supplied in surplus. On the other hand, condition (4.6$'$) represents the aggregate budget constraint of consumers in an open-economy situation. A positive (respectively negative) component of $\bar{e}$ in Eq. (4.6$'$) represents the import (respectively export) of a commodity.

[10] In particular, we have in mind an economy similar to the Arrow–Debreu model for the existence of competitive equilibria. See Debreu (1959) and Nikaido (1968, Chapter 5). McKenzie (1959) allows for negative equilibrium prices, the possibility of which we exclude by assumption in this chapter. The demonstration of an existence theorem is, however, outside the scope of the present analysis. The reader interested in this line of inquiry in the context of the present model is referred to Sontheimer (1971).

4.3 Introduction of Welfare Criterion

The stage is now set to discuss the fundamentals of the present study. To initiate the argument, consider two distinct situations, such as S' and S'', say. Evidently, situation S' can be distinct from situation S'' in many different ways. We shall assume, however, that the set of consumers is given and invariant between the two situations. This implies, among other things, that the set of consumers can be independent of the other elements of economic situation such as the government's taxes and subsidies and the foreign environment.[11] With this assumption in hand, we wish to compare, from the consumers' point of view, the welfare of the two situations, S' and S''. For this purpose, a brief detour is first necessary to pronounce on the criterion under which we plan to carry out the comparison.

Let us indicate the equilibrium vectors and other symbols relating to S' by single primes, and those relating to S' by double primes, and, henceforth, omit bars on equilibrium vectors. Let $E(S; V)$ be the set of multiples of equilibrium vectors $(p_c\, x, \ldots)$ for a situation S, and a distribution V.

Definition: welfare criterion. Situation S'' is said to be preferable to situation S' if condition $p_c''x'' \geq p_c''x'$ is satisfied for all multiples $(p_c'x', \ldots) \in E(S'; V')$, $(p'', x'', \ldots) \in E(S'', V'')$, and for all relevant distributions V' and V''.

In a similar vein, the transition from situation S' to situation S'' will be occasionally said to be *beneficial* and the reverse transition *harmful* under the same condition. Thus, a policy change, say, is beneficial if it brings about an increase (or at worst non-decrease) in the aggregate real income in the so-called Paache backward index measure for all relevant distributions.

Caveats are necessary concerning the scope of all *relevant* situations. Needless to say, the relative desirability of a distribution for any situation can only be determined by the specification of one firm or another of social value judgment involving the interpersonal comparison of utility. Thus, in the absence of such a specification, we must identify the set of relevant distributions with the set of all potentially feasible distributions. In this case, our definition is equivalent to the conventional Samuelson–Kennedy criterion.

Lemma 4.1 *Let $p''x'' \geq p''x'$ for all tuples $(p_c'x', \ldots) \in E(S'; V')$, $(p'', x'', \ldots) \in E(S'', V'')$, and for all relevant distributions V' and V'' Then, given any distribution V' (respectively V''), there can be no distribution V'' (respectively V') such that some are strictly better off, while others are not worse off, in the situation S' than they are in situation S'.*[12]

[11] It should be understood that some trade in labor is in no way at variance with the given set of consumers. At the present level of abstraction, we should be ready to account for the possibility that some kind of labor is traded internationally without affecting the set of consumers and the country's endowment of leisure. For example, some laborers are able to offer their services for a foreign firm located inside the country.

[12] This result is first observed by Samuelson (1950) and later generalized by Kennedy (1954). Kemp (1962) employs essentially the same reasoning in his discussion of gains from trade.

Proof Consider a partition of the set of indices K of all consumers into two non-empty subsets K_1 and K_2 such that, for some distributions V' and V'',

$$x^{k_1'} \succ^{k_1} x^{k_1''} \text{ for } k_1 \in K_1$$

and

$$x^{k_2'} \succ^{k_2} x^{k_1''} \text{ for } k_2 \in K_2$$

where $x^{k'}$ (respectively $x^{k''}$) is an equilibrium consumption vector chosen by the kth consumer in situation S' (respectively S''). Then, from Eq. (4.5), we must have

$$p_c''x^{k_1''} \leq p_c''x^{k_1'} \text{ for } k_1 \in K_1$$

and

$$p_c''x^{k_2''} < p_c''x^{k_2'} \text{ for } k_2 \in K_2$$

(Otherwise, the choice of $x^{k''}$ would be contradicted.) But this implies

$$\sum_{k \in K} p_c''x^{k''} < \sum_{\in K} p_c''x^{k'},$$

or

$$p_c''x'' < p_c''x'$$

which contradicts the hypothesis.

The message is somewhat unsatisfactory in light of the compensation principle. Under the same condition, one may wish to establish the unambiguous proposition that, given any feasible distribution V', there exists a feasible distribution V'' such that none is worse off in situation S'' than in situation S'. The latter proposition is certainly true in the special case in which all consumers have identical tastes and identical shares in all income sources as the only feasible distribution. In general, however, we cannot make this point without investigating the problem of the existence of competitive equilibrium, which lies outside the scope of the present study.

Alternatively, it is often assumed that there exists a certain social value judgment ordering the set of feasible distribution for each situation, and that the government redistributes income accordingly so as to achieve a best feasible distribution. In this case, the set of relevant distribution reduces to the set of best feasible distributions. Thus, if the set of feasible distribution V'' contains the set of feasible distribution V', the condition given in our definition of welfare criterion evidently implies the non-deterioration of social welfare as a result of the transition from situation S' to situation S'. It is, however, only under some further assumptions that the use of a well-behaved social indifference map is known to be legitimate. Once we assume the existence of a social indifference map, we are able to abstract from individual consumers and concern ourselves only with the social consumption set X, which is convex and completely preordered by a social preference relationship (denoted by $\succsim$). Relevant distribution V is then uniquely determined for each situation S, and the set of consumers is represented simply by the consumption set and preference x' relationship, $(X; \succ)$..[13] In this context, it is worthwhile to call attention to a possible property of preference relationship $\succsim$ and its implications.

Definition: convexity of preference relationship. Preference relationship $\succsim$ is said to be strongly convex if $x'' \succ x'$ for distinct x', $x'' \in X$ implies $\lambda x'' + (1-\lambda)x' \succ x' (0 < \lambda < 1)$.[14]

Lemma 4.2 *Suppose that preference relationship $\succsim$ is strongly convex. Then, p_c'' $x'' \geq p_c'' x'$ implies $x'' \succ x'$, where x' (respectively x'') is an equilibrium aggregate consumption vector in situation S' (respectively S'').*

Proof In contrast, suppose $x' \succ x''$. Then, by the strong convexity of $\succsim$, we have $\lambda x' + (1-\lambda)x'' \succ x'$, where $\lambda x' + (1-\lambda) \in X$ by the convexity of X. But $p_c'' x'' \geq p_c''$ x' implies $p_c'' x'' \geq p_c'' \left[\lambda x' + (1-\lambda)x''\right]$, thereby contradicting the choice of x'' (see Eq. (4.5)).

Thus, if a social indifference map is assumed to exist with surfaces strictly convex toward the origin, our welfare criterion can be seen to give a sufficient (but by no means necessary) condition for a strict increase of social welfare from

---

[13] See Samuelson (1956) and Negishi (1963). Chipman (1965) gives an extensive survey of the related literature. Consider a limiting case where there is an additive social utility function with every consumer possessing an identical, linear homogeneous utility function. Write the social utility as

$$F(p_c) = \sum_{k \in K} u\left(x^k(p_c)\right)$$

where u denotes the utility function common to all consumers and $x^k(p_c)$ the consumption vector chosen by the kth consumer at price p_c. Because u is linear homogeneous, we obtain

$$F(p_c) = u(x(p_c)) \text{ where } x(p_c) = \sum_{k \in K} x^k(p_c).$$

At each price, p_c, $u(p_c)$ is maximized over the set of the aggregate consumption vectors x such that $p_c x \leq p_c x(p_c)$. In this case, we have a social indifference map regardless of the state of distribution. In fact, all distributions are deemed equally good. Thus, our welfare criterion degenerates to the crude convention of measuring social welfare in terms of per capita real income with no reference to distribution.

[14] For a discussion of the convex preference relationship, see, for example, Debreu (1959, pp. 59–61).

situation S' to situation S''. This conclusion may also be extended to the economy with nonconsumable commodities provided that the preference relationship is strongly convex in the space of consumable commodities, and that there is no surplus in the supply of nonconsumable commodities. In any case, it is vital to bear the foregoing result in mind in interpreting the forthcoming propositions in proper relationship to the traditional analyses of trade and welfare.

4.4 A General Theorem on Welfare Comparison

Leaving the discussion of welfare criterion, let us now turn to the central theme of this study. To avoid unnecessary repetition of similar reasoning, we wish to provide here a general theorem of welfare comparison focusing upon a basic formula comparing the welfare of two situations, S' and S''. Simple as it is, the formula contains most of the important results in the area with which we are concerned and will serve as a cornerstone of the subsequent analyses.

Suppose that S'' represents a situation under trade. Our strategy is to break down into several meaningful constituents the expression $p_c''(x'' - x')$, that is, the change in aggregate real income in the Paache sense involved in the transition from situation S' to situation S''. To carry this out, first recall the definition of excess demand:

$$e = x - y - a. \tag{4.7}$$

Applying Eqs. (4.1), (4.2), and (4.3) to situation S'', we get

$$p_c'' = q''\left(I + T''\right)\left(I + C''\right); \tag{4.8}$$

$$p_r'' = q''\left(I + T''\right)\left(I + R''\right). \tag{4.9}$$

From Eqs. (4.7) and (4.8), we are able to write

$$\begin{aligned} p_c''(x'' - x') &= q''(I + T'')(I + C'')\{(e'' + y'' + a'') - (e' + y' + e')\} \\ &= q''(e'' - e') + q''T''(e'' - e')q''(I + T'')C''(x'' - x') \\ &\quad + q''(I + T'')\{(y'' - y') + (a'' - a')\} \end{aligned} \tag{4.10}$$

In light of Eqs. (4.1), (4.2), and (4.9), we find

$$q''\left(I + T''\right) = p'' = p_r'' - p''R''. \tag{4.11}$$

Substituting Eq. (4.11) into (4.10), we obtain the desired decomposition as follows:

$$p''\left(x'' - x'\right) = q''\left(e'' - e'\right) + q''T''\left(e'' - e'\right) + p''C''\left(x'' - x'\right) + p''R''\left(y' - y''\right) + p''\left(\boldsymbol{a}'' - \boldsymbol{a}'\right) \tag{4.12}$$

Theorem 4.1: Welfare Comparison *If condition*

$$q''\left(e'' - e'\right) + q''T''\left(e'' - e'\right) + p''C''\left(x'' - x'\right) + p''R''\left(y' - y''\right) + p_r''\left(y'' - y'\right) + p''\left(a'' - a'\right) \geq 0 \tag{4.13}$$

is satisfied for $(p_c', x', \ldots) \in E(S'; V')$, $(p_c'', x'', \ldots) \in E(S'', V'')$, *and for relevant distributions* V' *and* V'',, *situation* S'' *is preferable to situation* S'.

Proof Straightforward from the definition of welfare criterion and Eq. (4.12).

Each term in condition (4.13) can be interpreted as a component of the real income change in the Paache sense. Thus, the term, $q''(e'' - e')$, if positive, shows the gain in the trade deficit from situation S' to situation S'' if world prices remain unchanged, or $q' = q''$. Similarly, the terms, $q''T''(e'' - e')$, $p''C''(x'' - x)$, and $p''R''(y' - y'')$ indicate in turn the gain in the government's net revenue arising from tariffs, taxes, and subsidies on consumption, and taxes and subsidies on production, on the assumption that $q' = q''$, $p' = p''$, $C' = C''$ and $R' = R''$. The terms $p_r''(y'' - y')$ and $p''(a'' - a')$ show, respectively, the gain in producers' profits and the income from endowment if $p' = p''$ and $p_r' = p_r''$.

The lengthy expression of condition (4.13) may obscure its intrinsic usefulness for analytical purposes. In what follows, however, we shall often (but not always) assume that the set of producers and the aggregate endowment are constant between situations S' and S''.[15] This implies

$$a' = a''; Y' = Y''.$$

Under this assumption, the profit maximization condition (4.4) implies

$$p_r''\left('' - y'\right) + p''\left(a'' - a'\right) = p_r''\left(y'' - y'\right) \geq 0. \tag{4.14}$$

Furthermore, we shall examine the effect of tariffs and other kinds of taxes and subsidies in isolation to focus upon its feature in sharp relief. Therefore, it will be convenient to have the simplified version of the previous theorem on hand.

[15] Again, this should not be regarded as inconsistent with trade in primary factors.

Theorem 4.2: Welfare Comparison Abridged *Assume that* $a' = a''$ *and* $Y' = Y''$.

(i) *Let* $C'' = R'' = 0$. *Then, if condition*

$$q''\left(e'' - e'\right) + q''T''\left(e'' - e'\right) \geq 0 \tag{4.15}$$

is satisfied, situation S'' *is preferable to situation* S'.

(ii) *Let* $T'' = R'' = 0$. *Then, if condition*

$$q''\left(\left(e'' - e'\right) + p''C''\left(x'' - x'\right) \geq 0 \tag{4.16}$$

is satisfied, situation S'' *is preferable to situation* S'.

(iii) *Let* $T'' = C'' = 0$. *Then, if condition*

$$q''\left(e'' - e'\right) + p''R''\left(y' - y''\right) \geq 0 \tag{4.17}$$

is satisfied, situation S'' *is preferable to situation* S'.

Proof Straightforward from Theorem 4.1 and Eq. (4.14).

Note that, in the statement of Theorem 4.1, we have tacitly avoided the complete enumeration of conditions as found in Theorem 4.1. To alleviate scholastic wordiness, we shall follow this convention hereafter in the belief that no confusion is thereby incurred.

Now, suppose that S', as well as S'', represents an open-economy situation. By virtue of Eq. (4.6′), we can then write

$$q''\left(e'' - e'\right) = \left(b'' - b'\right) + \left(q' - q''\right)e', \tag{4.18}$$

where the term $\left(b'' - b'\right)$ indicates the gain in the net aggregate transfer from abroad, and the term $\left(q' - q''\right)e'$ the terms of trade improvement in the Laspeyres sense, from situation S' to situation S'.[16] In this case, we are able to rewrite condition (4.13) accordingly. In particular, conditions (4.15, 4.16, 4.17) become

[16] Note that if the price of an export (respectively import) commodity increases (respectively decreases) from situation S'' to situation S', the term $\left(q' - q''\right)e'$ will have to be, ceteris paribus, positive.

$$\left(b^{''}-b^{'}\right)+\left(q^{'}-q^{''}\right)e^{'}+q^{''}T^{''}\left(e^{''}-e^{'}\right)\geq 0; \quad (4.15')$$

$$\left(b^{''}-b^{'}\right)+\left(q^{'}-q^{''}\right)e^{'}+p^{''}C^{''}\left(x^{''}-x^{'}\right)\geq 0; \quad (4.16')$$

$$\left(b^{''}-b^{'}\right)+\left(q^{'}-q^{''}\right)e^{'}+p^{''}R^{''}\left(y^{'}-y^{''}\right)\geq 0. \quad (4.17')$$

We discuss the more important implications of these results in detail in the following pages.

4.5 The Gains from Trade Revisited

Some trade is preferable to no trade. Although this is one of the most familiar dicta in economics, one must be careful about the exact bearing of the adjective "some." For instance, Bhagwati (1968a) elucidates a distinction between trade restricted by tariffs and trade restricted by taxes and subsidies on domestic consumption and production. Let us start out by restating the celebrated theorem, originally formalized by Kemp (1962) and Samuelson (1962). We use:

Definition: free trade. Free trade is an open-economy situation with neither tariffs nor domestic taxes and subsidies: $T = C = R = 0$.

With this in mind, we are able to state:

Proposition 4.1: Gains from Free Trade *Free trade is preferable to no trade; (ii) trade restricted by taxes on imports and for exports is preferable to no trade.*[17]

But we can in fact establish a more general proposition that applies to trade under tariffs comprising subsidies as well as taxes. Let us introduce:

Definition: self-financing tariffs. Tariffs are said to be self-financing if the net tariff revenue is nonnegative.

Needless to say, there are self-financing tariffs when trade subsidies are virtually financed out of the proceeds from trade taxes. To isolate the gains from trade, we assume that the net aggregate transfer is null.

Proposition 4.2: Gains from Trade Under Self-Financing Tariffs *Trade under self-financing tariffs is preferable to no trade.*

Proof We identify no trade with situation S' and trade under self-financing tariffs with situation S'' in Theorem 2 – (i). As we assume $b^{''} = q^{''}e^{''} = 0$, we can rewrite condition (4.15) as

$$q^{''}T^{''}e^{''} - p^{''}e^{'} \geq 0.$$

Note that $q''T''e''$ is the net tariff revenue, which is assumed to be nonnegative. From Eq. (4.6) $e^{'} \leq 0$. Because $p^{''} \geq 0$, condition (4.16) is satisfied.

[17] By the same token, trade restricted by quotas is preferable to no trade. See Kemp (1964), p. 166.

Proposition 4.1 follows at once as a corollary of Theorem 4.1. Clearly, the proof remains valid even if some commodities are free and some others are not available in the pre-trade situation. Thus, Proposition 4.1 covers trade arising from "vent for surplus" (see Mynt 1958) as well as trade based upon availabilities (see Kravis 1956). To our knowledge, this is the most comprehensive result ever obtained on the gains from trade.[18]

Let us turn to trade restricted by taxes and subsidies on consumption or production. It differs from trade restricted by tariffs in that it creates a discrepancy between consumer price and producer price in the domestic market. In the words of Bhagwati and Ramaswami (1963), trade restricted by domestic taxes and subsidies brings in perverse distortions along with trade, whereas trade restricted by tariffs simply opens up the country. This point generates a subtle, but definite, dissimilarity between the two situations because consumer price *counts* in the ultimate analysis of welfare economics, as discussed earlier (Sect. 4.3).

Now, let autarky correspond to situation S', and trade restricted by domestic taxes and subsidies to situation S'', in Theorem 4.1-(ii) or 4.2-(iii). We then obtain:

Proposition 4.3: Taxes and Subsidies on Consumption *If condition*

$$\boldsymbol{p}^{''}\boldsymbol{C}^{''}\left(\boldsymbol{x}^{''} - \boldsymbol{x}^{'}\right) \geq 0 \tag{4.19}$$

is satisfied, trade restricted by taxes and subsidies on consumption is preferable to no trade.

Proposition 4.4: Taxes and Subsidies on Production *If condition*

$$\boldsymbol{p}^{''}\boldsymbol{R}^{''}\left(\boldsymbol{y}^{'} - \boldsymbol{y}^{''}\right) >= 0 \tag{4.20}$$

is satisfied, trade restricted by taxes and subsidies on production is preferable to no trade.[19]

The proofs are straightforward from Theorem 4.1-(ii) or 4.2-(iii) and omitted here. Concerning Proposition 4.2, we may presume

$$c_i^{''} \geq 0 \, \text{if} \, e_i^{''} > 0 \, c_i^{''} \leq 0 \, \text{if} \, e_i^{''} < 0$$

because taxes and subsidies are supposed to restrict trade. Thus, for instance, condition (4.19) will be satisfied if $x_i^{''} \geq x_i^{'}$ for all i such that $e_i^{''} > 0$, and if $x_i^{''} \leq x_i^{'}$ for all i such that $e_i^{''} < 0$. An interesting special case is the situation in which

[18] Both Kemp and Samuelson avoid the discussion of trade with subsidies.

[19] These two propositions correspond to the result of Kemp and Negishi (1970, theorems 3 and 4), which came to our notice after the completion of this study. They interpret conditions (4.19) and (4.20) rather narrowly assuming that the same tax subsidy scheme exists before and after trade. As is clear from the derivation of these conditions, this assumption is not necessary. We can freely identify situation S' with any autarkic situation in regard to the domestic taxes and subsidies.

taxes are levied only on the consumption of foreign luxuries unavailable in autarky. Another less interesting special case is an exchange economy in which production has no role. Generally speaking, however, the sign restriction on the matrix C'' is not sufficient to exclude the possibility that condition (4.19) fails to hold. A similar conclusion will apply to Proposition 4.3. To push this point further, Bhagwati (1968a) constructs examples in which no trade is preferable to trade restricted by domestic tax subsidy schemes.

Thus, it is not correct to presume that restricted trade is preferable to no trade regardless of the manner of restriction. A fortiori, it is fallacious to say that *any* trade is preferable to no trade. Consider, for example, a predatory trade that involves free transfer of nationally scarce resources. We have ruled this out in this section by assuming the absence of (negative or positive) income transfer to consumers, but we have not thereby eliminated situations not quite dissimilar to a predatory trade. Take, for instance, trade saddled with tariffs that are not self-financing. It occurs only if the government finances the net tariff cost by lump-sum taxes and therefore resembles a combination of trade and negative income transfer. The autarkic situation may well be better than such trade.

4.6 The Terms of Trade Improvement and Price Divergence

It is a common presumption that the gains from trade will be greater the more the external prices "diverge" from those of the autarkic state. Samuelson (1939) muses over the problem, but quickly leaves it, only asserting that his answer is in the affirmative. Kemp (1964) suggests a useful concept of price divergence; Krueger and Sonnenschein (1967) adopt Kemp's concept to substantiate the price divergence conjecture to some extent; and yet Kemp (1969, p. 266) finally concludes that this speculation is false. In this section, we generalize Kemp's definition of price divergence and argue that the classical conjecture is not entirely unfounded.

We wish, however, first to clarify the welfare implication of the terms of trade improvement, which turn out to be fundamental to the price divergence thesis. Let q' and q'' be the external price vectors found in two different trading situations, S' and S''. Suppose that there are no tariffs and no domestic taxes and subsidies in both situations, and that an autonomous improvement of the terms of trade in the Laspeyres sense takes place in the transition from S' to S'', with everything else being unchanged. It is then immediate to reestablish the noted Krueger–Sonnenschen theorem in the present general context.

Proposition 4.5: Terms of Trade Improvement *If free trade prevails, the terms of trade improvement in the Laspeyres sense are beneficial.*[20]

[20] See Krueger and Sonnenschein (1967), pp. 123–124, and also Kemp (1969), pp. 262–265. Our Theorem 4.2 gives a more general result regarding a trading situation with tariffs or other taxes and subsidies.

Proof By hypothesis, Theorem 4.1 is applicable. Let $T'' = C'' = R'' = 0$ and $b' = b''$. Then, conditions (4.15′, 4.16′, 4.17′) reduce to $(q' - q'')e' \geq 0$. As already noted, the terms of trade improvement from S' to S'' means $(q' - q'')e' > 0$, and the condition is satisfied with strict inequality.

To proceed to a rehabilitation of the price divergence thesis, we want to be able to compare alternative external prices in their relationship to the autarkic price in an appropriate manner. For this purpose, we propose to normalize all price vectors such that their components add up to unity. This procedure is necessary only for the rest of this section in which we continue to concern ourselves with free trade situations vis-a-vis the autarkic situation.[21] Let p^0 be the autarkic price vector. For any external price vector q, one can define a diagonal matrix D such that

$$q = p^0(I + D) \tag{4.21}$$

Denoting by d_i the ith diagonal entry of D, we then have
$d_i = (q_i - p_i^0)/p_i^0$.

In the following, we shall associate D (respectively d_i) consistently with q (respectively q_i). For example, we shall write

$$q' = p^0\left(I + D'\right) q'' = p^0\left(I + D''\right),\ d_i' = \left(q_i' - p_i^0\right)/p_i^0,\ d_i'' = \left(q_i'' - p_i^0\right)/p_i^0 \text{ etc}$$

Let us consider:

Definition: price divergence. An external price vector q'' is said to diverge more from the autarkic price vector p^0 than does q' if

1. $d_i'' \leq d_i'$ for all i such that $d_i' < 0$;
2. $d_i'' \geq d_i'$ for all i such that $d_i' > 0$;
3. $d_i'' = d_i'$ for all i such that $d_i' = 0$

with at least one strict inequality.

This definition seems intuitively natural as a characterization of the notion of price divergence, and contains the concept of Kemp (1969, p. 266) as a special case. According to Kemp, q'' is said to diverge from p^0 by more than does q' if q' can be expressed as a convex combination of q'' and p^0, that is,

$$q' = \lambda q'' + (1 - \lambda)p^0\ (0 < \lambda < 1)$$

Obviously, this condition is satisfied if and only if $\lambda d_i'' = d_i'$ for all i in our definition.

Given the autarkic price vector p^0, let us now define a binary relationship "ν" such that $q'' {}^{\nu} q'$ means "q'' is more divergent from p^0 than is q'." One can easily show

[21] The price normalization is permissible when we assume away all taxes and subsidies.

that the relationship "ν" satisfies transitivity. Given a reference external price vector q^0 in addition, we may define a set of external prices:

$$Q(p^0, q^0) = \{q \mid q^{\nu} q^0\} \cup \{q^0\}$$

For $q \in Q(p^0, q^0)$, we introduce the hypothesis:

$$\begin{aligned} d_i &< 0 \text{ for all } i \text{ with } e_i > 0 \\ d_i &> 0 \text{ for all } i \text{ with } e_i < 0 \end{aligned} \tag{H}$$

where e_i is the ith component of excess demand vector e associated in equilibrium with price vector q, which means that the autarkic prices of importables are higher and those of exportables are lower than the corresponding external prices. It also implies

$e_i \gtrless 0$ according as $e_i^0 \gtrless 0$

where e_i^0 is the ith component of vector e^0 associated with the reference price vector q^0, which means that the import–export pattern remains invariable for all $q \in Q(p^0, q^0)$. [22] The price divergence conjecture may now be formalized as follows.

Proposition 4.6: Price Divergence and Gains from Trade *Under hypothesis (H), for any $q', q'' \in Q(p^0, q^0)$ such that $q''^{\nu} q'$, free trade under price vector q'' is preferable to free trade under q'.*

Proof Let S' represent free trade under q', and S'' free trade under q''. By hypothesis, we then have

$$\begin{aligned} d_i' - d_i'' &\geq 0 \text{ for all } i \text{ such that } e_i' > 0 \\ d_i' - d_i'' &\leq 0 \text{ for all } i \text{ such that } e_i' < 0 \end{aligned}$$

Hence, from Eq. (4.21)

$$\left(q' - q''\right)e' = p^0\left(D' - D''\right)e' > 0$$

That is, q'' represents a terms of trade improvement in relationship to q', and the desired conclusion follows from Proposition 4.4.

Note that Proposition 4.4 is stated so as to capture "the greater, the more" property of the price divergence thesis. In fact, we may suppose $q'' \nu q^0$ and conclude that free trade under q' is preferable to free trade under q^0, and that because $q''^{\nu} q'$,

[22] These assumptions are not at all novel in the literature on the pattern of trade. They reflect the doctrine of comparative advantage that a country's pattern of trade is determined by its autarkic cost structure vis-a-vis the external cost structure. As Inada (1967) demonstrates, however, the possibility of locally unique multiple equilibria undermines their intuitive plausibility.

free trade under q'' is *more* preferable than free trade under q' to free trade under q^0. In this case, we also note

$(q^0 - q'')e^0 > (q^0 - q')e^0 > 0.$

In words, q'' means a greater terms of trade improvement over q^0 than does q'. The converse of this relationship is, however, generally untenable, as illustrated by Krueger and Sonnenschein (1967, p. 127). But consider a subset $\overline{Q}$ of $Q(p^0, q^0)$ such that either $q' \nu q''$ or $q'' \nu q'$ must hold for $q', q'' \in \overline{Q}$. The set $\overline{Q}$ is not empty because, given p^0 and q^0, one can always find a pair of price vectors for which the specification is satisfied. Now suppose $(q^0 - q'')e^0 > (q^0 - q')e^0$ and $q' \nu q''$. The former implies

$$\left(q' - q''\right)e^0 > 0$$

But, under hypothesis (H), the latter implies $q_i' - q_i'' \leq 0$ for $e_i^0 > 0$ and $q_i' - q_i'' \geq 0$ for $e_i^0 < 0$, yielding a contradiction. Thus, we can generalize the transitivity theorem entertained by Krueger and Sonnenschein as follows.

Proposition 4.7: The Greater the Terms of Trade Improvement, the Greater the Gains from Trade
Given p^0 and q^0, *and under hypothesis (H), more of the terms of trade improvement is preferable to less of it if brought about by a shift within a subset* $\overline{Q}$ *of the price set* $Q(p^0, q^0)$.

To illustrate the purpose of this seemingly pedantic section, let us consider a small country that exports a few primary goods (e.g., tea and textiles), and imports a large number of intermediate goods and factor inputs (e.g., machines and oil) unavailable in the autarkic state. For such a country, the higher the world prices of tea and textiles, or the lower those of machines and oil, the greater will be, ceteris paribus, the gains from free trade *unambiguously*. The country's technology and preference structure are such that it cannot change its obvious import–export pattern under all circumstances. The price divergence thesis is perhaps meant to convey this kind of message, and there is no reason to disregard the grain of truth it carries.

4.7 Ranking of Policies Under Trade

Tariffs and other forms of government intervention in the economy have furnished one of the most exciting topics for economists. For example, using the two-by-two model of international trade, trade theorists have rigorously established that, under certain fundamental conditions, an increase in the level of tariffs will improve the country's terms of trade but will diminish the volume of exports.[23] In the present study, however, we are not directly concerned with the result of comparative statics per se. Rather, the burden of this section is to derive, from our general theorem, some additional welfare statements regarding ranking of policies under trade.

We compare here two situations under trade that differ from each other only in the government's taxes and subsidies, (T, C, R). Thus, Theorem 4.1 is applicable with $b' = b''$, and conditions (4.15′, 4.16′, 4.17′) simplify to

$$\left(q' - q''\right)e' + q''T''\left(e'' - e'\right) \geq 0 \tag{4.15′}$$

$$\left(q' - q''\right)e' + p''C''\left(x'' - x'\right) \geq 0 \tag{4.16′}$$

$$\left(b'' - b'\right) + \left(q' - q''\right)e' + p''R''\left(y' - y''\right) \geq 0 \tag{4.17′}$$

To refresh memory, the first term on the left-hand side of each condition represents the terms of trade change occurring in the transition from S' to S''. The second term, on the other hand, expresses the complicated effect of the change in the volume and composition of trade, consumption, or production. When the change in profits $p_r''\left(y'' - y'\right)$ is of the second-order magnitude, conditions (4.15′, 4.16′, 4.17′) correspond to the dichotomy of welfare change a la Meade (1955a).

It is conceivable and often likely that the two effects work in opposite directions. First, consider free trade as situation S'. The introduction of, say, some protective tariffs may contract the country's volume of trade but improve the terms of trade. Consider the latter situation with tariffs as situation S'', and suppose that, in the presence of a well-behaved social indifference map, condition (4.15′) is satisfied. Then, in view of Theorem 4.1-(i), the tariffs will be said to be beneficial. Given such tariffs, one may proceed to examine the welfare effect of successive increases (or decreases) in the level of tariffs, each time applying Theorem 4.1-(i) as above, until condition (4.15′) is no longer tenable. This process of searching for the *optimal* level of tariffs underlies the reasoning of the MacDougal–Jasay cases for curtailing foreign investment, as well as the Bickerdike–Edgeworth argument for protective tariffs, envisioned in the simpler models of trade.[24] The same conjecture will also be applied to the restriction of trade by means of taxes and subsidies on domestic consumption or production.[25]

The country may, however, be too small to affect the terms of trade significantly via a change in the government's taxes and subsidies. For simplicity, suppose that the world price of tradeable commodities is completely independent of the country's imports and exports. On this assumption of a *price-taking country*, we

---

[23] See, for example Mundell (1960), pp. 86–90, and Jones (1969).

[24] Jones (1967) presents a synthesis of the two cases in a capital-mobile, Heckscher–Ohlin model.

[25] Provided, of course, that there is a non-empty set of domestic tax subsidy schemes preferable to free trade, not to mention the autarkic state.

shall investigate various policy problems for the rest of this section. To start with, consider Kemp's argument (1964) that the lower the level of tariffs, the greater will be the gains from trade in this special case. As Bhagwati (1968a, b)) points out, this conclusion is not generally supportable. From Theorem 4.1-(i), we can instead state:

Proposition 4.8: Small Country's External and Internal Policies *If condition*

$$q''T''\left(e'' - e'\right) \geq 0 \tag{4.22}$$

is satisfied, a change in tariffs (and the abolition of domestic taxes and subsidies if any) from situation S' to situation S'' is beneficial for a price-taking country.

Proof Because the world price of tradeable commodities is constant, we have $q'e' = q''e'$. Therefore, condition 4.15′) reduces further to Eq. (4.22).

Consider, in particular, a uniformly proportionate variation of tariffs on the assumption that situation S' is possessed of some tariffs T'. In this case, we have

$$T'' = \alpha T' \; (\alpha > 0)$$

Condition (4.22) can therefore be rewritten as

$$q''T''e'' \geq \alpha q'T'e'$$

That is, the rate of increase (respectively decrease) in the net tariff revenue is not less (respectively greater) than the uniform rate of tariff increase (respectively decrease).

We can simplify conditions (4.16′) and (4.17′) in a similar fashion. If $T'' = C'' = R'' = 0$, these conditions are all satisfied by equality. Hence, we are able to state:

Proposition 4.9: Free Trade Is Optimal for a Price-Taking Country *Free trade is preferable to any manner of restricted trade for a price-taking country.*

In practice, the government often pursues policies to achieve specific objectives of its own.[26] For instance, it may wish to raise a fixed amount of revenue by means other than lump-sum taxes.[27] The commodity tax structure that minimizes the harm to consumers in such a case is investigated by Dixit (1970). One of his results can be extended to the present model with considerable gains in generality as well as in interpretation.

[26] Bhagwati (1971) gives a detailed taxonomic account of some of such policies.

[27] Perhaps for the purpose of reparation payment or economic aid to the rest of the world.

Proposition 4.10: Efficient Policy to Achieve a Given Government Revenue *Given a fixed amount of government revenue, trade with appropriate uniform-rate taxes on consumption is preferable, for a price-taking country, to a situation with tariffs and/or other domestic taxes and subsidies.*

Proof Let S'' be the trading-situation with uniform-rate taxes on consumption, and S' any other situation. Because a fixed amount of government revenue is raised in both S' and S'', we have $b' = b'' = q''e'' = q'e'$. For a price-taking country, we observe

$$\begin{aligned} p''C''\left(x'' - x'\right) &= p''C''\left(e'' + y'' + a'' - e' - y' - a'\right) \\ &= c''q''\left(e'' - e'\right) + c''q''\left(y'' - y'\right) = c''p''_r\left(y'' - y'\right) \end{aligned}$$

where c'' is the common rate of taxes on consumption such that $c''p''x'' = -b''$. Hence, from conditions (4.4) and 4.16′ follows the assertion.

This result shows that if the government of a price-taking country is to raise a fixed amount of revenue, a uniform rate consumption tax scheme is the appropriate policy optimal among all possible mixes of tariffs and domestic taxes and subsidies. Aside from its allowance for intermediate and non-tradeable commodities, Proposition 4.9 is, therefore, more comprehensive than the statement that a uniform consumption tax structure is better than differentiated consumption tax structure as a means to provide the government with a given sum of purchasing power.[28]

On occasions the government may also wish to restrict the value of certain imports or exports, the value of certain consumptions, and the value of certain outputs or inputs at some fixed levels other than those of free trade. The policy problems that arise under such circumstances are discussed by Johnson (1964). Our method enables us again to give a thoroughgoing treatment of these issues.

Proposition 4.11: Efficient Policy to Achieve a Target Value of Imports *Given a fixed value of certain imports (respectively exports), trade with appropriate uniform-rate taxes or subsidies on those imports (respectively exports) is preferable, for a price-taking country, to a situation with other tariffs and/or domestic taxes and subsidies.*

Proof Consider trade with appropriate uniform-rate tariffs as S'', and any other situation as S'. Let t'' be the common rate of tariffs applied to the group of imports or exports the value of which is to be restricted. Let $\widehat{q}''$ be an n-vector obtained from q'' by merely replacing the prices of nonrestricted commodities with zeros. By hypothesis, we then get

[28] Dixit considers this problem in the context of a closed economy on the assumption that all supply prices are constant and that there is a positive net transfer of purchasing power to consumers from somewhere resembling manna from the heaven. For a closed economy in which we have no terms of trade effect to worry about, Dixit's restrictive assumption is in fact unessential to the desired result.

$$q''T''\left(e'' - e'\right) = t''\left(\widehat{q}''e'' - \widehat{q}''e'\right)$$

where $\widehat{q}''e''$ and $\widehat{q}'e'$ indicate the given value of imports or exports of the commodities under restriction. Because $\widehat{q}'e' = \widehat{q}''e'$ for a price-taking country, condition (4.22) is satisfied by equality.

Similarly, we can establish the following.

Proposition 4.12: Efficient Policy to Achieve a Target Value of Consumption *Given a fixed value of consumption of certain tradeable commodities, trade with appropriate uniform-rate taxes or subsidies on the consumption of those commodities is preferable, for a price-taking country, to a situation with tariffs and/or other domestic taxes and subsidies.*

Proposition 4.13: Efficient Policy to Achieve a Target Value of Outputs *Given a fixed value of output (respectively input) of certain tradeable commodities, trade with appropriate uniform-rate taxes or subsidies on the output (respectively input) of those commodities is preferable, for a price-taking country, to a situation with tariffs and/or other domestic taxes and subsidies.*[29]

Finally, it is most conceivable that tariffs and other forms of restrictive measures are invoked by the government to fix the volume of certain imports or exports, the volume of certain consumptions, and the volume of certain outputs or inputs at some assigned levels other than those of free trade. Working with a two-commodity model, Johnson (1964) illustrates the principle that tariffs are superior to domestic taxes and subsidies for the purpose of restricting the volume of imports. Similarly, Corden (1957) shows that a production subsidy is less costly than a tariff in achieving a given level of the import-competing production. Bhagwati and Srinivasan (1969) study the case in which the use of a factor in production is restricted as well as the case in which the consumption of a commodity is the constrained variable. It is an easy matter to generalize these diverse results and place them in the common analytical perspective of this chapter.[30]

Proposition 4.14: Efficient Policy to Achieve a Target Value of Exports *Given a fixed volume of certain imports (respectively exports), trade with appropriate tariffs on those imports (respectively exports) is preferable, for a price-taking country, to a situation with other tariffs and/or domestic taxes and subsidies.*

Proof Let the trading situation with appropriate tariffs be represented by S'', and any other situation by S'. Because the volume of restricted imports or exports is given

[29] Note that these two propositions are concerned only with the case where the constrained variable is the value of consumption or production of *tradeable* commodities. The result does not extend to the case with restricted value of consumption or production of non-tradeable commodities.

[30] Tan (1971) also extends these results to three special models that allow for inter-industry linkages, the use of intermediate goods, and non-tradeable commodities. Our method provides an alternative and more general treatment of the problem.

and invariable for both S' and S'', we have $e_i' = e_i''$ for $t_i'' \neq 0$, implying that condition (4.22) is satisfied by equality.

Similarly, we can prove:

Proposition 4.15: Efficient Policy to Achieve Target Volume of Consumption *Given a fixed volume of certain consumptions, trade with appropriate taxes or subsidies on those consumptions is preferable, for a price-taking country, to a situation with tariffs and/or other domestic taxes and subsidies.*

Proposition 4.16: Efficient Policy to Achieve Target Volume of Outputs *Given a fixed volume of certain outputs (respectively inputs), trade with appropriate taxes or subsidies on those outputs (respectively inputs) is preferable, for a price-taking country, to a situation with tariffs and/or other domestic taxes and subsidies.*

Propositions 4.13 through 4.15 confirm the point recognized by Bhagwati (1971) that when distortions have to be introduced into the economy to constrain the value of certain variables, the optimal (or least-cost) method of doing this is to choose that policy intervention that creates the distortion affecting directly the constrained variable. In a controversial article, Lipsey and Lancaster (1956–1957) claim that there is no a priori way to judge between suboptimal situations. Their claim is valid only if little is known a priori. In fact, our results suggest that policy makers should be able to survive by the help of their wisdom and expert knowledge.[31]

4.8 Economic Growth and Unilateral Transfer

We have so far confined our attention to the economy with immutable technology and constant endowment. From the standpoint of this study, however, there is no special reason for us to adhere to this convention. After all, technology, as well as endowment, is just one of the structural determinants of the economy such as the foreign environment, the government taxes and subsidies, etc. Technological progress, along with endowment expansion, serves as a major factor in economic growth that is supposed to increase economic welfare under ordinary circumstances.[32] Nonetheless, they can be actually harmful to a country engaged in external trade. It is because of this ambiguity that we wish to discuss economic growth and also touch upon the comparable transfer problem.

---

[31] Similarly, Bhagwati and Ramaswami (1963) asserts that a tariff is not necessarily superior to free trade in the presence of domestic distortions. But this assertion is also misleading. Using the same model, Ohyama (1972), along with Kemp and Negishi (1969), demonstrates the existence of a tariff superior to free trade.

[32] In this statement, we consider endowment expansion as phenomena such as the natural growth of cattle and timber woods. Naturally, we must except population growth, which affects the set of consumers.

Let us consider here trading situations with only tariffs because our method will apply readily to other cases. Suppose that economic growth has changed situation S' into situation S''. The difference between the two is assumed to consist only of some technological progress and endowment expansion giving rise to the economic growth. Thus, we have to leave the hypothesis of Theorem 4.1 and instead postulate

$$a'' \geq a' a'' \neq a'), Y'' \supset Y' \left(Y'' \neq Y'\right)$$

From Theorem 4.1, we obtain:

Proposition 4.17: Condition for Beneficial Growth *If condition*

$$\left(q' - q''\right)e' + q''\left(e'' - e'\right) + p''\left\{\left(y'' - y'\right) + \left(a' - a'\right)\right\} \geq 0 \tag{4.23}$$

is satisfied, the economic growth is beneficial.

Proof By assumption, we have $C'' = R'' = 0$, and therefore, $p_r'' = p''$. Also, $b' = b''$ implies $q''\left(e'' - e'\right) = \left(q' - q''\right)e'$. With these relationships, condition (4.13) simplifies to (4.23).

Note that the third term on the left-hand side of condition (4.23) contains the gain from the growth and is assumed to be positive. We cannot, however, be so sure of the sign of the first and second terms. Bhagwati (1958), for instance, argues that economic growth may lead to sufficiently acute terms of trade deterioration, imposing a loss of real income to override the primary gain from the growth itself. He aptly names this phenomenon "immiserizing growth."[33] Appropriately reinterpreting Theorem 4.1, we readily obtain:

Proposition 4.18: Condition for Harmful Growth *If condition*

$$\left(q'' - q'\right)e'' + q'T''\left(e' - e''\right) - p'\left\{\left(y'' - y'\right) + \left(a'' - a'\right)\right\} \geq 0 \tag{4.24}$$

is satisfied, the economic growth is harmful.

Now, the term $\left(q'' - q'\right)e''$, if positive, measures the terms of trade deterioration in the Paache sense as a result of the economic growth. On the other hand, the term $p'\left\{\left(y'' - y'\right) + \left(a'' - a'\right)\right\}$ measures the gain in profits and endowment income in the Laspeyres sense. In the absence of tariffs, immiserizing growth will occur if

[33] Earlier economists were as well aware of this possibility. For instance, Edgeworth (1894, p. 40) discussed the possible adverse consequence of technological progress in the export industries, attributing the paradox to John S. Mill.

$$\left(q'' - q'\right)e'' \geq p'\left\{\left(y'' - y'\right) + \left(a'' - a'\right)\right\}$$

that is, if the unfavorable terms of trade effect outweigh the growth effect. Thus, an export-biased expansion may not be felicitous when the world is not ready to absorb the additional output only with a moderate fall in price.

Consider now a small growth in a price-taking country that docs not affect the world price of tradeable commodities. Under free trade there can be no diminution of the growth gain. If there are tariffs, however, even a country without any monopoly power in world trade is not completely exempt from immiserizing growth. Because we assume $T' = T''$, sufficient condition for that eventuality is written as

$$q'T'e' - q'T''e'' \geq p'\left\{\left(y'' - y'\right) + \left(a'' - a'\right)\right\}$$

The left-hand side of this condition, if positive, represents a reduction in the net tariff revenue brought about by the economic growth. Johnson (1967) shows that a technological progress in the domestic production of a protected import-competing industry can actually hurt the country's economic welfare through a decrease in the tariff revenue.[34]

Receiving a unilateral transfer *in kind* from abroad resembles, at first sight, an autonomous expansion of the country's endowment. In fact, the condition for a beneficial transfer will take the same form as condition (4.23). This resemblance is, of course, rather superficial, and fades away as soon as one realizes that a transfer receipt in kind gives rise simultaneously to the contraction of endowment in the rest of the world. Its welfare effect will differ depending on the nature of the commodities that are transferred.[35] In case of a transfer in purchasing power, it is established in the context of a simpler model of trade that if certain fundamental assumptions are satisfied, "immiserizing" transfer receipt will never take place under free trade.[36] This, however, does not seem to be the case in the presence of tariffs.

Suppose that S' now corresponds to a situation with no foreign transfer and S'' to the same situation except for a transfer receipt b''. We may reinterpret Theorem 4.1 to obtain:

[34] Bhagwati (1968b) extends this possibility to the case of domestic distortions such as external economies and diseconomies and inter-industry factor reward differentials, which we assume to not be used in this chapter. The underlying logic is, however, the same as in the case of tariffs.

[35] One must distinguish the transfer of tradeable commodities from that of non-tradeable commodities.

[36] See, for example Mundell (1960), pp. 79–80.

Proposition 4.19: Transfer and Tariff Revenue *If condition*

$$\left(q'' - q'\right)e'' + q'T''\left(e' - e''\right) + p'\left(y' - y''\right) \geq 0 \tag{4.25}$$

is satisfied, the transfer receipt is harmful.

If world prices happen to be unchanged in the face of the transfer, condition (4.25) becomes

$$q'T'e' - q''T''e'' \geq b''$$

which means that the reduction in the tariff revenue is at least as large in value as the transfer receipt itself.[37] This condition may be fulfilled if some tariff-free tradeables are inferior in social consumption. From a practical point of view, however, it is more interesting to observe that a transfer receipt produces an additional welfare effect in the form of changing tariff revenue on top of the obvious direct effect and the much-discussed terms of trade effect. This point is hardly recognized in the literature on the transfer problem.[38]

We have so far assumed that tariffs are unchanged in the face of economic growth or unilateral transfer. But suppose that the sole objective of tariffs is to restrict the volume of imports or exports at some assigned level. Then, tariffs are to be modified so as to achieve this objective as economic growth or transfer receipt tends to affect the country's external trade. So far as this modification of tariffs is appropriately carried out, economic growth, as well as transfer receipt, is bound to be beneficial for a price-taking country. To see this point, note that the first two terms of condition (4.23) vanish to zero under such a circumstance. The same conclusion will also hold for a price-taking country with domestic taxes and subsidies designed to restrict the volume of certain consumptions, outputs, and inputs at some target level.

4.9 The Infant Industry Argument

We have already established that free trade is preferable to any other situation for a price-taking country. Underlying this free trade proposition, however, is the assumption that the productive capacity of the country is unaffected by the volume and composition of its foreign trade. This assumption is at best questionable at

[37] In this special case, the term $p'\left(y' - y''\right)$, as well as $\left(q'' - q'\right)e''$, vanishes to zero. In fact, $p'y' \geq p''y$, but $p'y' = p''y' \leq p''y'' = p'y''$.

[38] See Samuelson (1952, 1954), which investigates the terms of trade effect of a transfer payment. Ohyama (1974) provides a supplementing analysis pointing out the tertiary effect through a change in the volume and composition of trade under tariffs.

times: it has indeed invited persistent challenges since the days of Hamilton and List. These challenges have culminated in a legitimate case for protection. The infant industry argument, as it is so called, maintains that, in some industries, producers (or the firms) learn from experience, thereby adding to efficiency and expanding the basis of national productive capacity through time. If free trade is expected to damage or extirpate such industries in their "infantile" stage through foreign competition, gains from trade must be weighed against the future benefit of the learning processes to be foregone. The free trade proposition is no longer tenable without qualifications.

Following Kemp (1960), let us digress to classify the relevant learning processes into two familiar categories. A learning process is internal to the firm if it helps to remunerate only the firm that actually carries on production. In this case, we shall speak of dynamic internal economies. Correspondingly, a process is external to the firm if the experience is not appropriate and necessarily benefits other firms inside (and perhaps also outside) the industry. We shall then speak of dynamic external economies. Kemp asserts that, under certainty and perfect markets, the existence of dynamic *internal* economies can never be the pretext for protection. But as Negishi (1968) points out,[39] Kemp's conclusion hinges crucially on his interpretation of Bastable's test for the legitimacy of infant industry protection. According to his interpretation, Bastable's test requires that the future gain accruing to the matured industry be sufficient to compensate present cost falling on the infant industry during the learning period. Kemp thus views Bastable's test only in terms of the producers' profitability in the long run. No wonder that the profit incentive is enough to carry out the venture that passes such a test. It is, however, not the producers' profitability, but the consumers' welfare that counts in deciding upon the propriety of protection. We wish to reconsider the infant industry argument as yet another application of our methodology supporting, in particular, the position taken by Negishi.

For simplicity, let us consider a two-period model of the economy. A commodity in the first (present) period and the same commodity in the second (future) period are, then, *different* economic objects. We have to reinterpret our vectors so that they now represent the quantities of the two periods:

$$x = \left({}^1x\,,\,{}^2x\right),\; y = \left({}^1y\,,\,{}^2y\right), p = \left({}^1p\,,\,{}^2p\right) \text{ etc}\,.$$

where the left-hand superscripts indicate the period of the vectors. In a two-period equilibrium, the rate of interest is implicitly determined by the price vector, $p = \left({}^1p\,,\,{}^2p\right)$. Assume that there exists a certain (positive) level of the infant industry output below which it cannot generate internal or external dynamic economies, and that the level is not achieved without protection in the first period. Because learning is a time-consuming process, dynamic economies are assumed to

[39] Negishi considers the infant industry argument from the point of view of the world. We shall return to this problem later in Sect. 4.11 to discuss the world gains from trade.

materialize only in the second period given the appropriate protection in the first. To sharpen the argumentative edge, let us further assume that there are no dynamic economies in the non-infant industries. As we have shown, the desirable level of the infant industry output is best achieved by appropriate subsidies on those outputs.

Now suppose that situation S' stands for free trade without any protection and S'' for the state with protection in the form of production subsides in the first period.

Proposition 4.20: Infant Industry Subsidization *If condition*

$$p_r^{''}\left(y^{''}-y^{'}\right)+p^{''}\left(a^{''}-a^{'}\right)\geq p^{''}R^{''}\left(y^{''}-y^{'}\right) \tag{4.26}$$

is satisfied, the infant industry promotion by means of production subsidies is beneficial for a price-taking country.

Proof Let $T''=C''=0$ and $q^{''}\left(e^{''}-e^{'}\right)=0$. Then, condition (4.13) in Theorem 4.1 reduces to Eq. (4.26).

According to Kemp's criterion, the protection is not to be recommended if there are only internal dynamic economies, for the desired level of infant industry outputs are assumed to be unprofitable. To discuss this point, let w and z be n-vectors of aggregate production of infant and non-infant industries. Thus,

$$y=w+z$$

and we can rewrite condition (4.26) as

$$p_r^{''}\left(z^{''}-z^{'}\right)+p''\left(a^{''}-a^{'}\right)\geq p^{''}\left(w^{'}-w^{''}\right)$$

based on the assumption that there are no taxes or subsidies on the production of non-infant industries. In particular, if $w^{'}=0$, the right-hand side of this condition is positive because production $w^{''}$ is unprofitable without protective subsidies, or $p''w^{''}<0$. On the other hand, the left-hand side may as well be positive in the presence of non-tradeable commodities because of the profit maximization condition for non-infant industries and the possible augmentation (in efficiency units) of factors of production *specific* to the firms of infant industries. Despite the unprofitability assumption, condition (4.26) may be satisfied, and therefore protection justified even though the available learning processes are all internal to the firms.[40] At any rate, condition (4.26) may or may not hold irrespective of the nature of dynamic economies occurring in the infant industries.[41]

---

[40] At this point, it should be recalled that, under the convexity of social preference relationship, condition (4.26) is merely sufficient (and not necessary) for the justification of infant industry protection.

[41] Haberler (1950) provided a diagrammatic demonstration of the essential argument, which was somehow neglected in later controversies.

On the other hand, if there are neither dynamic external economies nor non-tradeable commodities, we obtain

$$p'\left(z' - z''\right) + p'\left(a' - a''\right) = 0 > p'w''$$

because, in this case, we must have $p' = p''$ and $a' = a''$. It implies that the protection of unprofitable infant industries is harmful for a price-taking country.[42] Kemp's argument is therefore valid in the special case in which all commodities are tradeable.

Finally, protection may take the form of import taxes in spite of the fact that they are more costly than production subsidies. To consider this case, let S'' now represent the state with protective tariffs. Proposition 4.18 is no longer relevant. From Theorem 4.1, we instead obtain:

Proposition 4.21: Infant Industry Protection by Tariffs *If condition*

$$p'\left\{\left(y'' - y'\right) + \left(a'' - a'\right)\right\} \geq q'T''\left(e' - e''\right) \tag{4.27}$$

is satisfied, the infant industry protection by means of tariffs is beneficial for a price-taking country.

4.10 The Customs Unions Issue

Up to this point we have made no attempt to go beyond the aspect of a single country trading with the rest of the world, which is of course the result of the nature of our model as described at the outset. A little reflection, however, will reveal that we can at times reinterpret the single country's point of view so as to handle the problem of many countries. Our method remains indeed applicable whenever a group of several countries acts like a single country providing a common set of prices to measure and compare the sum of national consumption bundles of two situations. The customs unions issue provides a shining example of such a circumstance, and certainly deserves a separate treatment on its own right. Let us assume that the customs unions (1) abolish all tariffs among the member countries; (2) set up common external tariffs; and (3) fully coordinate distributional policies inside the union. Introducing picturesque concepts of trade creation and trade diversion,

[42] If $w' = 0$, we have

$$p''\left(x' - x''\right) = p'\left(y' - y''\right) + p'\left(a' - a''\right) = p'\left(z' - z'' - w''\right) + p'\left(a' - a''\right).$$

Viner (1950) aptly illustrates the generally ambiguous nature of the effect of the customs union. In fact, similar to many other statements on trade and welfare, it is only conditional that the customs union will augment the welfare of any concerned party.

Suppose that there are v countries in the world, and that $s\,(< v)$ countries formed a customs union. We indicate the countries by putting left-hand subscripts to all symbols. Let S' and S'' represent the pre- and post-union situations wherein domestic taxes and subsidies are assumed to be nonexistent.

Proposition 4.22: Beneficial Customs Union *If condition*

$$\left(q' - q''\right)\sum_{h=1}^{s} {}_{h}e'^{h} + q''T''\left(\sum_{h=1}^{s} {}_{h}e''^{h} - \sum_{\bar{h}1}^{s} {}_{h}e'^{h}\right) \geq 0 \qquad (4.28)$$

is satisfied, the post-union situation is preferable to the pre-union situation for the customs union as a whole.

Proof We may consider the members of the customs union as if they were a single country because of the distributional coordination available in the post-union situation. Condition (4.15') is then applicable with $b'' = \sum_{h=1}^{s} {}_{h}b'^{h}$, and may be rewritten as Eq. (4.28).

The first term on the left-hand side of condition (4.28) indicates the terms of trade effect, and the second term, the trade expansion (contraction) effect on the welfare of the customs union. If the terms of trade effect are negligible, and free trade prevails in the rest of the world, we can discuss the gain from the formation of the union solely in terms of the trade expansion (contraction) effect along the line made popular by Meade (1955a). For example, the expansion of the tariff-protected *net* imports will be, ceteris paribus, sufficient to suggest an increase of the world real income as well as the union's welfare. Note, however, that the much-discussed trade creating effect does not appear explicitly in condition (4.28). In fact, it is buried in the omitted expression

$$p''\left(\sum_{h=1}^{s} {}_{h}y''^{h} - \sum_{h=1}^{s} {}_{h}y'^{h}\right) \geq 0$$

and yet it certainly affects the condition indirectly through its expansive effect on external trade. In general, condition (4.28), together with condition (4.15′), provides a complete set of references for testing the welfare effect on the union itself as well as on each country in the outside world.

Criticizing Viner's pioneering analysis, Meade (1955a), Gehrels (1956–1957), and Lipsey (1957, 1960) demonstrate that the purely trade-diverting union may just easily be beneficial in the presence of a convex social preference relationship. To exclude trade creation and the terms of trade effect, they focus upon a customs unions of exchange economies with no monopoly power in world trade. Suppose as a limiting case that there is no trade diversion either. Then, condition (4.28) is satisfied by equality, and the members' welfare is shown to increase after the union (recall Lemma 4.2). By continuity, we may conclude that the union remains beneficial even with some trade diversions. In fact, their simple example relates to the case that fails to meet condition (4.28) and serves to remind us once again of the *sufficiency* nature of our welfare criterion under the convexity of consumers' preference relationships.

More recently, Kemp (1964) and Vanek (1965) advocate an interesting scheme of the tariff-compensating customs union. We may define it as the union that sets its common external tariffs so as to preserve the same volume and composition of net trade with the rest of the world as occurred before it was formed.

Proposition 4.23: Tariff-Compensating Customs Union *A tariff-compensating customs union is bound to benefit itself and the world as a whole.*

Proof Referring back to Proposition 4.22, we find

$$\sum_{h=1}^{s} {}_h e'^{\,h} = \sum_{h=1}^{s} {}_h e''^{\,h}$$

for a tariff-compensating customs union. Hence,

$$\left(q' - q''\right) \sum_{h=1}^{s} {}_h e'^{\,h} = q' \sum_{h=1}^{s} {}_h e'^{\,h} - q'' \sum_{h=1}^{s} {}_h e''^{\,h} = 0.$$

Thus, both the first and the second terms in condition (4.28) vanish to zero. Clearly, a tariff-compensating union does not hurt the rest of the world. Therefore, it is also beneficial for the world as a whole. As Vanek suggests, it may be useful to think of a customs union as adopting the compensating tariffs in the first step, and then shifting to the final tariffs in the second: this amounts to a conceptual device of splitting up the welfare effect of the union conveniently into two parts to examine them separately. The first step is necessarily beneficial. The second step is analytically equivalent to a single country's act of tariff reform.[43]

[43] A single country's tariff reform, say a reduction of tariffs, however, will not be unambiguous in its effect on the welfare of the tariff-ridden world. See Meade (1955b, pp. 511–520) and also Ozga (1955).

4.11 The World Gains from Trade

There seems to be little literature along the line of the present study that adequately considers the world gains from trade. Because we have already set out to consider the situations explicitly involving several countries, we shall follow the logic to its end, and fill the void to some extent. The familiar free trade doctrine immediately follows from condition (4.28). Suppose that $s = v$. In other words, imagine that all the countries get together and form the world customs union: that is, free global trade. We may now rewrite Eq. (4.28) simply as

$$\left(q' - q''\right) \sum_{h=1}^{v} {}_h e'^h = -q'' \sum_{h=1}^{v} {}_h e'^h \geq 0.$$

But this condition necessarily holds because $q'' \geq 0$ and $\sum_{h=1}^{v} {}_h e'^h \leq 0$. If the set of free commodities is identical for the two situations, the condition is to be satisfied by equality. Thus, free trade is preferable to any other situation for the world as a whole provided that there is a proper redistributional arrangement among nations.

In view of Proposition 4.3, we may also note that trade restricted by tariffs is preferable to no trade for all countries, that is, for the world. Clearly, we cannot obtain the same unconditional statement for trade restricted by domestic taxes and subsidies.[44] To proceed further, let us assume the presence of the world government coordinating all the functions of national governments. First, we can apply Theorem 4.1-(ii) to obtain the following.

Proposition 4.24: Global Free Trade with Tax and Subsidies on Consumption *Let $T'' = R'' = 0$. Then, if condition*

$$q''C'' \sum_{h=1}^{v} \left({}_h x''^h - {}_h x'^h\right) \geq 0 \tag{4.29}$$

is satisfied, situation S'' is preferable to situation S'.

Proof Note that C'' represents the common taxes and subsides applied throughout the world in situation S''. Consequently, all consumers are supposed to face the same price, which makes Theorem 4.1-(ii) applicable to the world. It then suffices to rewrite condition (4.16) and note $\left(q' - q''\right) \sum_{h=1}^{v} {}_h e'^h \geq 0$.

Similarly, from Theorem 4.1-(iii) we can derive:

[44] Similarly, trade may not be conducive to the world real income if non-self-financing tariffs are prevalent. This point generalizes Jones' observation (1961, pp. 173–174) about a Grahamesque, multi-country, multi-commodity model.

Proposition 4.25: Global Free Trade with Taxes and Subsidies on Production *Let* $T'' = C'' = 0$. *Then, if condition*

$$q'' \sum_{h=1}^{v} R'' \left({}_h y'^h - {}_h y''^h \right) \geq 0 \tag{4.30}$$

is satisfied, situation S'' *is preferable to situation* S'.

In the case there are only taxes and subsidies on production in situation S'', they can be different from country to country because consumers' price is identical throughout the world. In view of conditions (4.29) and (4.30), we find that there is a striking correspondence between the world envisioned here and a price-taking country with no external tariffs. In each case, we are able to disregard the cumbersome term $(q' - q'')e'$ reflecting the terms of trade effect. Thus, a number of welfare propositions that are valid for a price-taking country are also applicable to the world.

First, Proposition 4.8 corresponds to the free trade doctrine that we have just established. Similarly, Propositions 4.9, 4.13, 4.14, and 4.18 can be readily reformulated to fit in with the present context. For example, we can state the following.

Proposition 4.26: Global Free Trade with Taxes and Subsidies on Outputs *Given a fixed volume of certain outputs (respectively inputs) in certain countries, trade with appropriate taxes or subsidies on those outputs (respectively inputs) is preferable, for the world as a whole, to a situation with tariffs and/or other taxes and subsidies.*

In correspondence to Proposition 4.14, this result tells us that, from the point of view of the world, a national scheme of production taxes and subsidies is the optimal way of achieving a target level of any output or input in any country. We may then proceed to consider the global scheme of infant industry promotion by means of national production subsidies just as we considered it for a price-taking country.

Proposition 4.27: Global Subsidization of Infant Industries *If condition*

$$\sum_{h=1}^{\nu} {}_h p''_r \left({}_h y''^h - {}_h y'^h \right) + q'' \left(\sum_{h=1}^{\nu} {}_h a''^h - \sum_{h=1}^{\nu} {}_h a'^h \right)$$
$$\geq q'' \sum_{h=1}^{\nu} {}_h R'' \left({}_h y''^h - {}_h y'^h \right) \tag{4.31}$$

is satisfied, the infant industry protection by means of national production subsidies is beneficial for the world as a whole.

Generally speaking, if tariffs are nonexistent, and if taxes and subsidies on consumption are common to all countries, we find a correspondence in the above sense between the world and a price-taking country.[45] We may refer to this fact as a "correspondence principle" in trade and welfare. It is specifically pertinent to the familiar notion of the "ideal" world economy where free trade prevails among countries, except some national schemes of production subsidies designed to foster infant industries under the auspices of a world government.[46]

4.12 Concluding Remarks

We have derived numerous propositions from our basic theorem of welfare comparison, thereby showing that most of the welfare propositions obtained in simple models of trade are viable in the presence of trade in intermediate goods and factor services as well as in the presence of any number of non-traded commodities. Some of our propositions may be considered to be worthwhile from a puristic aspect, although many of the conditional statements will only satisfy non-purists. But we wish to emphasize the simplicity and the methodological uniformity of our approach, which compares two situations that may differ from each other in any manner and respect except in the set of consumers. If employed with enough caution, it may serve further useful purposes.

The lack of analysis of external economies and diseconomies may be pointed out as a major qualification of this study. When we consider the government as a producer or a consumer of *public goods*, this qualification may appear particularly restrictive: the external effect of public goods is often too obvious to escape one‘s eyes.[47] As is well known, externalities among economic agents will give rise to interdependence among their behaviors and invalidate the equilibrium conditions for producers and consumers. To remedy such a situation, it would be necessary to set up a system of artificial markets for externalities so that both external economies and diseconomies are properly counted as commodities.[48] Note, however, that external *diseconomies* are comparable to the supply of labor and their absence to

---

[45] Strictly speaking, this correspondence fails to apply to the propositions on a price-taking country that depend not only on the absence of the terms of trade effect but also on the *constancy* of the price of each tradeable commodity. Thus, Propositions 4.11 and 4.11 cannot be held valid for the world.

[46] An adept blueprint of such a world economy is found in Tinbergen (1962).

[47] As in the case of public goods that are not subject to the exclusion principle, the consumption or production of some commodities by an economic agent may affect a number of other economic agents at the same time. In such an event, it would be necessary to establish an agreement among those affected on the individual shares in the price of the externalities. For closely related concepts, see Musgrave (1959).

[48] But for the governmental intervention in the economy as a law-enforced broker between potential sellers and buyers, the scheme would be largely impractical because of the thinness of many markets for externalities. In fact, it would be economically equivalent to an alternative remedy by means of domestic taxes and subsidies if both are administered properly.

the endowment of leisure.[49] In fact, external diseconomies are not themselves commodities, but rather losses of the commodities which, in their full endowment, represent perfect freedom from external diseconomies. No one is, therefore, able to *supply* his external diseconomies beyond the tolerable degree of their irksomeness. This point is indeed essential to the workability of artificial markets for externalities. But so long as externalities are assumed to be internalized through such a scheme, the present model remains applicable without any formal modification.

References

Baldwin, R. E. (1952). The new welfare economics and gains in international trade. *The Quarterly Journal of Economics, 66*, 90–101.

Bhagwati, J. (1958). Immiserizing growth: A geometrical note. *The Review of Economic Studies, 25*, 201–205.

Bhagwati, J. (1964). The pure theory of international trade: A survey. *The Economic Journal, 74*, 1–81.

Bhagwati, J. (1968a). The gains from trade once again. *Oxford Economic Papers, 20*, 137–148.

Bhagwati, J. (1968b). Distortions and immiserizing growth: A generalization. *The Review of Economic Studies, 35*, 481–485.

Bhagwati, J. (1971). The generalized theory of distortions and welfare. In J. Bhagwati et al. (Eds.), *Trade, balance of payments and growth, papers in international economics in honor of Charles P. Kindleberger*. Amsterdam: North-Holland.

Bhagwati, J., & Ramaswami, V. K. (1963). Domestic distortions, tariffs, and the theory of optimum subsidy. *The Journal of Political Economy, 71*, 44–50.

Bhagwati, J., & Srinivasan, T. N. (1969). Optimal intervention to achieve non-economic objectives. *The Review of Economic Studies, 36*, 27–38.

Chipman, J. S. (1965). A survey of international trade: Part 2, the neo-classical theory. *Econometrica, 33*, 685–760.

Corden, W. M. (1957). Tariffs, subsidies, and the terms of trade. *Econometrica, 24*, 235–242.

Debreu, G. (1959). *Theory of value*. New York: Wiley.

Diamond, P. A., & Mirrlees, J. A. (1971a). Optimal taxation and public production I: Production efficiency. *The American Economic Review, 61*, 8–27.

Diamond, P. A., & Mirrlees, J. A. (1971b). Optimal public production II: Tax rules. *The American Economic Review, 61*, 261–278.

Dixit, A. K. (1970). On the optimal structure of commodity taxes. *The American Economic Review, 60*, 107–116.

Edgeworth, F. Y. (1894). The theory of international values. *The Economic Journal, 4*, 35–50.

Gehrels, F. (1956–1957). Customs unions from a single country viewpoint. *Review of Economic Studies, 24*(1), 61–64.

Inada, K. (1967). A note on the Heckscher–Ohlin theorem. *The Economic Record, 43*, 88–96.

Johnson, H. G. (1960). The cost of protection and the scientific tariff. *The Journal of Political Economy, 68*(4), 327–354.

[49] For example, consider a fisherman who suffers from a water-polluting factory only in business aspects. He is not in the position to *supply* his diseconomies beyond the degree of water pollution at which he goes out of business. Otherwise, he would supply an infinite amount of diseconomies at any positive price.

Johnson, H. G. (1964). Tariffs and economic development: Some theoretical issues. *Journal of Development Studies, 1*, 3–30.
Johnson, H. G. (1967). The possibility of income losses from increased efficiency or factor accumulation in the presence of tariffs. *The Economic Journal, 77*, 151–154.
Jones, R. W. (1961). Comparative advantage and the theory of tariffs: A multi-country, multi-commodity model. *The Review of Economic Studies, 28*, 161–175.
Jones, R. W. (1967). International capital movements and the theory of tariffs and trade. *The Quarterly Journal of Economics, 81*, 1–38.
Jones, R. W. (1969). Tariffs and trade in general equilibrium: Comment. *The American Economic Review, 59*, 418–424.
Kemp, M. C. (1960). The Mill–Bastable infant industry dogma. *The Journal of Political Economy, 68*, 65–67.
Kemp, M. C. (1962). The gains from international trade. *The Economic Journal, 72*, 803–819.
Kemp, M. C. (1964). *The pure theory of international trade*. Englewood Cliffs: Prentice-Hall.
Kemp, M. C. (1968). Some issues in the analysis of trade gains. *Oxford Economic Papers, 20*, 149–161.
Kemp, M. C. (1969). *The pure theory of international trade and investment*. Englewood Cliffs: Prentice-Hall.
Kemp, M. C., & Negishi, T. (1969). Domestic distortions, tariffs, and the theory of optimum subsidy. *The Journal of Political Economy, 77*, 1014–1016.
Kemp, M. C., & Negishi, T. (1970). Variable returns to scale, commodity taxes, factor market distortions and their implications for trade gains. *The Swedish Journal of Economics, 1*, 1–11.
Kennedy, C. (1954). An alternative proof of a theorem in welfare economics. *Oxford Economic Papers, 6*, 98–99.
Kravis, I. B. (1956). Availability and other influences on the commodity composition of trade. *The Journal of Political Economy, 64*, 143–155.
Krueger, A. O., & Sonnenschein, H. F. (1967). The terms of trade, the gains from trade, and price divergence. *International Economic Review, 8*, 121–127.
Leontief, W. W. (1933). The use of indifference curves in the analysis of foreign trade. *The Quarterly Journal of Economics, 47*, 493–503.
Lipsey, R. G. (1957). The theory of customs unions: Trade diversion and welfare. *Economica, 24*, 40–46.
Lipsey, R. G. (1960). The theory of customs unions: A general survey. *The Economic Journal, 70*, 496–513.
Lipsey, R. G., & Lancaster, K. J. (1956–1957). The general theory of second best. *Review of Economic Studies, 24*(1), 11–32.
McKenzie, L. W. (1959). On the existence of general equilibrium for a competitive market. *Econometrica, 27*, 54–71.
Meade, J. E. (1952). *A geometry of international trade*. London: Allen & Unwin.
Meade, J. E. (1955a). *The theory of customs unions*. Amsterdam: North Holland.
Meade, J. E. (1955b). *Trade and welfare (the theory of international economic policy)* (Vol. II). Oxford: Oxford University Press.
Mundell, R. A. (1960). The pure theory of international trade. *The American Economic Review, 50*, 67–110.
Musgrave, R. A. (1959). *The theory of public finance*. New York: McGraw-Hill.
Mynt, H. (1958). The classical theory of international trade and the underdeveloped countries. *The Economic Journal, 68*, 317–337.
Negishi, T. (1963). On social welfare function. *The Quarterly Journal of Economics, 77*, 156–158.
Negishi, T. (1968). Protection of the infant industry and dynamic internal economies. *The Economic Record, 24*, 56–57.
Nikaidô, H. (1968). *Convex structures and economic theory*. New York: Academic.
Ohyama, M. (1972). Domestic distortions, and the theory of tariffs. *Keio Economic Studies, 9*(1), 1–14.

Ohyama, M. (1974). Tariffs and the transfer problem. *Keio Economic Society, 11*, 29–45.
Ozga, S. A. (1955). An essay in the theory of tariffs. *The Journal of Political Economy, 63*, 489–499.
Samuelson, P. A. (1939). The gains from international trade. *Canadian Journal of Economics and Political Science, 5*, 195–205.
Samuelson, P. A. (1950). Evaluation of real national income. *Oxford Economic Papers, 2*, 1–29.
Samuelson, P. A. (1952). The transfer problem and transport costs: The terms of trade when impediments are absent. *The Economic Journal, 62*, 278–304.
Samuelson, P. A. (1954). The transfer problem and transport costs, II: Analysis of effects of trade impediments. *The Economic Journal, 64*, 264–289.
Samuelson, P. A. (1956). Social indifference curves. *The Quarterly Journal of Economics, 70*, 1–22.
Samuelson, P. A. (1962). The gains from international trade once again. *The Economic Journal, 72*, 820–829.
Scitovsky, T. (1942). A reconsideration of the theory of tariffs. *The Review of Economic Studies, 9*, 89–110.
Sontheimer, K. C. (1971). An existence theorem for the second best. *Journal of Economic Theory, 3*, 1–22.
Tan, A. H. H. (1971). Optimal trade policies and non-economic objectives in models involving imported materials, inter-industry flows and non-traded goods. *The Review of Economic Studies, 38*, 105–111.
Tinbergen, J. (1962). *Shaping the world economy: Suggestions for an international economic policy*. New York: Twentieth Century Fund.
Vanek, J. (1965). *General equilibrium of international discrimination: The case of customs unions*. Cambridge: Harvard University Press.
Viner, J. (1950). *The customs union issue*. New York: Carnegie Endowment.
von Haberler, G. (1950). Some problems in the pure theory of international trade. *The Economic Journal, 60*, 223–240.

Chapter 5
Domestic Distortions and the Theory of Tariffs

5.1 Introduction

The theory of tariffs, which evolved from the classical controversy over free trade and protectionism, occupies an important position in the study of trade and welfare. Early in the present century Bickerdike (1906, 1907a, b) formalized the proposition that a country is able to increase its real income by imposing a tariff on imports. The theme, labeled by Edgeworth (1908) as "poison," was later revived by Kaldor (1940) and thus achieved general recognition in the literature. Known today as the optimal tariff argument, it postulates fully competitive conditions, and relies crucially upon the assumption that the tariff-imposing country is potentially capable of affecting the international prices by restricting the volume of trade. In the absence of such national monopoly power, however, the argument ends up in endorsing the doctrine of free trade as the best policy for the country.

On the other hand, the explicit introduction of distortions in the domestic market has given rise to independent cases for tariff protection. Hagen (1958) popularized the idea of Manoilesco's pioneering work (1931) on the consequence of wage differentials between manufacturing and agriculture. Haberler (1952) provided a diagrammatic interpretation of Graham's earlier study (1923) concerning the implications of external economies. Despite the skepticism expressed in Bhagwati and Ramaswami (1963), these lines of thinking indeed serve to justify tariff protection for a country without monopoly power. This point was made clear by the companion papers by Kemp and Negishi (1969) and Bhagwati et al. (1969).

Although the literature on the subject is bulky, there seems to be no thoroughgoing algebraic treatment of the theory of tariffs for a general case in which elements of domestic distortions may be present. Perhaps as a result of the traditional distinction between the positive and normative aspects of the theory, the

---

This chapter is adapted from "Domestic Distortions and the Theory of Tariffs," *Keio Economic Studies*, Vol. 9, No.1, 1–15, 1972.

© Springer Japan 2016

M. Ohyama, *Macroeconomics, Trade, and Social Welfare*, Advances in Japanese Business and Economics 14, DOI 10.1007/978-4-431-55807-1_5

analysis of the subject, until recently, was not made fully explicit even for the case of ideally competitive conditions.[1] In this chapter we intend to fill in this gap in the literature, primarily with a view to synthesizing the standard optimal tariff argument and the distortion-oriented causes of protectionism. We first describe our model which, as in Jones (1969), incorporates the real incomes of trading countries among its endogenous variables, then followed in Sect. 5.3 by the positive analysis of tariffs in the presence of domestic distortions. All the qualitative results of the standard theory will be shown to remain valid for our general case, provided that the supply of a commodity is a positive function of its relative price and that no commodities are inferior in social consumption. Finally, in Sect. 5.4, we investigate the real income effect of tariffs and combine alternative arguments for a protective tariff in a generalized formula for the optimal tariff.

5.2 Tariffs in Trade Equilibrium

We select as the vehicle of our discussion the simple model of trade wherein two countries, home and foreign, produce and consume two commodities. The supply of productive resources is fixed and fully utilized in production in each country. The home country is assumed to export commodity 1 and the foreign country commodity 2. To clarify the make-up of this prototype, let us first concern ourselves with the home country. We define the home *excess* demand, e_i for commodity i, as the difference between the domestic demand x_i and the domestic supply y_i:

$$e_i = x_i - y_i \, (i = 1, 2) \tag{5.1}$$

The supply of commodities is supposed to be determined directly or indirectly by the competitive firms' efforts to maximize profits. For the moment we merely characterize y_i as a function of the domestic relative price of commodity 2.

$$y_i = y_i(p) \, (i = 1, 2) \tag{5.2}$$

We shall return to the discussion of this formulation in the next section.

The home country is assumed to impose a tariff on the import of commodity 2, creating a discrepancy between the home relative price p and the international relative price q of commodity 2. We write

$$p = tq \tag{5.3}$$

where t represents unity plus the ad valorem rate τ of the tariff, or

[1] See Sodersten and Vind (1968), pp. 394–395; they provide an explicit account of the general equilibrium model appropriate for the theory of tariffs. By way of comment on their paper, Jones (1969) achieves an alternative development of algebra of tariffs.

$$t = 1 + \tau \tag{5.4}$$

The tariff proceeds are assumed to be reimbursed to the home consumers in the form of lump-sum subsidies. The values of excess demand in the domestic price must always add up to the tariff proceeds. Thus, the aggregate budget constraint is written as

$$e_1 + pe_2 = (t - 1)qe_2 \tag{5.5}$$

In what follows, we abstract from complications caused by distributional changes, and define the index u of the home country's welfare as a strictly concave, differentiable function of consumption demands.

$$u = u(x_1, x_2) \tag{5.6}$$

Note that any function

$$v = v(u), v^{'}(u) > 0$$

formed by a monotonic transformation of u also serves as a valid index of welfare.

Competitive consumers are supposed to maximize u insatiably subject to the budget constraint (Eq. (5.5)); this implies that, for each level of welfare achieved, the consumers minimize their expenditure, that is, the value of the consumption bundle in the domestic price. Otherwise, there would be a consumption bundle costing less and yielding the same level of welfare. Consumers could choose it and buy more of both commodities without violating the budget constraint. This is a contradiction unless consumers are satiated. The minimization of expenditure for a given level of welfare, in its turn, implies that the demand for each commodity is a function of p and u. Therefore, we are able to write

$$x_i = x_i(p, u)\,(i = 1, 2) \tag{5.7}$$

Although this formulation of demand functions is neither conventional nor operational, it will prove useful for our analytical purposes.

For the foreign country we posit exactly symmetrical assumptions. We put an asterisk to each symbol to indicate the corresponding foreign variable. The foreign excess demand e_i^* is the difference between the foreign demand x_i^* and the foreign supply y^*:

$$e_i^* = x_i^* - y_i^*\,(i = 1, 2) \tag{5.8}$$

Without reiterating the explanation, we may write

$$y_i^* = y_i^*(p^*)\ (i = 1, 2) \tag{5.9}$$

$$x_i^* = x_i^*(p^*, u^*)\ (i = 1, 2) \tag{5.10}$$

where

$$u^* = u^*(x_1^*, x_2^*) \tag{5.11}$$

The foreign country imposes a tariff on the import of commodity 1. With t^* signifying unity plus the foreign ad valorem rate of tariff, we have the relationship

$$\pi = p^* t^* \tag{5.12}$$

The foreign aggregate budget constraint is written

$$e_1^* + p^* e_2^* = \left(\frac{t^* - 1}{t^*}\right) e_1^*. \tag{5.13}$$

The demand functions given in Eq. (5.10) reflect the welfare maximization of foreign consumers in conformity with the budget constraint.[2]

The familiar condition for an international trade equilibrium states

$$e_1{}^* = q e_2{}^* \tag{5.14}$$

where

$$e_1^* > 0,\ e_2 > 0 \tag{5.15}$$

In words, the value of foreign imports is equal to that of home imports when expressed in the international price; this is equivalent to the market clearance condition for all commodities because of the budget constraints, Eq. (5.5) and Eq. (5.13). Given t and t^*, we have so far 19 independent equations to determine the equilibrium value of the same number of variables.

Recall, however, that welfare functions u and u^* are uniquely given only up to a monotonic transformation. Needless to say, their choice does not affect the equilibrium values of other variables. Without loss of generality, let us assume

[2] To understand (5.3), (5.5), (5.12) and (5.13), note the definitions

$p = \frac{p_2}{p_1}, p^* = \frac{p_2^*}{p_1^*}, \pi \equiv p_2^*/p_1$

where p_i and p_i^* denote the domestic price of the ith commodity in unit of account in the home and foreign countries, respectively. For example, we can write the budget constraint of the foreign country first as

$p_1^* e_1^* + p_2^* e_2^* = (t^* - 1) p_1 e_1^*.$

Dividing through both sides by p_1^* and noting $p_1^* = t^* p_1$, we obtain Eq. (5.13).

$$\frac{\partial u}{\partial x_1} = 1, \ \frac{\partial u^*}{\partial x_1^*} = 1 \tag{5.16}$$

where the partial derivatives are evaluated at the equilibrium position. One can best see the significance of this normalization in the following variational forms:

$$du = dx_1 + \left(\frac{\partial u}{\partial x_2}\right) dx_2 = dx_1 + p dx_2, \tag{5.17}$$

$$du^* = dx_1^* + \left(\frac{\partial u^*}{\partial x_2^*}\right) dx_2^* = dx_1^* + p^* dx_2^*. \tag{5.18}$$

A small change in u (respectively u^*) is expressed as a price-weighted sum of changes in x_1 and x_2 (respectively x_1^* and x_2^*). If the welfare functions are linearly homogeneous, we observe

$$u = x_1 + p x_2,$$
$$u^* = x_1^* + p^* x_2^*.$$

The index u (respectively u^*) of the home (respectively foreign) country welfare is tantamount to the home (respectively foreign) consumption expenditure. In this light we propose to call u (respectively u^*) the real income of the home (respectively foreign) country. Thus, demand functions, Eqs. (5.7) and (5.10), state that the demand for each commodity is a function of the domestic relative price and real income in each country.

5.3 The Positive Effects of Tariffs

In the description of the model given in the preceding section, the supply of each commodity is assumed to be a function of the domestic relative price. One can best justify this assumption for a competitive model with a strictly convex production set, exempt from all sources of market failures: the production of each commodity is then related by the transformation schedule to the production of the other, and, for a given relative price, a point on the schedule is chosen such that the marginal rate of transformation is equal to the relative price. The dependence of the supply of commodities on the relative price is certainly conceivable in a more general situation possibly saddled with domestic distortions such as external economies and factor–reward differentials between sectors. In this broader context, however, we have to take into account at least two additional problems. First, an increase in a commodity's relative price may now result in a decrease in the quantity of that commodity produced. The possibility of this anomalous phenomenon has been extensively discussed for the case of intersectoral factor–reward differentials.[3] In the present study, we choose to eliminate this possibility arbitrarily and assume that the supply of commodities is *normally* responsive to a change in the relative price. As a matter of fact, this assumption is implicit in Haberler's analysis of external economies, as well as Hagen's treatment of factor reward differentials, each intended to rationalize tariff protection.

In the second place, with distortions in production, the marginal rate of transformation is no longer expected to be equal to the relative price. We propose to express this fact as

$$\alpha p = -\frac{dy_1}{dy_2}\ (\alpha > 0) \tag{5.19}$$

for the home country. The value of α will generally depend upon the choice of production point, (y_1, y_2). The social marginal opportunity cost of commodity 2 falls short of its relative price if α is less than one, and the former exceeds the latter if α is greater than one. Needless to say, the standard special case obtains if and only if α is equal to one.[4] For simplicity, we suppose that there are no domestic distortions in the foreign country.

Assuming the differentiability of all functions, we now wish to investigate the effect of an increase in the level of the home country's tariff on the key variables of the model. To ease notation, let a circumflex $(\widehat{\ })$, indicate the relative change in a variable or a parameter. For example, $\widehat{t}$ denotes dt/t and $\widehat{p}$ denotes dp/p. Totally differentiating the home excess demand for commodity 2 in the light of Eqs. (5.2), (5.3), and (5.7), we obtain

$$\hat{e}_2 = -(\xi_2 + \varphi_2)\hat{q} - (\varepsilon_2 + \varphi_2)\hat{t} + m_2\left(\frac{1}{pe_2}\right)du \tag{5.20}$$

where

$$\xi_2 = -\frac{p}{e_2}\frac{\partial x_2}{\partial p},\ \varphi_2 = -\frac{p}{e_2}\frac{\partial y_2}{\partial p}\ m_2 = p\partial x_2 \ \partial u\ .$$

The common coefficient $-(\xi_2 + \varphi_2)$ of $\hat{q}$ and $\hat{t}$ is the income compensated elasticity of the home country's import demand. The term ξ_2 is positive by the assumption of utility maximization. As noted earlier, we assume

A1. $\varphi_2 > 0$

[3] This and some other interesting implications of factor market distortions are largely outside the scope of the present study. We refer the reader to Magee (1969), Herberg and Kemp (1969), and Jones (1971).

[4] Thus, α may be taken to constitute "distortions parameters" discussed by Fishlow and Davis (1961).

that is, that the supply of commodity 2 increases as a result of an increase in its relative price. The coefficient m_2 of $(1/pe_2)du$ represents the home country's marginal propensity to consume the imported commodity. We assume

A2. $0 \leq m_2 \leq 1$

that is, that no commodity is inferior in home consumption. The role of assumptions A1 and A2 will be made clear momentarily.

From Eqs. (5.8), (5.9), (5.10), and (5.12), we similarly obtain

$$\hat{e}_1{}^* = -(\xi_1{}^* + \varphi_1{}^*)\hat{q} + m_1{}^*\left(\frac{1}{e_1{}^*}\right)du^* \tag{5.21}$$

where

$$\xi_1^* \equiv \frac{p^*}{e_1^*};\ \psi_1^* \equiv -\frac{p^*}{e_1^*}\frac{\partial y_1^*}{\partial p^*},\ m_1^* \equiv \frac{\partial x_1^*}{\partial u^*}.$$

In the derivation of Eq. (5.21), the foreign country's tariff is assumed to be constant, that is, $\hat{i} = 0$. To obtain an appropriate expression for the change in home real income du, we note Eq. (5.17), and differentiate the home budget constraint to discover

$$du = (dy_1 + pdy_2) - qe_2\hat{q} + qe_2(t-1)\hat{e}_2. \tag{5.22}$$

From Eq. (5.3), Eq. (5.19), and the definition of φ_2, we find

$$dy_1 + pdy_2 = qe_2\varphi_2 t(1-\alpha)(\hat{q} + \hat{t}). \tag{5.23}$$

When there are no domestic distortions, the price-weighted sum of output changes $(dy_1 + pdy_2)$ vanishes to zero because of the tangency condition that the marginal rate of transformation is equal to the relative price. The introduction of domestic distortion serves to destroy this elegant property of the model. Equations (5.22) and (5.23) demonstrate the fundamental fact that if α differs from one, output changes give rise to a change in real income. Substituting Eq. (5.23) into Eq. (5.22) and collecting terms, we get

$$du = -\pi e_2\left\{[1-\psi_2 t(1-\alpha)]\widehat{\pi} - \psi_2 t(1-\alpha)\widehat{t} - (t-1)\widehat{e}_2\right\} \tag{5.24}$$

In a similar fashion, we obtain the corresponding expression for du^* from Eqs. (5.12), (5.13), and (5.18) as

$$du^* = e_1{}^*\left[\left(\frac{1}{i^*}\right)\hat{q} + \left(\frac{t^*-1}{t^*}\right)\hat{e}_1{}^*\right]. \tag{5.25}$$

The relative simplicity of the expression for du^* is attributable to the assumption that there are no domestic distortions in the foreign country. Equation (5.20), together with Eq. (5.24), yields

$$\hat{e}_2 = -\varepsilon_2\hat{q} - \overline{\varepsilon}\hat{t} \tag{5.26}$$

where

$$\varepsilon_2 \equiv \frac{t}{t - m_2(t-1)}\left\{\xi_2 + [1 - m_2(1-\alpha)]\psi_2 + \left(\frac{1}{t}m_2\right)\right\},$$
$$\overline{\varepsilon}_2 = \frac{t}{t - m_2(t-1)}\{\xi_2 + [1 - m_2(1-\alpha)].\varphi_2$$

Now, $\varepsilon_2(\overline{\varepsilon}_2)$ is the (compensated) elasticity of the home country's offer curve. Assumptions A1 and A2 ensure that both ε_2 and $\overline{\varepsilon}_2$ are positive, irrespective of the value of α. Therefore, the presence of domestic distortions does not affect the standard result that a rise in the level of the home country's tariff brings about an inward shift of the home offer curve. This intermediate conclusion will suffice to enable the reader acquainted with the geometry of international trade to anticipate the terms of trade effect of a tariff reform. We shall, however, follow the present logic to its end. In a similar fashion, Eq. (5.21), together with Eq. (5.25), results in

$$\hat{e}_1{}^* = \varepsilon_1{}^*\hat{q} \tag{5.27}$$

where

$$\varepsilon_1{}^* = \frac{t^*}{t^* - m_1{}^*(t^*-1)}\left\{\xi_1{}^* + \varphi_1{}^* + \left(\frac{1}{t^*}\right)m_1{}^*\right\}$$

The equilibrium condition, Eq. (5.14), is shown in rates of change as

$$\hat{e}_1{}^* = \hat{q} + \hat{e}. \tag{5.28}$$

From Eqs. (5.26), (5.27), and (5.28), we obtain

$$\widehat{\pi} = -\overline{\varepsilon}_2\left(\frac{1}{\Delta}\right) \tag{5.29}$$

where

$$\Delta \equiv \varepsilon_1^* + \varepsilon_2 - 1$$

As is easily seen, the stability condition of the system requires that the generalized Marshall–Lerner expression Δ be positive. Hence, we can state:

Proposition 5.1: Tariffs and the Terms of Trade *Under assumptions A1 and A2, an increase in the home level of tariffs gives rise to an improvement in the home country's terms of trade.*

In the standard special case, assumptions A1 and A2 are not required for the validity of this proposition. So long as assumption A1 is acceptable, the price of generalization is probably not so demanding because the inferiority of a commodity is always considered to be aberrant in a highly aggregated model such as the present one.

The substitution of Eq. (5.29) back into Eq. (5.27) gives the effect of a tariff increase upon the home country's export.

$$\widehat{e}_1^* = -\varepsilon_1^* \overline{\varepsilon}_2 \left(\frac{1}{\Delta}\right) \widehat{t}. \tag{5.30}$$

From Eqs. (5.28), (5.29), and (5.30), we obtain the relationship between a change in the tariff and a change in the home country's import.

$$\widehat{e}_2 = -\overline{\varepsilon}_2 \left(\varepsilon_1^* - 1\right) \left(\frac{1}{\Delta}\right) \widehat{t}. \tag{5.31}$$

We have established:

Proposition 5.2: Tariffs and the Volume of Trade *Under assumptions A1 and A2, the home country's export diminishes as a result of a tariff increase: Its import diminishes as a result of a tariff increase if and only if the foreign country's offer curve is elastic.*

Increasing tariffs is said to be protective if it brings about an expansion of the import-competing production. Under the present assumption of positive ψ_2, the effect of a tariff increase upon the domestic price is the key reference as to whether a given tariff increase is in fact protective. Using Eqs. (5.3) and (5.29), we obtain

$$\widehat{p} = \left(\frac{1}{\Delta}\right) (\Delta - \overline{\varepsilon}_2) \widehat{t}. \tag{5.32}$$

From the definition of Δ, ε_2, and $\overline{\varepsilon}_2$, we can easily calculate the relationship

$$\Delta - \overline{\varepsilon}_2 = \varepsilon_1^* - 1 + \frac{m_2}{t - m_2(t-1)}. \tag{5.33}$$

This is nothing but the famous Metzler expression.

Proposition 5.3: Tariffs and Protection *Under assumption A1, an increase in the home level of a tariff is protective if and only if the Metzler condition*

$$\varepsilon^{*} > 1 - \frac{m_2}{t - m_2(t-1)} \tag{5.34}$$

is satisfied.

Note that the Metzler expression is completely independent of the value of α. The introduction of domestic distortions does not affect the condition for a protective tariff under assumption A1. This result is of course not surprising. In fact, a rise in the rate of tariff will be protective if there exists a positive world excess demand for commodity 2 when the home relative price is fixed at the initial level. But so long as the home relative price is fixed, there will be no output changes, and therefore no real income change associated with them. Thus, the crucial real income effect of output changes has no part in determining the condition for a positive world excess demand to arise for the initial home relative price.[5]

5.4 Tariffs and the Real Income

We have so far concerned ourselves with the "positive" aspect of the theory of tariffs. It is shown that all the clear-cut outcomes of the standard special case carry over to the present general setting under the rather simple assumptions A1 and A2. The propositions obtained, however, would be of little significance if they were in no way related to the question of how tariffs affect the real incomes in trading countries. In fact, their relevance is evident for the present model, positing the real incomes as endogenous variables. We are now in the position to investigate the "normative" aspect of the theory of tariffs and trade.

Let us substitute Eqs. (5.29) and (5.31) into Eq. (5.24) to connect a change in the home country's real income directly with a change in the tariff.

$$du = \frac{qe_2t}{\Delta}\left\{\left[1 - \left(\frac{t-1}{t}\right)\varepsilon_{1*}\right]\overline{\varepsilon}_2 + \varphi_2(1-\alpha)(\Delta - \overline{\varepsilon}_2)\right\}\hat{t}. \tag{5.35}$$

Consider the case $\alpha < 1$, in which the social marginal opportunity cost of commodity 2 is less than its domestic relative price, and therefore its marginal rate of substitution in the domestic consumption. Under such a circumstance, an increase in the output of commodity 2 is expected to improve the home country welfare because the increment is more valuable than the amount to be foregone of commodity 1. This consideration is justified by the second term $\psi_2(1-\alpha)(\Delta - \overline{\varepsilon}_2)$ in the bracket of the right-hand side of Eq. (5.35). So long as an increase in the home

[5] See Metzler (1939).

level of tariff is protective, it contributes to the country's real income by that account alone. If there is no tariff in the initial situation, that is, if $t = 1$, Eq. (5.35) simplifies to

$$du = \frac{qe_2}{\Delta}\{\overline{\varepsilon}_2 + \psi_2(1-\alpha)(\Delta - \overline{\varepsilon}_2)\}\hat{t}. \tag{5.36}$$

This situation leads us to the following.

Proposition 5.4: Tariffs and Real Income *Let $\alpha < 1$. Under assumptions A1 and A2, a small tariff starting from free trade increases the home country's real income if the tariff is protective.*[6]

Now, as the initial rate of tariff increases, the term $[1 - (t - 1/t)\varepsilon_1^*]\overline{\varepsilon}_2$ will eventually become nonpositive over the elastic portion of the foreign offer curve and may at some point exactly cancel out the nonnegative term $\psi_2(1-\alpha)(\Delta - \overline{\varepsilon}_2)$. In view of Eq. (5.35), it is at this point that the optimal tariff obtains. Recalling Eq. (5.4), we may characterize the optimal position by

$$\tau = \frac{\overline{\varepsilon}_2 + \varphi_2(1-\alpha)(\Delta - \overline{\varepsilon}_2)}{\overline{\varepsilon}_2(\varepsilon_1{*} - 1) - \varphi_2(1-\alpha)(\Delta - \overline{\varepsilon}_2)}. \tag{5.37}$$

Note that if $\alpha = 1$, Eq. (5.39) gives the familiar optimal tariff formula for the standard special case:

$$\tau = \frac{1}{\varepsilon^* - 1}. \tag{5.38}$$

When α is strictly less than one, the term $[1 - (t - 1/t)\varepsilon_1^*]\overline{\varepsilon}_2$ must be strictly negative at the optimal point. Hence, everything else being unchanged, the presence of domestic distortions is expected to push up the level of the optimal tariff.

Let us briefly consider the case $\alpha > 1$. In this case, the social marginal opportunity cost of commodity 2 is greater than its marginal rate of substitution in the domestic consumption. Therefore, an increase in the output of commodity 2 brings about a loss in the home country's real income. Starting from free trade, the imposition of a small tariff improves the home country's terms of trade, but if it is protective, it increases the output of commodity 2 at the same time. In the presence of two opposing forces thus set loose, there is no a priori way to determine the net effect of the protective tariff on the real income. In consequence, the usual

---

[6] This summarily expresses various arguments for a protective tariff. Bhagwati, Ramaswami, and Srinivasan (1969) argue that if there exist domestic distortions and national monopoly power, a tariff may not increase the country's real income above the free trade level. Without contradicting their result, we have here established that a protective tariff, if possible at all, will always increase the country's welfare in the case that α is less than one.

optimal tariff argument breaks down in this case. A small tariff, however, improves the home country's welfare unambiguously whenever it fails to be protective.

Now suppose that the home country is very small compared to the foreign country, and that the home export of commodity 1 plays only a negligible role in the foreign consumption. Consider the definition:

$$\xi_1{}^* = \frac{p^*}{e_1{}^*}\frac{\partial x_1{}^*}{\partial p^*} = \frac{x^*}{e_1{}^*}\left(\frac{p^*}{x_1{}^*}\frac{\partial x_1{}^*}{\partial p^*}\right);$$

$$\varphi_1{}^* = -\frac{p^*}{e_1{}^*}\frac{\partial y_1{}^*}{\partial p^*} = -\frac{y_1{}^*}{e_1{}^*}\left(\frac{p^*}{y_1{}^*}\frac{\partial y_1{}^*}{\partial p^*}\right).$$

One can approximate such a state by letting ξ_1^* and ψ_1^* to infinity because terms x_1^*/e_1^* and y_1^*/e_1^* are considered to be practically as large as desired. Note also that ε_1^* tends to infinity as ξ_1^* and ψ_1^* tend to infinity. Therefore, letting ξ_1^* to infinity in Eq. (5.37), we obtain

$$du = \pi e_2 t\left[\psi_2(1-\alpha) - \left(\frac{t-1}{t}\right)\overline{\varepsilon}_2\right]\hat{t} \tag{5.39}$$

which approximates the relationship between a change in the home country's real income and a change in the tariff for the present special case. If there is initially no tariff, Eq. (5.39) reduces to

$$du = \pi e_2[\psi_2(1-\alpha)]\hat{t} \tag{5.40}$$

The right-hand side of this equality is positive or negative according as whether α is less or greater than one. Hence, we have the following.

Proposition 5.5: Tariffs and Real Income *Assume that the home country is sufficiently small.*

1. *Let $\alpha < 1$. Under assumption A1, a small tariff starting from free trade increases the home country's real income.*
2. *Let $\alpha > 1$. Under assumption A1, a small (export or import) subsidy starting from free trade increases the home country's real income.*

Once the initial rate of tariff or subsidy departs from zero, we must revert to Eq. (5.39). Notice that the two terms in the right-hand side bracket are of opposite signs for each case. The term $\psi_2(1-\alpha)$ is positive, but the term $-(t-1/t)\overline{\varepsilon}_2$ is negative if α is less than one and there is initially a tariff. The converse is true if α is greater than one and there is initially a subsidy. Thus, the optimal tariff or subsidy obtains when the two terms are exactly equal in absolute value. The rate of the optimal tariff or subsidy is therefore given by

$$\tau = \frac{\varphi_2(1-\alpha)}{\overline{\varepsilon}_2 - \varphi_2(1-\alpha)} \tag{5.41}$$

One can easily check that τ is positive if α is less than one and negative if α is greater than one.

In their 1963 paper, Bhagwati and Ramaswami cast a strong doubt on the validity of the conjecture that there exists a tariff or subsidy superior to free trade in the presence of domestic distortions. Except for the explicit statement of assumption A1, the conjecture is later rehabilitated, in the form similar to Proposition 5.5, by Kemp and Negishi (1969) and Bhagwati et al. (1969). The principal historic interest of Proposition 5.5 consists in its first part, which elaborates in a single procedure the Haberler–Graham case, as well as the Manoilesco–Hegen case, for a protective tariff.

5.5 Concluding Remarks

Throughout the foregoing analysis we have adhered to the assumption A1 that the output of a commodity expands as its relative price increases. As noted here, this is no longer an innocuous assumption in the presence of domestic distortions. We must therefore be well aware of the consequences of its failure. First, note that the sign of $\overline{\varepsilon}_2$ is crucial for the conclusion of Propositions 5.1, 5.2, and 5.4. Although the positivity of φ_2 is not necessary for the positivity of $\overline{\varepsilon}_2$, nothing can be said as to the sign of $\overline{\varepsilon}_2$ if φ_2 is negative. Second, the Metzler condition for a protective tariff must be reversed if the output of a commodity decreases as its domestic prices increases. Propositions 5.3 and 5.5 are accordingly to be modified. If the foreign country is sufficiently large relative to the home country, the value of $\varepsilon_1{}^*$ will be such that condition (5.34) is always satisfied. However, this now implies that a subsidy is protective, but it is not a tariff.

It may be worth dwelling for a moment upon some of these anomalous implications of the failure of assumption A1. Let us first reconsider the significance of Proposition 5.5 in relation to the Manoilescu–Hagen case for protection. Suppose that there are two factors of production, say, labor and capital. In the case that there are factor–reward differentials between sectors, assumption A1 holds if and only if the factor-intensity ranking of sectors in a value sense coincides with the ranking in a physical sense.[7] Hagen argues that wages in manufacturing are typically higher than in agriculture in an economy in which per capita income is rising secularly. If this is the case, and if agriculture is more labor intensive than manufacturing in a physical sense, then the latter may as well be more labor intensive in a value sense because of the wage premium paid to the labor hired in manufacturing. Therefore,

[7] Jones (1971) gives a most lucid account of this condition.

assumption A1 may fail to hold, and the case may have to be made for subsidy protection rather than tariff protection.

There are also some points of interest concerning the reevaluation of the message contained in Proposition 5.1. Early in the twentieth century, Marshall (1903) pondered the possibility that a tariff on wheat might turn the terms of trade against England when the "Giffen" paradox seemed to operate in respect to imports of wheat into England.[8] In view of Eq. (5.29) and the definition of $\overline{\varepsilon}_2$, Marshall's conjecture may be justified if assumption A1 fails to hold *and* the social marginal opportunity cost of the import commodity is smaller than its relative price ($\alpha < 1$). It should be noted, however, that, in the standard special case in which there are no domestic distortions and the output of a commodity expands as its relative price rises, an increase in the home level of tariff turns the terms of trade against the home country if and only if

$$m_2 > \frac{t}{t-1} > 1.$$

This point implies that the export commodity (and not the import commodity) is inferior in the home country's consumption.

Finally, it is well established that a tariff is *not* the best policy instrument available for a country subject to domestic distortions (see Bhagwati and Ramaswami 1963)). Although we have confined ourselves to the theory of tariffs, we can likewise develop the theory of other (indirect) forms of intervention in foreign trade. The use of a tariff in combination with a corrective production tax-cum-subsidy is capable of yielding the best solution and is superior to the use of a tariff alone. This consideration, however, will not discount the significance of the present exercise as a study of the piecemeal economic policy.

References

Bhagwati, J., & Ramaswami, V. K. (1963). Domestic distortions, tariffs, and the theory of optimum subsidy. *Journal of Political Economy, 71*, 44–50.

Bhagwati, J., Ramaswami, V. K., & Srinivasan, T. N. (1969). Domestic distortions, tariffs, and the theory of optimum subsidy: Some further results. *Journal of Political Economy, 77*, 1005–1010.

Bickerdike, C. F. (1906). The theory of incipient taxes. *Economic Journal, 16*, 529–535.

Bickerdike, C. F. (1907a). Protective and preferential import duties: Book review. *Economic Journal, 17*, 98–102.

Bickerdike, C. F. (1907b). Relation of the general supply curve to a particular expenses curve. *Economic Journal, 17*, 583–585.

Edgeworth, F. Y. (1908). Appreciations of mathematical theories: III. *Economic Journal, 18*, 392–403, 541–556

[8] Marshall (1903), pp. 382–383. Kemp (1966) gives a reexamination of the Marshallian conjecture on the assumption that the government consumes out of the tariff revenue.

Fishlow, A., & David, P. A. (1961). Optimal resource allocation in an imperfect market setting. *Journal of Political Economy, 69*, 529–546.

Graham, F. D. (1923). Some aspects of protection further considered. *Quarterly Journal of Economics, 37*, 199–227.

Haberler, G. v. (1952). Some problems in the pure theory of international trade. *The Economic Journal, 60*, 223–240.

Hagen, E. E. (1958). An economic justification of protectionism. *Quarterly Journal of Economics, 72*, 496–514.

Herberg, H., & Kemp, M. C. (1969). Factor market distortions, the shape of the locus of competitive outputs, and the relation between product prices and equilibrium outputs. In J. Bhagwati et al. (Eds.), *Trade, balance of payments, and growth: papers in honor of Charles P. Kindleberger*. Amsterdam: North-Holland.

Jones, R. W. (1969). Tariffs and trade in general equilibrium: Comment. *American Economic Review, 59*, 418–424.

Jones, R. W. (1971). Distortions in factor markets and the general equilibrium theory of production. *Journal of Political Economy, 79*, 437–459.

Kaldor, N. (1940). A note on tariffs and terms of trade. *Economica, 7*, 377–380.

Kemp, M. C. (1966). Note on a Marshallian conjecture. *Quarterly Journal of Economics, 80*, 481–484.

Kemp, M. C., & Negishi, T. T. (1969). Domestic distortions, tariffs, and the theory of optimum subsidy. *Journal of Political Economy, 77*, 1011–1013.

Magee, S. P. (1969). *Factor market distortions and the pure theory of international trade*. Ph.D. thesis, Massachusetts Institute of Technology (M.I.T.), Cambridge

Manoilescu, M. (1931). *The theory of protection and international trade*. London: King & Son.

Marshall, A. (1903) Memorandum on fiscal policy of international trade. Official policy of international trade. In: *Official Papers by Alfred Marshall*. London: Macmillan, 1926.

Metzler, L. A. (1939). Tariffs, international demand and domestic prices. *Journal of Political Economy, 57*, 345–351.

Sodersten, B., & Vind, K. (1968). Tariffs and trade in general equilibrium. *American Economic Review, 58*, 394–408.

Chapter 6
Tariffs and the Transfer Problem

6.1 Introduction

The transfer problem has attracted much attention in the literature of international trade theory since the famous controversy between Keynes and Ohlin in the late 1920s. Practically, the international transfer of purchasing power is widely observed in various guises such as private remittance, reparation, and economic aid. Theoretically, it poses an interesting question concerning the *real* income effect of income transfers between countries. This question lurks also in the analysis of currency devaluation, often conceived as an attempt to affect the international terms of trade to create a trade surplus. Discussing the German reparation problem, Keynes (1929) held the position that the expenditure of the German people will be reduced, not only by the amount of reparation, but also by a decrease in their gold-rate of earnings. As Ohlin (1929) pointed out quickly, however, Keynes thereby failed to pursue the logic of his own argument: "if £ 1 is taken from you and given to me and I choose to increase my consumption of precisely the same goods as those of which you are compelled to diminish yours, there is no transfer problem." (See Keynes 1929, p. 2.) Later analysis, notably Samuelson (1952, 1954) and Johnson (1955), elucidated the implications of this logic in the context of a two-country, two-commodity model of trade. They showed that the direction of change in the terms of trade depends crucially upon the relative magnitude of the marginal propensities to consume between the two countries. There is, however, no presumption about this relative magnitude under free trade with no trade impediments.

As Samuelson argued quite convincingly, we need either to remold the basic structure of the model or to introduce trade impediments into the picture if we are to give credit to the orthodox view held by Keynes and other classical economists on

This chapter is adapted from "Tariffs and Transfer Problem," *Keio Economic Studies*, Vol. 11, No. 1, 29–45, 1974.

© Springer Japan 2016

M. Ohyama, *Macroeconomics, Trade, and Social Welfare*, Advances in Japanese Business and Economics 14, DOI 10.1007/978-4-431-55807-1_6

the "additional" burden of a transfer. In this chapter, we intend to give a microscopic study of the transfer problem in relationship to tariffs, one of the typical trade impediments. Needless to say, tariffs create a divergence between the internal and external prices, thereby affecting the volume of trade and giving rise to tariff revenue. It is because of this obvious property of tariffs that we cannot disregard its special bearing on the transfer problem. Aside from Samuelson's celebrated studies, however, there seems to be little literature exploring the implications of this fundamental recognition.

The next section provides the analytical groundwork for our inquiry. In Sect. 6.3, we investigate the effect of an international transfer on the terms of trade and real incomes. As is emphasized, the change in a country's tariff revenue resulting from a transfer constitutes a genuine real income effect in addition to the change in the initial income and the terms of trade. Section 6.4 is devoted to the study of the anomalous case in which the transferor becomes better off or the transferee gets impoverished as a result of transfer. Finally, in Sect. 6.5, we consider the neglected issue of *tied* transfer, which may be regarded as a further aspect of the relevance of tariffs to the transfer problem.

6.2 The Model

To analyze the transfer problem in the presence of tariffs, we have to modify slightly the standard model of tariffs. As usual, let there be two countries, home and foreign, and two commodities, 1 and 2. Each country is assumed to produce and consume both of the two commodities under perfectly competitive conditions. There are no domestic distortions such as factor–rewards differentials between industries, or external economies. In each country, the domestic supply of productive resources is fixed in quality as well as in quantity. The home country is supposed to export commodity 1 and the foreign country commodity 2 in a trade equilibrium. The home country imposes a tariff on the import of commodity 2, and the foreign country on the import of commodity 1, and this produces a cleavage between the home prices $p_i (i = 1, 2)$ and the foreign prices $p_i{}^* (i = 1, 2)$[1]:

$$p_1{}^* = p_1 t^* = p_1(1 + \tau^*), \tag{6.1}$$

$$p_2 = p_2^* t = p_2^*(1 + \tau) \tag{6.2}$$

where t (respectively t^*) represents unity plus the home (respectively foreign) ad valorem rate τ (respectively τ^*). The tariff proceeds are assumed to be given away to the public in the form of lump-sum subsidies.

[1] We assume that the unit of home currency is adjusted such that the exchange rate is equal to unity. Thus, the unit of account is common between countries.

This setting is merely a reproduction of the standard model of tariffs. In addition, however, we assume that the home country pays an indemnity $b\,(>0)$ fixed in terms of the common unit of account. The home country raises this amount by lump-sum taxes, and the foreign country uses it as lump-sum subsidies. Under these conditions, the consumers' budget constraint implies

$$p_1 e_1 + p_2 e_2 = (t-1)p_2^* e_2 - b, \tag{6.3}$$

$$p_1^* e_1^* + p_2^* e_2^* = (t^* - 1)p_1 e_1^* + b \tag{6.4}$$

where e_i (respectively e_i^*) denotes the home (respectively foreign) excess demand for commodity i. In other words, the excess demand values in domestic prices sum up to the net value of lump-sum subsidies given to the public in each country. Note that the excess demand e_i is the difference between the demand x_i and the supply y_i, or

$$e_i = x_i - y_i \ (i = 1,\ 2). \tag{6.5}$$

Similarly,

$$e_i^* = x_i^* - y_i^* \ (i = 1, 2). \tag{6.6}$$

We assume that the demand is a function of internal prices and the country's real income, and that the supply is a function of internal prices. However, a uniform doubling of accounting prices should not affect the behavior of rational economic agents. For this reason, we may set the home price of commodity 1 at a certain fixed level.[2] Define

$$p = \frac{p_2}{p_1}, \tag{6.7}$$

$$p^* = \frac{p_2{}^*}{p_1{}^*}, \tag{6.8}$$

$$q = \frac{p_2{}^*}{p_1}. \tag{6.9}$$

Then, we may write

$$e_i = e_1(p, u) = x_i(p, u) - y_i(p) \tag{6.10}$$

$$e_i{}^* = e_i{}^*(p^*, u^*) = x_i{}^*(p^*, y^*) - y_i{}^*(p^*) \tag{6.11}$$

where u (respectively u^*) denotes the home (respectively foreign) country's real income. We can interpret q in Eq. (6.9) as the international terms of trade.

[2] This implies the constancy of the foreign prices of commodity 1 under the given exchange rate and the given rate of tariffs.

Following the convention in the literature, we say that if q increases (respectively decreases), the terms of trade deteriorates (respectively improves) from the home country's point of view.

An international trade equilibrium obtains if and only if the home country achieves the balance of trade surplus by the amount of the transfer payment when evaluated in international prices:

$$p_1 e_1^* - p_2^* e_2 - b = 0 \tag{6.12}$$

where

$$e_1^* > 0,\ e_2 > 0.$$

For the purpose of comparative statics, it is necessary to rewrite the system just described in variational form. We assume that there is no transfer payment in the initial equilibrium, or $b = 0$. This assumption is usually made to avoid unnecessary complications of the variational system. Let us express real income changes by

$$du = p_1 dx_1 + p_2 dx_2, \tag{6.13}$$

$$du^* = p_1^* dx_1^* + p_2^* dx_2^*. \tag{6.14}$$

This formula gives us the Laspeyres index of real income changes: but note that its sign also agrees with the sign of the Paache index for a sufficiently small variation.[3] To ease notation, let a circumflex ($\hat{\ }$) indicate the relative change in a variable. For example, $\hat{t}$ denotes dt/t and $\hat{p}$ denotes dp/p. We first totally differentiate the home excess demand function (6.10) for commodity 2. Rearranging terms in view of Eqs. (6.2), (6.7), and (6.9), we obtain

$$\hat{e}_2 = -\overline{\eta}_2 \hat{q} - \overline{\eta}_2 \hat{t} + m_2 \left(\frac{1}{p_2 e_2}\right) du \tag{6.15}$$

where

$$\overline{\eta}_2 = -\frac{p}{e_2}\frac{\partial e_2}{\partial p},\ m_2 = p_2 \frac{\partial x_2}{\partial u}.$$

The coefficient $\overline{\eta}_2$ of $\hat{q}$ and $\hat{t}$ is the "income compensated" elasticity of the home country's import demand, and the coefficient m_2 is the home country's marginal propensity to consume the import commodity. From Eqs. (6.1), (6.8), (6.9), and (6.11), we similarly obtain

[3] For this definition of real income changes, see also the discussion in Jones (1969).

$$\hat{e}_1^{\,*} = -\overline{\eta}_1^* \hat{\pi} - \overline{\eta}_1^* \hat{t}^{\,*} + m_1^* \left(\frac{1}{p_1^* e_1^*} \right) du^* \tag{6.16}$$

where

$$\overline{\eta}_1^* = \frac{p^*}{e_1^*} \frac{\partial e_1^*}{\partial p^*},\ m_1^* = p_1^* \frac{\partial x_1^*}{\partial u^*}.$$

We can interpret η^* and m^* as above except that they now pertain to the foreign country rather than to the home country. To rewrite Eqs. (6.15) and (6.17), we need to obtain appropriate expressions for du and du^*. For the home country, differentiate totally the budget constraint (Eq. (6.3)), taking notice of Eqs. (6.5) and (6.10). Then, we can rewrite the result in the light of definitions, Eqs. (6.2), (6.7), (6.9), and (6.13), as follows:

$$du = -p_2^* e_2 \hat{\pi} - db + (t-1) p_2^* e_2. \tag{6.17}$$

Here, the first term on the right-hand side represents the terms of trade effect of the variation on the home country's real income, the second term stands for the direct effect of a transfer payment, and the last term for the effect of a change in tariff revenue. Clearly, an increase in imports gives rise to an increase in tariff revenue under positive tariffs and an increase in subsidy expenditure under negative tariffs. In general, it is in the presence of some wedge between internal and external prices that this last effect appears to be reflecting some "arbitrage" loss or benefit for the country. For the foreign country, we similarly obtain

$$du^* = p_2^* e_2 \hat{\pi} + db + (t^* - 1) p_1^* e_1^* \hat{e}_1^*. \tag{6.18}$$

Now substitute Eq. (6.17) into Eq. (6.15) and collect terms. We get

$$\hat{e}_2 = -\varepsilon_2 \hat{\pi} - \overline{\varepsilon}_2 \hat{t} - \left(\frac{1}{p_2^* e_2} \right) \mu_2 db \tag{6.19}$$

where

$$\varepsilon_2 = \frac{t}{t - m_2(t-1)} \left(\overline{\eta}_2 + \frac{m_2}{t} \right),$$

$$\overline{\varepsilon}_2 = \frac{t\overline{\eta}_2}{t - m_2(t-1)},$$

$$\mu_2 = \frac{m_2}{t - m_2(t-1)}.$$

The symbol ε_2 (respectively $\overline{\varepsilon}_2$) signifies the (respectively "compensated") elasticity of the home country's offer curve. In a similar fashion, Eq. (6.17), together with Eq. (6.17), yields

$$\widehat{e}_1^* = \varepsilon_1^* \widehat{\pi} - \overline{\varepsilon}_1^* \widehat{t}^* + \left(\frac{1}{p_1 e_1^*}\right) \mu_1^* db \tag{6.20}$$

where

$$\varepsilon_1^* = \frac{t^*}{t^* - m_1^*(t^* - 1)} \left(\overline{\eta}^* + \frac{m_1^*}{t^*}\right),$$

$$\overline{\varepsilon}_1^* = \frac{t^* \overline{\eta}_1^*}{t^* - m_1^*(t^* - 1)},$$

$$\mu_1^* = \frac{m_1^*}{t^* - m_1^*(t^* - 1)}.$$

The equilibrium condition (6.12) is shown in variational form as

$$p_2^* e_2 (\hat{e}_2 - \hat{e}_1^*) + p_2^* e_2 \hat{\pi} + db = 0. \tag{6.21}$$

From Eqs. (6.15), (6.16), and (6.17), we obtain

$$\hat{q} = \frac{1}{\Delta}\left\{ (\overline{\varepsilon}_1 {*} \hat{t} {*} - \overline{\varepsilon}_2 \hat{t}) + \left(\frac{1}{p_2 {*} e_2}\right)(1 - \mu_1 {*} - \mu_2) db \right\} \tag{6.22}$$

where

$$\Delta = \varepsilon_1^* + \varepsilon_2 - 1$$

Note that by the stability condition the generalized Marshall–Lerner expression Δ is positive.

The groundwork is now complete. We shall proceed to examine the problems posed earlier in this chapter.

6.3 The Effect of Transfer Under Tariffs

There is no ambiguity about the direct effect of a transfer payment. The past literature is primarily concerned with the delicate terms of trade effect. If a transfer results in a deterioration of the paying country's terms of trade under free trade, it means an additional loss of the latter's real income and an extra gain for the receiving country. The so-called orthodox view suggests that this will in all probability indeed be the case. After examining the related literature exhaustively, Samuelson (1952, 1954) concludes that, in the absence of trade impediments such as tariffs and transport costs, the orthodox presumption turns out to fall completely to the side. In the tariff case, however, he shows by the technique of a box diagram that a transfer will tend to affect the terms of trade in favor of the receiving country when preferences are identical between the countries and representable by a set of homothetic indifference curves. We shall begin by examining this result in greater detail.

To focus upon the pure effect of an untied transfer, let us assume in this section that the tariffs are invariable, viz.

$$\widehat{t} = 0, \widehat{t^*} = 0.$$

Then, from Eq. (6.21) we immediately obtain

$$\hat{q} = \frac{1}{p_2^* e_2 \Delta}\left(1 - \mu_1^* - \mu_2\right) db. \tag{6.23}$$

because the home country imports commodity 2, e_2 is positive. As noted, the stability condition requires that Δ be positive. Hence,

$$\hat{q} \gtreqless \text{ according as } \mu_1^* + \mu_2 \lesseqgtr 1. \tag{6.24}$$

For simplicity, suppose that $t^* = 1$, or the foreign country imposes no tariffs. Then, the orthodox view holds true if and only if

$$m_1^* + \frac{m_2}{t - m_2(t-1)} < 1 \tag{6.25}$$

in view of Eq. (6.23) and the definition of μ_1^* and μ_2. Note that if the home country imposes no tariffs as well, then Eq. (6.24) reduces to the familiar agnostic condition for the orthodoxy. We can state:

Proposition 6.1: Orthodox Presumption *Suppose all commodities are normal in social consumption, or* $0 < m_1^*$, $m_2 < 1$. *Then, the higher the rate of tariffs, the stronger is the presumption that a transfer payment from the home to the foreign country will shift the terms of trade against the former. For given values of* m_1^* *and* m_2, *there is a critical rate of tariffs*

$$\overline{\tau} = \frac{m_1^* + m_2 - 1}{\left(1 - m_1^*\right)\left(1 - m_2\right)} \tag{6.26}$$

such that the presumption holds if and only if $\tau > \overline{\tau}$.

The proof is straightforward. The critical rate is of course negative if $m_1^* + m_2 < 1$.

Corollary 6.1: Samuelson (1954)
If preferences are representable by a set of homothetic indifference curves with identical taste between the two countries, the orthodox view is valid under any positive tariffs.

In such a case, m_1^* and m_2 add up to unity, so that the critical rate of tariffs given by Eq. (6.25) becomes zero.

The basic relationship (6.23) can be interpreted as follows. Suppose for the moment that the terms of trade are unchanged in the face of the payment db, which is that nowhere does a price change take place, and only income effects are at work. In the home country, the value of imports declines by $(m_2/t)db$ in the first round,[4] but this immediately causes a reduction in the tariff revenue by $(t-1)(m_2/t)db$. So, the "multiplier" process will go on, with each new round decreasing the value of imports by $(t-1)(m_2/t)$ of the previous round reduction. If $(t-1)(m_2/t)<1$, the upshot will be the total contraction of the import value by $m_2/(t - m_2(t-1))db$ or $\mu_2 db$. Similarly, in the absence of price changes, there will be in the foreign country the total expansion of the import value by $\mu_1^* db$ at the termination of its tariff-import multiplier process. Now, the value $(\mu_1^* + \mu_2)db$ represents the net trade surplus accruing to the home country under our supposition. If $(\mu_1^* + \mu_2)db < db$, there will be a deficit in the home country's balance of payments. To remove the deficit, the terms of trade must eventually deteriorate against the home country in a stable market. In contrast, if $(\mu_1^* + \mu_2)db > db$, the home country's terms of trade must eventually improve.

In the present setting, more interesting than the terms of trade effect per se is the ultimate change in real incomes consequent upon an international transfer. As we shall see in a moment, there is, under the tariffs, a further impact on real incomes through import contraction or expansion. To capture this point in precise terms, we substitute Eq. (6.18) and Eq. (6.22) into Eq. (6.16), and Eq. (6.19) and Eq. (6.22) into Eq. (6.17). After some manipulations, we obtain

$$du = -\frac{1}{\Delta}\{\bar{\varepsilon}_1^* + \bar{\varepsilon}_2 + (t-1)\left[\mu_2\bar{\varepsilon}_1^* + (1-\mu_1^*)\bar{\varepsilon}_2\right]\}db, \tag{6.27}$$

$$du^* = \frac{1}{\Delta}\{\bar{\varepsilon}_1^* + \bar{\varepsilon}_2 + (t^*-1)\left[(1-\mu_2)\bar{\varepsilon}_1^* + \mu_1^*\bar{\varepsilon}_2\right]\}db. \tag{6.28}$$

If free trade prevails, or $t = t^* = 1$, these simplify to

[4] The value of imports (measured in international price) is given by $p_2^* e_2$. Because $m_2 = \frac{\partial(p_2 e_2)}{\partial b} = t\frac{\partial(p_2^* e_2)}{\partial b}$, we find $d(p_2^* e_2) = \left(\frac{m_2}{t}\right)db$.

$$du = -\frac{1}{\Delta}(\overline{\eta}_1^* + \overline{\eta}_2)db, \tag{6.27'}$$

$$du^* = \frac{1}{\Delta}(\overline{\eta}_1^* + \overline{\eta}_2)db. \tag{6.28'}$$

The usual assumption is that the "income-compensated" elasticities of import demand are positive, or

$$\overline{\eta}_1^* > 0, \overline{\eta}_2 > 0.$$

Thus, Eqs. (6.29′) and (6.30′) confirm the familiar proposition that under free trade the home country (the transferor) is bound to become worse off, and the foreign country (the transferee) better off as a result of transfer.

In the presence of tariffs, we need to reconsider the simple free trade result. As is clear from Eqs. (6.24) and (6.25), a transfer under tariffs tends to exert a *tertiary* effect on the home and foreign real incomes in addition to the obvious primary effect and the terms of trade effect. As we have indicated, this tertiary effect is nothing but the change in each country's tariff revenue resulting from the transfer. It is, therefore, rather surprising that it has escaped closer attention in the controversies on the transfer problem. In each of the equations (6.24) and (6.25), the third term on the right-hand side gives a compressed expression to the tertiary effect of transfer. To study its implications, we must keep in mind the exact relationship between the pair of parameters, μ_2 and m_2, or μ_1 * and m_1 *. Figure 6.1 (i) and 6.1 (ii) are introduced to visualize this relationship for positive and negative rates of tariffs. Observe

$$0 < \mu_2 < 1 \text{ if and only if, } 0 < m_2 < 1,$$
$$0 < \mu_1^* < 1 \text{ if and only if } 0 < m_1^* < 1.$$

On the other hand, from the definition of $\overline{\varepsilon}_2$ and $\overline{\varepsilon}_1^*$,

$$\overline{\varepsilon}_2 > 0 \text{ if } 0 < m_2 < 1,$$
$$\overline{\varepsilon}_1^* > 0 \text{ if } 0 < m_1^* < 1.$$

This, together with Eqs. (6.24) and (6.25), establishes the following.

Proposition 6.2: Tertiary Effect of Transfer *Suppose all commodities are normal. Then, under positive tariffs, the tertiary effect of transfer is definitely negative for the paying country and definitely positive for the receiving country. Under negative tariffs (that is, import subsidies), it is definitely positive for the paying country and definitely negative for the receiving country.*

Note that the tertiary effect for each country does not directly depend on the other country's tariffs.

Fig. 6.1 The multiplier effect of tax increase on the home marginal propensity to import commodity 2. Case (i) $t > 1$. Case (ii) $0 < t < 1$

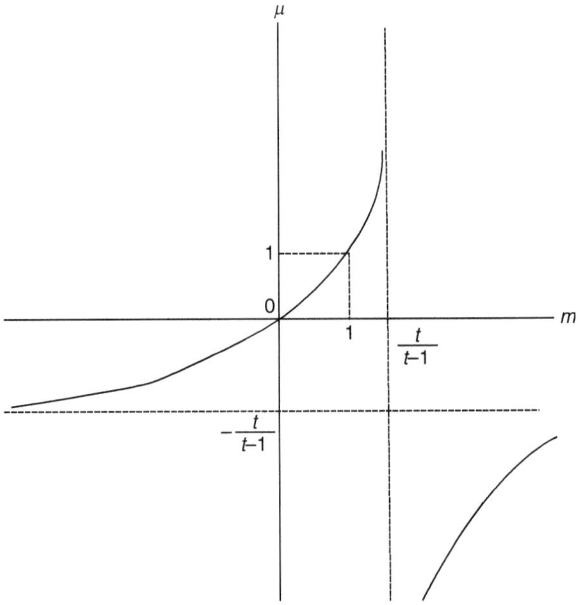

$t > 1$

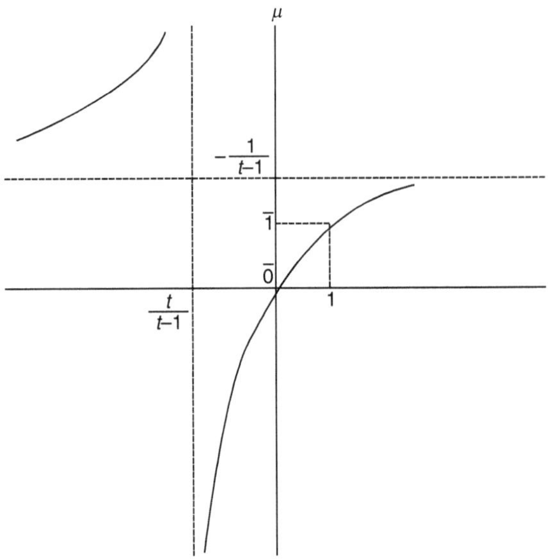

0;< t < 1

The results of Propositions 6.1 and 6.2 lead us naturally to the suspicion that the transferor will suffer from an additional burden and the transferee will enjoy an extra benefit under the conditions of heavy tariffs and superior commodities. In fact, we can approximate the *total* additional effect by

$$du + db = -\frac{1}{\Delta}\{(t-1)\left[\mu_2\bar{\varepsilon}_1^* + (1-\mu_1^*)\bar{\varepsilon}_2\right] + (1-\mu_1^* - \mu_2)\} \tag{6.29}$$

$$du^* - db = \frac{1}{\Delta}\{(t^*-1)\left[(1-\mu_2)\bar{\varepsilon}_1^* + \mu_1^*\bar{\varepsilon}_2\right] + (1-\mu_1^* - \mu_2)\} \tag{6.30}$$

The higher the rate of tariffs t (respectively t^*), the more likely is the right-hand side of Eq. (6.28′) (respectively 6.29) to assume a positive value unless parameters m_2 and $\bar{\eta}_2$ (respectively m_1^* and $\bar{\eta}_1^*$) are thereby significantly affected. Thus, we may conclude that the presence of tariffs lends a strong supporting hand to the orthodox presumption of "additional burden" under the normal circumstances. Let us turn to the examination of anomalous situations in which some commodities are inferior in consumption.

6.4 A Geometric Analysis of Anomalies

To simplify further analyses, let us assume in this section that $\mu_1^* + \mu_2 = 1$, or that the terms of trade are not affected by a transfer: this reduces Eqs. (6.28) and (6.27′) to

$$du = -db - (t-1)\mu_2 db_2 \tag{6.31}$$

$$du^* = db + (t^* - 1)\mu_2 db. \tag{6.32}$$

In each equation, the first term on the right-hand side represents the primary effect of a transfer on real income, and the second term the additional effect, or the change in tariff revenue. In the absence of price variations, a change in real income is synonymous with a change in nominal income, and the additional effect is equivalent to the "tertiary" effect. Here we assume that the rates of tariffs are positive, or $t>1$ and $t^*>1$. We drop the case of negative tariffs from our consideration because we can handle it easily in a similar fashion. From Fig. 6.1 (i), notice

$$\operatorname{sign}\mu_2 = \operatorname{sign} m_2 \text{ and } \mu_2 > -\frac{1}{t-1} \text{ if } m_2 < \frac{t}{t-1},$$

$$\operatorname{sign}\mu_1^* = \operatorname{sign} m_1^* \text{ and } \mu_1^* > -\frac{1}{t^*-1} \text{ if } m_1^* < \frac{t^*}{t^*-1}.$$

In view of Eqs. (6.33) and (6.34), this enables us to state the following.

Proposition 6.3: Transfer and Tariff Revenue *Suppose that a transfer from the home to the foreign country does not affect the terms of trade under positive tariffs. (i) Let* $m_2 < t/(t-1)$. *Then, if the home country's importable is normal, or* $m_2 > 0$, *there will be a decrease in the home tariff revenue. If* $m_2 < 0$, *there will be an increase in the home tariff revenue, but the increment will never exceed the value of transfer. (ii) Let* $m_1^* < t^*/(t^* - 1)$. *Then, if the foreign country's importable is normal, or* $m_1^* < 0$, *there will be an increase in the foreign tariff revenue. If* $m_1^* > 0$, *there will be a decrease in the foreign tariff revenue, but the decrement will never outweigh the value of transfer.*

For given values of m_1^* and m_2, the relative magnitude of changes in tariff revenue depends on the rate of tariffs. For $m_2 > 1/2$, the reduction of home tariff revenue overshadows the value of transfer if $\tau > 1/(2m_2 - 1)$. Similarly, for $m_1^* > 1/2$, the addition to the foreign country's tariff revenue is greater than the value of transfer if $\tau^* > 1/(2m_1^* - 1)$.

The common sense of this result is illustrated in Fig. 6.2 (i) for the home country (the transferor), which shows the home country's production possibilities schedule and the social indifference curves. Suppose that the equilibrium production is at *A*, given the rate of tariffs and the terms of trade indicated by the slope of the $q - q$ line. The social indifference curve *S* is tangential at the initial consumption equilibrium point *Q* to the $p - p$ line, whose slope represents the domestic relative price. Consider the impact of a transfer payment *AB* in terms of commodity 1 under the constant terms of trade. The vertical shift from *Q* to *C* on the lower $q - q$ line may be considered as the primary loss of home real income before there is any change in the import volume and therefore in the tariff revenue. The new consumption equilibrium must, however, be at a point on the lower $q - q$ line where an indifference curve has the slope of the $p - p$ line. The dotted, downward-sloping curve *gg* is drawn in to represent the Engel curve for the constant domestic relative price on the assumption that commodity 2 is inferior in the home country, or $m_2 < 0$. Hence, the new consumption equilibrium is at Q' to the right of *C* where the Engel curve cuts the lower $q - q$ line. The shift from *C* to Q' clearly involves an increase in the import volume and therefore in the tariff revenue. The indifference curve S' through Q' is indeed higher than the one through *C* (not drawn). Note that it is impossible for the Engel curve to have an intersection with the lower $q - q$ line to the right of *D* where the upper $p - p$ line cuts the lower $q - q$ line: that would simply contradict the assumption of inferiority. On the other hand, if commodity 2 had been assumed to be superior in the home country, we would have found the new consumption equilibrium to the left of *C* under the condition of Proposition 6.3.

So far, the result is merely reasonable. Let us consider the possibility that the paying country somehow ends up with an extra real income, or the receiving country becomes impoverished as a result of transfer. No such anomalies seem to obtain under usual circumstances. But Fig. 6.1 (i) indicates

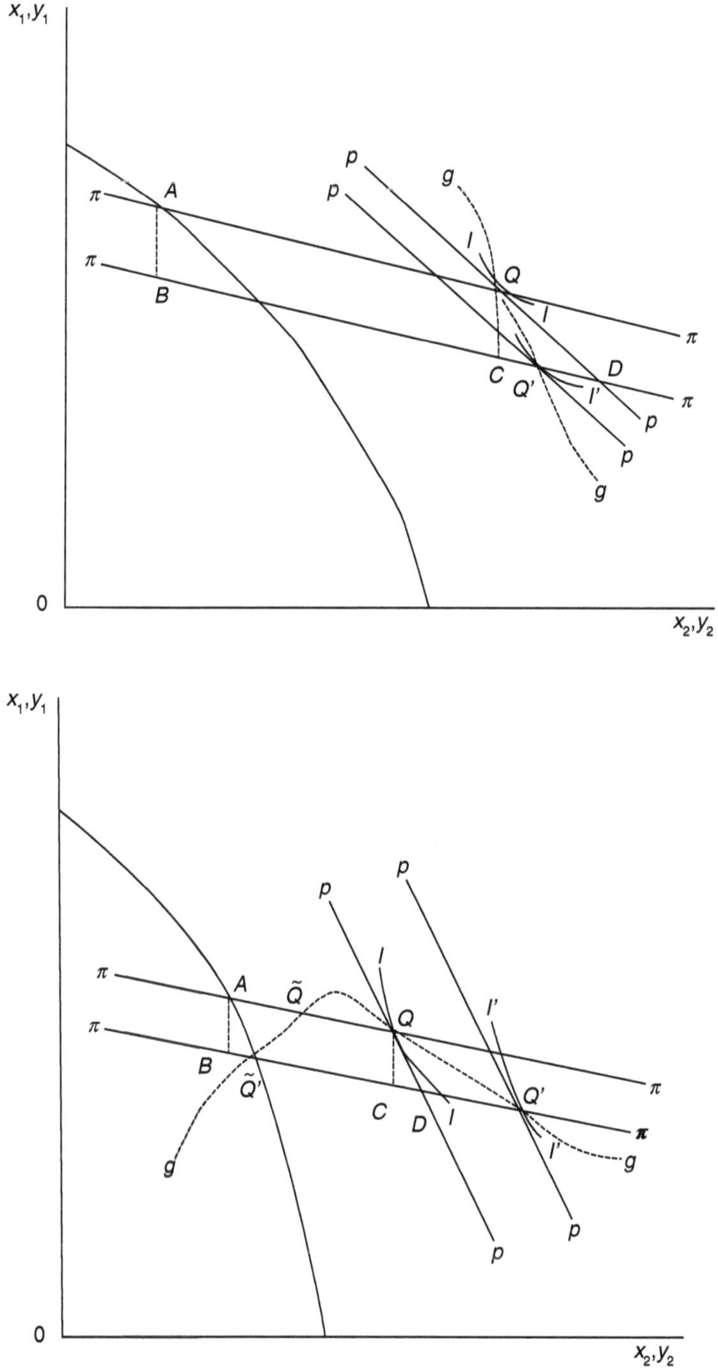

Fig. 6.2 (i) Normal real income effects of transfer with constant terms of trade. (ii) Anomalous real income effects of transfer with constant terms of trade

$$\mu_2 \left\langle -\frac{1}{t-1} \text{ if } m_2 \right\rangle \frac{t}{t-1},$$
$$\mu_1^* \left\langle -\frac{1}{t^*-1} \text{ if } m_1^* \right\rangle \frac{t^*}{t^*-1}.$$

This, along with Eqs. (6.33) and (6.34), leads to the following.

Proposition 6.4: Transfer Paradox *Suppose that a transfer from the home to the foreign country does not affect the terms of trade under positive tariffs. (1) Let* $m_2 > t/(t-1)$. *Then, the home country will increase its tariff revenue by the amount greater than the value of transfer. (2) Let* $m_1^* > t/\left(t^*-1\right)$. *Then, the foreign country will decrease its tariff revenue by the amount greater than the value of transfer.*

Note that (1) and (2) cannot hold at the same time because of the restriction $\mu_1^* + \mu_2 = 1$.

Because $t > 1$ and $t^* > 1$, the condition for this paradox involves the strong inferiority of each country's exportable commodity. It is shown, again for the home country, by Fig. 6.2 (ii), which is basically similar to Fig. 6.2 (i). Here, the Engel curve gg is given a flatter slope than the $p - p$ line in the neighborhood of the initial consumption equilibrium. This must be so under the condition $m_2 > t/(t-1)$ because

$$-\frac{dx_1}{dx_2} = -p\left(\frac{m_1}{m_2}\right) = -p\left(\frac{1-m_2}{m_2}\right) < \frac{1}{t}p.$$

As before, the vertical shift from Q to C represents the primary loss of home real income after transfer. With its slope as such, the Engel curve cuts the lower $q - q$ line at Q' to the right of D: this of course shows the existence of a new consumption equilibrium with a greater real income than before. A vigorous expansion of the home country's imports is, however, essential for this equilibrium to be realized.

Some may question the attainability of such an equilibrium. They will argue that if $m_2 > t/(t-1)$, the consumption equilibrium cannot be sustainable.[5] Consider a random departure of the country's income from the equilibrium position under constant terms of trade. As described earlier, this will set forth a tariff-import multiplier process. But this time, the process will be explosive rather than convergent as in every round the change of the country's import volume tends to overwhelm that of the previous round. In this connection, note that as home real income diminishes, the Engel curve must eventually approach the origin. As shown in Fig. 6.2 (ii), the curve must at some point turn round and cut the $q - q$ lines once more as at $\widetilde{Q}$ and $\widetilde{Q}'$: this is the well-known phenomenon of multiple equilibria under tariffs. According to the foregoing point of view, it is $\widetilde{Q}$ or $\widetilde{Q}'$ that represents

[5] See, for example, Kemp (1964, p. 37). A modified point of view is, however, found in Kemp (1969, p. 66).

the lasting choice of the people, but evidently there can be no paradox between $\widetilde{Q}$ and $\widetilde{Q}'$. This suspicion may seem to be reasonable at first, but turns out to be much less convincing in reflection. For after all, the real income position of $\widetilde{Q}$ or $\widetilde{Q}'$ is absolutely inferior to Q or Q'. This means that at $\widetilde{Q}$ or $\widetilde{Q}'$, the people are failing to achieve the maximum well-being for the given terms of trade, tariffs, and the consequent budget constraint. There is in fact no reason to justify such a myopic behavior on the part of the people except for ignorance and irrationality. Therefore, we may simply disregard a choice such as $\widetilde{Q}$ or $\widetilde{Q}'$ in favor of Q or Q'. In this instance, the real question is whether the international market can be stable in the usual sense under the condition of Proposition 6.4. From the definition of ε_2, $m_2 > t/(t-1)$ implies $\varepsilon_2 < 0$. Hence, the stability condition requires $\varepsilon_1^* > 1 - \varepsilon_2 > 1$, or that the foreign offer curve be sufficiently elastic. Because, under the restriction $\mu_1^* + \mu_2 = 1$, there is no upper limit for the possible values of ε_1^*, we should be able to provide an example of a stable equilibrium appropriate for the case under consideration.

In this section we have taken much advantage of the simplifying assumption that $\mu_1^* + \mu_2 = 1$, but the gist of our discussion will not be invalidated in the general case of variable terms of trade.

6.5 Notes on Tied Transfer

It is thus far taken for granted that a transfer from the home to the foreign country is completely untied. In other words, the latter is assumed to dispose of the transfer in the form of lump-sum subsidies without any restriction. This assumption is common in the standard discussions of the transfer problem and serves to isolate the effect of pure income transfer. In reality, however, genuine gifts are rare, and we find transfers tied in various ways. Consider, for example, international economic aids that are tied by source or end-use via specification of commodities or countries. Despite the intrinsic interest of the issue, the analysis of tied transfer has been largely neglected in the literature on the transfer problem. In this section, we shall make a small step to fill in this gap.

Generally speaking, a transfer is tied if accompanied by a contractual requirement that the recipient country spends the transferred purchasing power for promoting its import of specified commodities from specified countries. In our two-country, two-commodity model, however, there is evidently no degree of freedom of choice of specified commodities or countries. We can, however, think of several distinct ways of tying a transfer so as to expand the recipient country's imports. Let us confine ourselves to the following two typical cases. First, the home country grants an income transfer to the foreign country only on the condition that the latter agrees to increase its import value up to the amount of the transfer. Second, the foreign country agrees to employ the fund to subsidize its imports.

For simplicity, we assume that there were no tariffs before the transfer, or $t = t^* = 1$.

Case 1: tying the value of imports to the transfer.

The foreign country is supposed to subsidize its import to achieve the requirement

$$db = d\left(p_1 e_1^*\right) = p_1 e_1^* \widehat{e}_1{}^*. \tag{6.35}$$

Because we have agreed to regard p_1 as a constant, the right-hand side of Eq. (6.30) represents the *value* of the foreign import increment in the post-transfer equilibrium. Substitute Eq. (6.15) into Eq. (6.21), and let $\hat{t} = 0$ to obtain

$$\hat{q} = \frac{1}{\Delta}\left[\overline{\eta}_1^* \hat{t}^* + (1 - m_2)\ \hat{e}_1^*\right] \tag{6.35}$$

From Eq. (6.19) and Eq. (6.30), we find

$$\overline{\eta}_1^* \hat{t}^* = -\left(1 - m_1^*\right) \hat{e}_1^* + \overline{\eta}_1^* \hat{\pi}.$$

Substituting this back into Eq. (6.30) and collecting terms, we obtain

$$\hat{\pi} = -\frac{m_2}{\eta_2 - 1} \widehat{e}_1{}^*. \tag{6.36}$$

Because $\hat{e}_1^* = db / \left(p_1^* e_1^*\right) > 0$, the terms of trade improves for the home country provided that commodity 2 is normal and the home offer curve is elastic. The economic interpretation of this result is fairly straightforward. In the absence of the terms of trade variation, the value of the home country's imports will diminish by $m_2 db$, whereas that of the foreign imports expands by db because of the requirement (Eq. (6.30)). Thus, the net surplus in the home country's balance of payments is $(m_2 db + db) - db = m_2 db$. On the other hand, we know from the analysis of the offer curves that the value of the home country's imports increases as the terms of trade improves if and only if the home offer curve is elastic. Because the value of the foreign imports is frozen, the value of the home imports must increase to wipe out the surplus $m_2 db$: this will give rise to the terms of trade improvement if and only if $\overline{\eta}_2 > 1$.

The effect of the present case on the foreign real income can be readily obtained from Eqs. (6.17), (6.30), and (6.32):

$$du^* = \frac{\overline{\eta}_2 - 1}{\eta_2 - 1} db. \tag{6.37}$$

Clearly, the foreign real income gain is less than the face value of the transfer if the terms of trade moves against the foreign country. As no tariffs exist initially, the change in the home real income is simply given by $du = -du^*$. In summary, we may state as follows.

Proposition 6.5: Contrived Anomaly from Tied Transfer *Suppose that the foreign country agrees to increase its import value up to the amount of a transfer given by the home country. Suppose also the superiority of the home country's importable, or $m_2 > 0$. Then, the terms of trade will improve for the home country as a result of transfer if and only if the home offer curve is elastic. If there are no tariffs initially, the home country (transferor) will derive a real income gain, and the foreign country (transferee) will invite a real income loss from such an arrangement when condition*

$$\eta_2 > 1 > \overline{\eta}_2 \tag{6.38}$$

is satisfied.

Case 2: subsidizing the value of imports to match the transfer.

The foreign country is supposed to exhaust the transferred fund in subsidizing its imports:

$$db = -p_1 e_1{}^* d\tau^* = -p_1{}^* e_1{}^* \hat{t}^*. \tag{6.39}$$

With $\hat{t}^*$ being negative, the right-hand side of this equation shows the value of the foreign subsidies in the post-transfer equilibrium $t^* = 1$. As before, suppose $\hat{t} = 0$. The substitution of Eq. (6.37) into Eq. (6.21) yields

$$\hat{\pi} = -\frac{1}{p_2^* e_2 \Delta}\left(\eta_1^* + m_2 - 1\right) db. \tag{6.40}$$

Or the terms of trade improve for the home country if and only if the condition

$$\eta_1^* > 1 - m_2. \tag{6.41}$$

is satisfied. Note that this is none but the familiar Metzler condition for protective tariffs. Upon a little reflection, however, the result obtained is not at all surprising. The present form of tied transfer would be equivalent in its impact effect on the home country's subsidizing exports if we reinterpret the terms of trade as the domestic relative price in the home country. But by Lerner's symmetry theorem, export subsidies are equivalent to import subsidies or negative tariffs.

We can calculate the change in the foreign real income from Eq. (6.17) and Eq. (6.38) as

$$du^* = \frac{1}{\Delta}\overline{\eta}_2 \cdot db. \tag{6.42}$$

The change in the home real income is again given by $du = -du^*$. One can easily see that this is identical to the real income effect of the home export subsidies. After the transfer, the home country will be made definitely worse off, and the foreign country definitely better off, but not so much as in the case of untied pure transfer.

This simple conclusion suggests yet another equivalence relationship. Suppose that, in addition to the present scheme of tied transfer, the home country taxes imports so as to finance the transfer payment. Then, we obtain

$$db = p_1 e_1^* \cdot \hat{t}. \tag{6.43}$$

instead of $\hat{t} = 0$. From Eqs. (6.21), (6.37), and (6.41),

$$\hat{q} = -\frac{1}{p_1 e_1{}^*} db. \tag{6.44}$$

The terms of trade will certainly improve for the home country, and yet there will be no ultimate real income effect. To sum up, we have the following.

Proposition 6.6: Tied Transfer Versus Untied Transfer *Suppose no tariffs exist initially. A transfer from the home to the foreign country can be made equivalent in its real income effect to the home country's import subsidies by the agreement that the foreign country uses the transferred sum solely to subsidize imports. Consequently, a transfer tied in this way will have weaker effects on real incomes than the untied transfer of the same face value. Furthermore, consider a simultaneous introduction of import subsidies in the foreign country and import taxes in the home country such that the subsidy expenditure is of the same value as the tariff revenue; this will be equivalent in its real income effect to a transfer from the foreign to the home country amounting to the common value of the subsidy expenditure and the tariff revenue.*

6.6 Concluding Remarks

We have investigated the effect of an international income transfer in some detail in the context of a simple two-country, two-commodity model of trade with tariffs. The orthodox presumption about the terms of trade movement has been given a favorable judgment in the presence of positive tariffs. This finding confirms the conclusion obtained by Samuelson (1952, 1954) with some gain in clarity and insight because of the explicit introduction of the concept of real income change. Furthermore, we have been able to bring into strong relief the tertiary effect of transfer in the form of tariff revenue variation. Under normal conditions, the paying country suffers from a reduction in tariff revenue while the receiving country enjoys an increase in tariff revenue. Thus, when there are tariffs, the former is likely to experience extra losses, and the latter extra gains as a result of transfer on double accounts, that is, the terms of trade change *and* tariff revenue variation. To the best of our knowledge, the significance of the tertiary effect of transfer is largely ignored in the literature despite the universal presence of tariffs in the real world. In this connection, it should be noted that tariffs for revenue purposes are still popular among some developing countries because of the savings made possible in administrative costs of tax collection.[6] The changes in tariff revenue consequent upon a transfer should not be a matter of negligible concern for such countries.

The transfer problem takes on special interest in the tariff-ridden world because of the possibility that the paying country becomes better off and the receiving country worse off as a result of transfer. We have considered this rather improbable outcome in some length primarily as a theoretical curiosity. This point will be, however, of little practical importance save for the case of tied transfer, which attracts one's attention because of its relevance in reality rather than its value in theory. As a matter of fact, it is a common presumption that a tied transfer will be less costly to the transferor and less beneficial to the transferee than the untied transfer of the same face value. One can certainly go further and demonstrate that it is almost probable for the giver to benefit and the recipient to suffer from a certain type of arrangement of tied transfer. This is what we have tried to bring home in the last section by way of application of the model of tariffs and transfer.

References

Bangs, R. B. (1968). *Financing economic development: Fiscal policy for emerging country*. Chicago: The University of Chicago Press.

Johnson, H. G. (1955). The transfer problem: A note on criteria for changes in the terms of trade. *Economica, 22*, 113–121.

Jones, R. W. (1969). Tariffs and trade in general equilibrium: Comment. *The American Economic Review, 59*, 418–424.

Kemp, M. C. (1964). *The pure theory of international trade*. Englewood Cliffs: Prentice-Hall.

Kemp, M. C. (1969). *The pure theory of international trade and investment*. Englewood Cliffs: Prentice-Hall.

Keynes, J. M. (1929). The German transfer problem. *The Econometrics Journal, 39*, 1–7.

Ohlin, B. (1929). The reparation problem: A discussion. *The Econometrics Journal, 39*, 172–178.

Samuelson, P. A. (1952). The transfer problem and transport costs: The terms of trade when impediments are absent. *The Econometrics Journal, 62*, 278–304.

Samuelson, P. A. (1954). The transfer problem and transport costs. II: Analysis of effects of trade impediments. *The Econometrics Journal, 64*, 264–289.

[6] See, for example, Bangs (1968), pp. 121–126 and pp. 130–133.

Chapter 7
Innovations and International Trade

7.1 Introduction

Innovation plays a key role in the theory of economic growth, but it contains different elements. Roughly, these can be divided into two distinct categories: process innovations and product innovations. The former may also be named "cost-reducing innovations" in the sense that they take place through the discovery of new processes to produce the old products at lower costs. In contrast, the latter may be called "quality-improving innovations" because they occur through the creation of new products with higher qualities. Both categories of innovations are of course important as the engines of economic development, but their implications for economic welfare can be vastly different from time to time and from place to place. In poor economies in the early stage of development, process innovations in the daily necessities contribute significantly to the life of people. In affluent societies in the modem age, however, "it would be a terribly dull life if innovations only reduced costs of producing the same menu of goods and services that now populate their markets (Oi 1997, p. 134)." Product innovations are crucially important in such a situation. This chapter compares the welfare implications cost-reducing and quality-improving innovations in the context of modern international economies in which both poor and affluent countries coexist. Standard textbooks on trade theory teach that a growth in a country's export industry could be a curse rather than a blessing for its economic welfare. They argue that it brings about a deterioration of its terms of trade, thereby necessarily benefiting its trading partner but possibly damaging its own welfare when the direct gain from the innovation is relatively small.[1] This proposition is, however, based on the implicit assumption

This chapter is adapted from "Innovations and International Trade," *Keio Economic Studies*, Vol. 46, 1–15, 2010.

[1] The possibility of self-damaging innovations was aptly named "immiserizing growth" and made popular by Bhagwati (1957a, b).

© Springer Japan 2016

M. Ohyama, *Macroeconomics, Trade, and Social Welfare*, Advances in Japanese Business and Economics 14, DOI 10.1007/978-4-431-55807-1_7

that the growth occurs through a cost-reducing innovation and is definitely untenable if it is the outcome of a quality improving innovation. In fact, a quality-improving innovation in any product will generally increase its demand and lead to a rise in its relative price. The traditional literature on trade and growth has apparently overlooked this point because of its unwarranted preoccupation with cost-reducing innovations. In the real world, there are many important quality-improving innovations as well as cost-reducing innovations. For instance, the high rate of growth of the Japanese economy in the 1960s and 1970s may be explained by a series of both types of innovations achieved in important modern manufacturing industries such as steel, automobiles, electric machinery, precision and machine tool instruments, etc., originally imported from the West. The stagnation of the Japanese economy since the 1980s may be attributable to the decrease of quality-improving innovation after the completion of the process of catching up to the West. In the twenty-first century, however, we will perhaps witness a new surge of product innovations related to the conservation of energy and environment such as solar generators and electric vehicles.

In Sect. 7.2, we develop a simple general equilibrium model of innovations and international trade between the "home" and "foreign" countries. In Sect. 7.3, we begin by exploring the effects of a cost-reducing innovation in the home country's export industry and recapitulate the possibility of widely publicized "immiserizing growth." The necessary and sufficient condition for immiserizing growth in the present model is that the price elasticity of the world demand for the product is smaller than its export ratio (the share of export in the domestic output). In Sect. 7.4, we consider the effects of a quality-improving innovation in the home export industry. In sharp contrast to cost-reducing innovations, this type of innovation gives rise to an improvement of the home country's terms of trade and may impoverish its trading partner ("*inverse* immiserizing growth," say). Section 7.5 presents a necessary and sufficient condition for inverse immiserizing growth in a solvable example of the model. Loosely speaking, we may say that inverse immiserizing growth occurs when the quality improvement achieved by the innovation is not as highly regarded in the foreign country as in the home country. Finally, Sect. 7.6 discusses the significance and limitations of the model.

7.2 Product Quality and International Trade: The Model

Let us consider a simplest two-country, two-good model of international trade. There are two countries, home and foreign. The home country specializes completely in the production of good x and the foreign country in the production of good y. Perfect competition prevails in the home and foreign markets, and all factors are fully employed in both countries. Factors of production are not allowed to move internationally, implying that the supply of each good is fixed, given the product quality and production technology. On the other hand, goods are freely traded internationally, ensuring the international equalization of the prices of the goods.

The representative consumers in each country are assumed to possess a Marshallian, quasi-linear utility function with product y serving as "money." The utility function of the home consumers is written as

$$u = Y + \nu(X, \rho),\ \nu_1 > 0,\ \nu_2 > 0,\ \nu_{11} < 0,\ \nu_{22} < 0,\ \nu_{12} > 0 \tag{7.1}$$

where X and Y denote the consumption of good x and y, respectively, ρ indicates the quality of good x, ν_1, and ν_2 signify the partial derivative of function $\nu(X,\rho)$ with respect to X and ρ, respectively. Similarly, ν_{11} and ν_{12} denote the partial derivatives of $\nu(X,\rho)$, respectively. (In what follows, we shall use similar notation when necessary.) The marginal utilities of the home product x and that of its quality are positively decreasing, whereas the marginal utility of the foreign product or "money" is assumed to be constant. The foreign consumers also possess a similar utility function:

$$u^* = Y^* + \nu^*(X^*,\rho^*),\ \nu_1^* > 0,\ \nu_2^* > 0,\ \nu_2^* > 0,\ \nu_{11}^* < 0,\ \nu_{22}^* < 0,\ \nu_{12}^* > 0. \tag{7.2}$$

We follow the convention in trade literature (originated by Murray Kemp) to attach asterisks to the foreign variables for distinction from the home variables.

For simplicity, we assume that the home country produces good x only at the highest quality level under given technology. By assumption, the home and foreign consumers must satisfy the budget constraint

$$Y + pX = p\overline{X}, \tag{7.3}$$

$$Y^* + pX^* = \overline{Y}^*, \tag{7.4}$$

where $\overline{X}$ and $\overline{Y}^*$ denote the full-employment outputs of the home and foreign products, respectively, assumed to be fixed as of given factor endowments and technologies. The home and foreign consumers face the same international price, p, under free trade without any trade impediments.

The utility maximization of the home and foreign consumers subject to budget constraints (7.3) and (7.4) leads to

$$\nu_1(X,\rho) = p \tag{7.5}$$

$$\nu_1^*(X^*,\rho) = p \tag{7.6}$$

Solving Eqs. (7.5) and (7.6) for X and X^*, we obtain the home and foreign demand functions for product x:

$$X = x(p, \rho), \tag{7.7}$$

$$X^* = x^*(p, \rho). \tag{7.8}$$

Note that these are functions of only of p and ρ. Thus, the equilibrium condition for international product market may be written as

$$x(p, \rho) + x^*(p, \rho) = \overline{X}., \tag{7.9}$$

Given the quality of product x, Eq. (7.9) determines the free trade equilibrium price p as a function of q and $\overline{X}$.

In this equilibrium, the utility of each country depends upon its terms of trade (or the relative price of product x), the quality of product x, and the total supply of each product. Totally differentiating Eqs. (7.1), (7.2), (7.3), and (7.4) and rearranging terms in light of Eqs. (7.5) and (7.6), we obtain

$$du = -(Y - X)dp + \nu_2 d\rho + pd\overline{X}, \tag{7.10}$$

$$du^* = -X^* dp + \nu_2{}^* d\rho + d\overline{Y}^*. \tag{7.11}$$

A rise in the relative price of product x increases the utility of its exporter, or the home country, but decreases the utility of its importer, or the foreign country. An improvement in the quality of product generally increases the utility of both countries. Other things being equal, an increase in the total supply of the home product x increases the home country's utility and an increase in the total supply of the foreign product increases the foreign country's utility. Equations (7.10) and (7.11) have important functions in the following welfare analysis.

7.3 The Effects of a Process Innovation

To start with, let us consider process innovations as a benchmark. Suppose that an innovation occurred in the production process of the home country, reducing the cost of product x, but keeping its quality unchanged. In the present model, it simply gives rise to an increase in the total supply of product x. Differentiating Eq. (7.9) with respect to $\overline{X}$, we obtain

$$\frac{dp}{d\overline{X}} = \frac{1}{x_1 + x_1^*} \tag{7.12}$$

From Eqs. (7.5) and (7.6), we have

$$x_1 = \frac{1}{\nu_{11}}, \tag{7.13}$$

$$x_1{}^* = \frac{1}{\nu_{11}{}^*}. \tag{7.14}$$

The substitution of Eq. (7.15) and Eq. (7.16) into Eq. (7.12) yields

$$\frac{dp}{d\overline{X}} = \frac{\nu_{11}\nu_{11}{}^*}{\nu_{11} + \nu_{11}{}^*} < 0. \tag{7.15}$$

Naturally, the increase in the supply of product x as a result of the cost-reducing innovation in the home export industry brings about a decline of its relative price, thereby increasing its consumption in both countries and benefiting the importing foreign country. The question is whether this type of innovation is also beneficial to the home country. The increase in the supply of x would in itself benefit the home consumers, but the concurrent terms of trade deterioration would subtract from, or even overturn, the beneficial output effect. Generally, we cannot rule out the possibility of the well-known "immiserizing growth" (Bhagwati (1958a, b)). Setting $d\rho = 0$ in Eqs. (7.10) and (7.11), we get

$$\frac{du}{d\overline{X}} = p + \left(\overline{X} - X\right)\frac{dp}{d\overline{X}}, \tag{7.16}$$

$$\frac{du^*}{d\overline{X}} = -x^*\frac{dp}{d\overline{X}} > 0. \tag{7.17}$$

Equation (7.15), together with Eq. (7.17), shows that the foreign country unambiguously benefits from the innovation through its favorable effects on the terms of trade. Using Eq. (7.12), we can further rewrite Eq. (7.16) as

$$\frac{du}{d\overline{X}} = p\left(1 - \frac{\overline{X} - X}{X + X^*}\cdot\frac{1}{\eta}\right), \tag{7.18}$$

where η is the price elasticity of the world demand for x defined by

$$\eta = -\frac{p}{X + X^*}\cdot\left(x_1 + x_1^*\right) > 0. \tag{7.19}$$

Proposition 7.1: Immiserizing Growth *The necessary and sufficient condition for the immiserizing growth consequent upon a process innovation in the home export industry is*

$$\frac{\eta < \frac{\overline{X}-X}{X+X^{*}} = \overline{X} - X}{\overline{X},} \tag{7.20}$$

which means that the price elasticity of the world demand for x is smaller than the home country's export ratio, or export share in the total domestic supply of x.

It is likely to be satisfied in the case of a typical underdeveloped export economy specialized in a primary product for which the world demand is price inelastic.

Figure 7.1 illustrates the effects of a cost-reducing innovation in the production of x. The world demand curve for x is given by D_W and the home demand curve by D_H. (For simplicity, we assume that both home and world markets exhibit the same prohibitive price.) Suppose that the initial supply of x is shown by OA, and the corresponding initial equilibrium price by OB. The initial home consumption of x is conformably shown by BC and the export by CE. The initial home consumer's surplus is measured by the triangle BCD and the initial producer's surplus by rectangle $OBEA$, whereas the initial foreign consumer's surplus is triangle DCE. Starting from this initial situation, suppose that a cost-reducing innovation increases the home supply of x toward OA' and lowers the equilibrium price to OB'. In the subsequent new equilibrium, the foreign consumer's surplus increases to $DC'E'$ and the home consumer's surplus also increases to $DB'C'$. The home producer's surplus changes to $OB'E'A'$. Thus, the sum of home consumer's and producer's surplus increases or decreases, depending upon whether $CC'FE'$ is smaller or larger than $FAA'E'$ The condition that $CC'FE$ is larger than $FAA'E'$ coincides with the condition for immiserizing growth, that is, Eq. (7.20), when the increase in the supply of x is infinitesimally small. Clearly, the world social surplus, or the sum of the world consumer's surplus and producer's surplus, increases from $ODEA$ to $ODE'A'$.

7.4 The Effects of a Product Innovation: General Case

The possibility of immiserizing growth that a cost-reducing innovation in the home country's export industry may decrease its welfare is well known and well documented in the trade literature. Surprisingly, much less attention has been paid to the almost diametrically opposite welfare effects of quality-improving innovations. In this section, we employ the present simple model of international trade to show that a *quality-improving* innovation in the home country's export industry necessarily increases its welfare and may lead to the immiserization of the foreign country. Keeping $\overline{X}$ at a given level, we differentiate Eq. (7.9) with respect to ρ to obtain

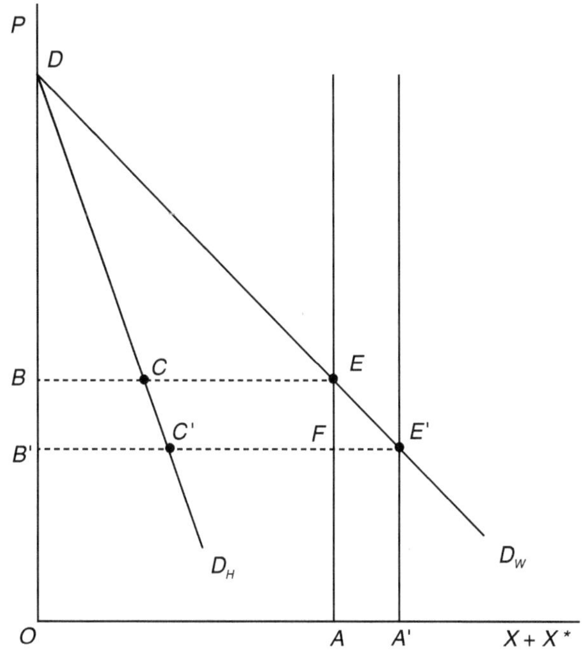

Fig. 7.1 The effects of a process innovation

$$\frac{dp}{d\rho} = -\frac{x_2 + x_2{*}}{x_1 + x_1{*}}, \tag{7.21}$$

where

$$x_2 = -\frac{\nu_{12}}{\nu_{11}}, \tag{7.22}$$

$$x_2{*} = -\frac{\nu_{12}{*}}{\nu_{11}{*}}, \tag{7.23}$$

In view of Eqs. (7.5) and (7.6) from Eqs. (7.22) and (7.23), we can rewrite Eq. (7.21) as

$$\frac{dp}{d\rho} = \frac{\nu_{11}\nu^{*}{}_{12} + \nu_{11}{*}\nu_{12}}{\nu_{11} + \nu_{11}{*}} > 0. \tag{7.24}$$

Note that the quality-improving innovation increases the demand for x, thereby raising its relative price. In particular, consider the special case in which the innovation increases $\nu_{12} = \nu_{12}{*}$. the marginal utility of the product equally both at home and abroad, or Eq. (7.26) then simplifies to

$$\frac{dp}{d\rho} = \nu_{12} = \nu_{12}^*. \tag{7.25}$$

In this case, the size of price increase equals the increase in the marginal utility of the product both at home and abroad. How about the consequent change in the foreign import as compared to its home consumption of x? It depends upon the comparative effects of the increase in the marginal utility of the product as perceived by the home and foreign consumers. Differentiating Eqs. (7.5) and (7.6) with respect to ρ, and making use of Eq. (7.26), we obtain

$$\frac{dX^*}{d\rho} = -\frac{\nu_{12}^*}{\nu_{11}^*}\left(1 - \frac{\nu_{11} + \nu_{11}^* \nu_{12}/\nu_{12}^*}{\nu_{11} + \nu_{11}^*}\right). \tag{7.26}$$

The foreign import of product x increases if and only if $\nu_{12}^* > \nu_{12}$.. Because the total supply of product x is unaffected by the innovation, the home consumption of x decreases under the same condition.

The effect of technological improvements of this type on the home consumer's utility is definitely positive because it improves both the quality of the product and its relative price. In fact, setting $d\overline{X} = 0$ in Eq. (7.10), we have

$$\frac{du}{d\rho} = \left(\overline{X} - x\right)\frac{dp}{d\rho} + \nu_2 > 0. \tag{7.27}$$

The first term on the right-hand side (the terms of trade effect) and the second term (the quality effect) are both positive. In contrast, its effect on the foreign consumer's utility becomes ambiguous. The quality improvement effect benefits the foreign consumers, but its terms of trade effect affects them perversely. Note, from Eq. (7.11),

$$\frac{du^*}{d\rho} = -X^*\frac{dp}{d\rho} + \nu_2^*, \tag{7.28}$$

where the first term on the right-hand side is negative, but the second term is not negative. The net effect is indeterminate, depending on the relative size of the opposing effects.

The phenomenon that the quality-improving innovation originated in the home export industry imposes a net welfare loss on the foreign country is rarely discussed in the trade literature. Here, let us focus on the possibility of such a phenomenon, naming it "inverse immiserizing growth." In practice, its relevance is widely recognized in the popular writings on the "competitiveness" of different countries.[2] Theoretically, suppose that a quality-improving innovation in a country's export good is highly regarded at home but deemed unimportant among foreigners, $\nu_2 > 0$

[2] For a sharp critique on the concept of international competitiveness, see Krugman (1994).

and $\nu_2{}^* = 0$. In view of Eqs. (7.26) and (7.28), this is clearly a typical case of inverse immiserizing growth.To be more precise, substitute Eq. (7.26) into Eq. (7.27) to get

$$\frac{du^*}{d\rho} = \nu_2{}^*\left(1 - \frac{\varepsilon^*\left(\nu_{11}{}^*\nu_{21}/\nu_{21}{}^* + \nu_{11}\right)}{\nu_{11} + \nu_{11}{}^*}\right), \tag{7.29}$$

where ε^* denotes the consumption elasticity of foreign utility increase from the quality improvement of x,:

$$\varepsilon^* = \frac{\nu_{21}{}^* X^*}{\nu_2{}^*} > 0. \tag{7.30}$$

From this, the necessary and sufficient condition for inverse immiserizing growth is

$$\varepsilon^* > \frac{\nu_{11} + \nu_{11}{}^*}{\nu_{11}{}^*\nu_{12}/\nu_{21}{}^* + \nu_{11}} \tag{7.31}$$

Given the magnitude of ε^*, this condition is likely to be satisfied when the marginal utility increase from the quality improvement of x perceived by the foreign consumers (indicated by $\nu_{21}{}^*$) is small compared to that perceived by the home consumers (indicated by ν_{21}). It simplifies to $\varepsilon^* > 1$ in the case where it affects both consumers equally, or $\nu_{21} = \nu_{21}^*$. Note also that if $\varepsilon^* = 1$, the innovation is neutral to the foreign consumer's well-being in the sense that it leaves the foreign consumer's utility totally unaffected. Suppose that $\nu_{21} = \nu_{21}{}^*$. The condition ε^* > 1 can then be written as

$$\frac{\nu_2{}^*}{X^*} < \nu_{21}{}^*. \tag{7.32}$$

It means that the average utility increase from the quality improvement falls short of the marginal utility increase from the quality improvement. As pointed out earlier, the relative price increase of product x from the quality improvement imposes a utility loss on the foreign consumers, which is exactly matched by the marginal utility increase from the quality improvement in this special case (see Eq. (7.27)). Thus, condition (7.32) clearly shows that the foreign consumer's utility declines as a result of the quality improvement. To sum up, we can put forward the following:

Proposition 7.2: Inverse Immiserization *A quality-improving innovation in the home export industry immiserizes the foreign country if and only if*

$$\varepsilon^* > \frac{\nu_{11} + \nu_{11}^*}{\nu_{11}^*\nu_{21}/\nu_{21}^* + \nu_{11}}. \tag{7.33}$$

Specifically, inverse immiserization occurs if $v_{21} > v_{21}^*$ *and* $\varepsilon^* = 1$, *or if* $v_{21} = v_{21}^*$, *and* $\varepsilon^* > 1$.[3]

Figure 7.2 illustrates the condition that $\varepsilon^* > 1$ when $\nu_{21} = \nu_{12}*$. The curve OV depicts ν_2*, the increase of the foreigner's marginal utility from the quality improvement as a function of $X*$. Assuming $\nu_2*(0, \rho) = 0$,, it goes through the origin and upward rising.[4] $\varepsilon^* > 1$ implies that the curve is strictly convex below. Suppose that the initial consumption of x is given at OA. The increase in the foreign consumer's utility from the quality-improving innovation of the product is shown by the area OAB, or the integration of ν_2* along segment OA. In the present special case where $\nu_{12} = \nu*_{12}$, the increase in the price of x equals $\nu_{12}*$, or the slope of OV at point B. The loss of the foreign consumer's utility from this price hike is given by the triangle OAC, which is greater than the area the below the curve OV along segment OA. Thus, the total increase in the foreigner's utility is negative. On the other hand, the foreigners will become better off in the special case in which $\varepsilon^* < 1$ and $\nu_{12} = \nu*_{12}$.

In passing, it should be noted that the rise in the price of product x consequent upon its quality improvement does not necessarily mean the deterioration of the foreign country's terms of trade. In fact, the gain from the quality improvement may outweigh the loss from the price increase, making the foreigners better off in the ultimate analysis. In general, the price of a country's export good in terms of its import good is not a good indicator of the terms of trade in the true sense of the word when the quality-improving innovation is taking place. Let $q*$ denote the foreign terms of trade in distinction from the relative price p of product x. The differential change of $q*$ with respect to ρ may be defined by

$$\frac{dq*}{d\rho} = -\frac{dp}{d\rho} + \frac{\nu_2*}{X*}. \tag{7.34}$$

The first term on the right-hand side may be taken as the relative price effect and the second term as the direct effect of a quality improvement of product x on the terms of trade. Note that the foreign country enjoys gains amounting to $\frac{\nu_2*}{X*}$ per unit of its import from the quality improvement of product x even in the absence of relative price change. In view of Eq. (7.11), the foreign country's utility depends on the terms of trade improvements as defined earlier, as well as on the supply of its national product.

Similarly, let q denote the home country's terms of trade. Its differential change with respect to ρ may be written as

---

[3] Examples of utility functions that satisfy $\varepsilon^* = 1$ or $\varepsilon^* > 1$ are given and discussed in the next section.

[4] $v_2^*(0, q) = 0$ means that the quality improvement of x does not affect utility, when there no consumption of x. Note that $\varepsilon^* > 1$ if and only if $v_{211}^* > 0$, which is often employed in the policy analysis of product quality. For instance, see Spence (1976) and Krishna (1987).

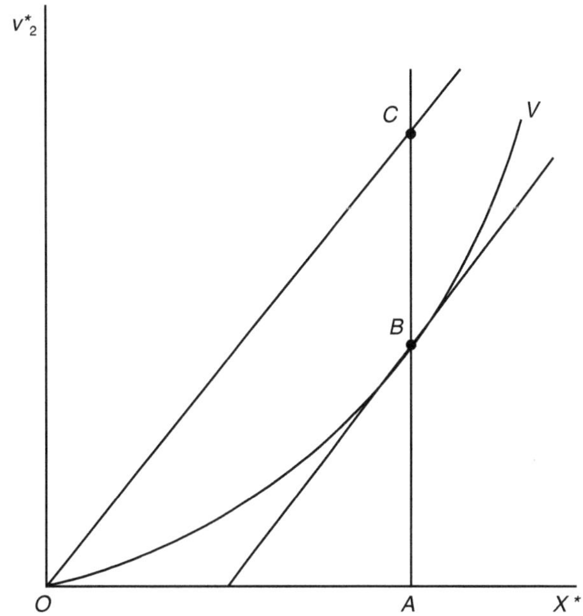

Fig. 7.2 Foreign utility change from a product innovation

$$\frac{dq}{d\rho} = \frac{dp}{d\rho} - \frac{\nu_2}{X^*}. \tag{7.35}$$

The home country's terms of trade may be said to deteriorate if there is a quality improvement of x at the unchanged relative price of product x.

7.5 Product Innovation: An Example

The foregoing analysis of product innovation introduced a condition for "inverse-immiserizing growth." It contains a somewhat unfamiliar concept of the consumption elasticity of utility increase from quality improvement, denoted by ε. To exemplify this concept, let us consider here some specific cases of relevant utility functions such as

$$\nu(X,\rho) = -\frac{aX^2}{2} + \rho bX, \tag{7.36}$$

$$\nu^*(X^*,\rho) = -\frac{aX^{*2}}{2} + \beta\rho bX^*, \tag{7.37}$$

$$a, b > 0, \beta \geq 0$$

The corresponding demand functions are linear:

$$p = -aX + \rho b, \tag{7.38}$$

$$p = -aX^* + \rho\beta b. \tag{7.39}$$

Note that the implied demand curves have the same slope and different intercepts. We can easily show that $\varepsilon^* = 1$ in the example. A quality-improving innovation in product x shifts up these functions upward and in a parallel fashion. Parameter β indicates differential evaluation of a given quality improvement between the home and foreign consumers. For instance, $\beta < 0$ means that the foreign consumers do not marginally evaluate the innovation as highly as the home consumers. In this case, Eq. (7.27) simplifies to

$$\frac{dp}{d\rho} = \frac{(1+\beta)b}{2}, \tag{7.40}$$

A quality-improving innovation of product x leads to a rise in the price of x and an increase in the home consumer's utility. We can also specify Eq. (7.29) as

$$\frac{du^*}{d\rho} = \beta b X^* \left(1 - \frac{1+\beta}{2\beta}\right) \tag{7.41}$$

The consumption elasticity of foreign utility increase from quality improvement is unity, or $\varepsilon^* = 1$ and the condition for inverse immiserizing growth becomes $\beta < 1$. An improvement in the quality of the home product decreases the foreign utility when the induced shift of the foreign demand curve is smaller than that of the home demand curve. Here, Eq. (7.34) can be written as

$$\frac{dq^*}{d\rho} = \frac{(\beta - 1)b}{2}. \tag{7.42}$$

Adjusted for the quality improvement, the foreign country's terms of trade deteriorates if $\beta < 1$..

Figure 7.3 illustrates the effect of a product innovation on the foreign utility when $\beta = 1.$, so that demand functions are identical. D_H and D_W show the single-country and world demand curves for product x, respectively. The total supply of x is given at the level of OA. At the initial equilibrium, each country consumes B C $(= CE)$ of x at the price of OB. The social surplus of the home country's is the sum of areas $OAEB$ (producer's surplus) and DBC (consumer's surplus), and that of the foreign country is equal to the area DCE (consumer's surplus). By virtue of the subsequent quality improvement of x, the demand curves shift upward toward D_H' and D_W' by the amount of $BB' = EE'$. At the new equilibrium, the price rises to OB', and both countries consume the same amount $B'C' = BC$ of x as before. In this special case, the effects of quality improvement and price hike on the quantity consumed cancel each other completely. As a result, the home country's social surplus increases by the area $BEE'B$, but the foreign country's surplus remains unchanged at $D'C'E' = DCE$. Needless to say, this is the borderline case. The foreign country's surplus increases when $\beta > 1.$ and decreases when $\beta < 1$.

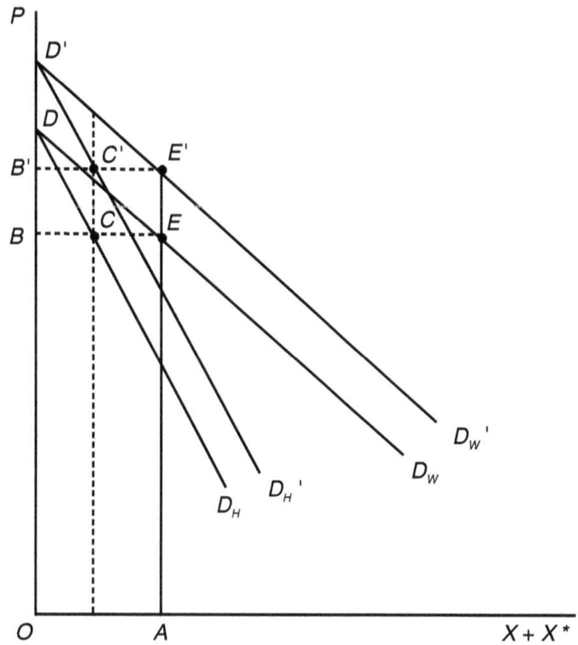

Fig. 7.3 The effects of a product innovation: an example

As pointed out earlier, $\varepsilon^* = 1$ in the present example. Consider another example of utility functions:

$$\nu(X,\rho) = -\frac{a}{\rho}X^{\beta} + bX,\ \beta > 0. \tag{7.43}$$

$$\nu*(X*,\rho) = -\frac{a}{\beta\rho}X*^{\beta} + bX*,\ \beta > 0. \tag{7.44}$$

where $\varepsilon^* = \beta$. To save space, we omit the detailed analysis of this example.

7.6 Concluding Remarks

The foregoing analysis shows that a product innovation in the home export industry increases the utility of the foreign country only if it is at least as well received in the foreign country as in the home country. We may roughly conclude that a quality-improving innovation in the home export industry benefits the home consumer presumably at the expense of the foreign consumer, in sharp contrast to the standard textbook teaching that a cost-reducing innovation in the same industry is generally beneficial to the foreigners. Thus, we should carefully take account of the differential effects of product and process innovations in evaluating the controversies over international distribution of gains from trade.

First, let us consider the vertical trade between industrialized and agricultural countries. In advanced industrialized countries with large domestic markets, product innovations are likely to introduce quality improvements that cater to the home consumer's preference rather than to the foreign consumer's taste. Thus, their product innovations tend to benefit themselves more than agricultural countries irrespective of the adverse terms of trade effects. In contrast, agricultural countries with small domestic markets tend to introduce quality improvements suitable for the large foreign markets and benefit the industrialized countries more than themselves through the resulting terms of trade deterioration. This analysis helps us to reconsider the time-honored "Prebisch–Singer thesis" to the effect that the long-term rise in the price of manufactures relative to agricultural product has diminished the trade gains of developing agricultural countries vis-à-vis developed industrialized countries [see Prebisch (1949) and Singer (1950)]. The foregoing analysis indeed suggests that the quality-improving innovations in industrialized countries may be responsible for the adverse terms of trade movements (in the usual sense of the word) against agricultural countries. As argued here, however, the terms of trade deterioration do not necessarily mean loss of trade gains for agricultural countries because the beneficial effects of the quality-improving innovations may more than compensate the adverse terms of trade effects. For instance, Lipsey (1994) shows that there have been no long-term trends toward rising prices of manufactures relative to primary product prices during the 1980s when the price indices of manufactures are adjusted for quality change and other influences.

Quality-improving innovations in manufactures are also important in the horizontal trade between industrialized countries. Krugman (1994, 1995) criticized what he called "pop internationalism," that popularized the concept of national "competitiveness" as a keyword for understanding international economic relationships in the 1990s. He argued that the definition of national competitiveness is much more problematic than corporate competitiveness. If a corporation fails to compete with rivals, it must go out of business, but countries do not go out of business even if they are unhappy with their economic performance. For example, suppose that a cost-reducing innovation occurs in the home country's export industry in the absence of any innovation in foreign country. Does it mean that the home country gets prosperous at the sacrifice of the foreign country? On the contrary! The foreign countries will benefit from the innovation in the home country through its terms of trade effect. Moreover, the home country may become worse off from its own innovation. Thus, in the case of international competition in cost-reducing innovation, the winner may not gain after all, while the loser is bound to gain. In contrast, suppose that a quality-improving innovation occurs in the home country's export industry in the absence of any innovation elsewhere. As shown in this chapter, it will definitely benefit the home country's welfare but may hurt foreign countries through its effects on the terms of trade. The abuse of the word "competitiveness" is certainly confusing, but it should be meaningful to talk about competitiveness in quality-improving innovative capacity.[5]

[5] Krugman (1994, 1996) considered-only cost-reducing competition but apparently overlooked quality-improving competition.

Finally, a few words for the limitations of the present model may be in order. First, it is a general equilibrium model under the special assumption that the representative consumers exist with Marshallian quasi-linear utility functions. This assumption implies that the demand for the product in question depends only on its relative price independent of the consumer's income. It is misleadingly named the "partial equilibrium" model more often than not. This assumption does not essentially affect the conclusion that a quality-improving innovation in the home country's export industry raises its relative price and increases its welfare, while it may decrease the trading partner's welfare. Second, it is assumed that the home country specializes completely in the production of product x (ordinary good) and the foreign country in the production of y (Marshallian "money"). This assumption is also essentially innocuous in deriving the message of the present analysis that quality-improving innovations and cost-reducing innovations in the home export industry exert asymmetrical effects on the terms of trade and the well-being of the home and foreign consumers. Relaxing this assumption and stepping into the world where the home and foreign countries specialize incompletely in the production of the two goods, we would have to take into account the differentiation of home and foreign non-money products and consider the quality-improving innovations in each of them. The essential message of the original model, that a quality-improving innovation in any industry will lead to a rise in its relative price, would remain intact. We would be able to infer its welfare implications roughly on the basis of this message as in the preceding analysis.

References

Bhagwati, J. (1958a). Immiserizing growth: A geometrical note. *Review of Economic Studies, 25*, 201–205.

Bhagwati, J. (1958b). International trade and economic expansion. *American Economic Review, 48*, 941–953.

Krishna, K. (1987). Tariffs versus quota with endogenous quality. *Journal of International Economics, 23*, 97–122.

Krugman, P. R. (1994). Competitiveness: A dangerous obsession. *Foreign Affairs*, 28–44.

Krugman, P. R. (1996). *Pop internationalism.* Cambridge, MA: MIT Press.

Lipsey, R. E. (1994). *Quality change and other influences on measures of export prices of manufactured goods and the terms of trade between primary products and manufactures* (NBER Working Paper 4611). Cambridge, MA: National Bureau of Economic Research.

Oi, W. Y. (1997). The welfare implications of invention. In T. F. Bresnahan & R. J. Gordon (Eds.), *The economics of new goods.* Chicago: University of Chicago Press.

Prebisch, R. (1949). *The economic development of Latin America and its principal problems.* United Nations.

Singer, H. W. (1950). The distribution of gains between investing and borrowing countries. *American Economic Review, 40*, 473–485.

Spence, A. M. (1976). Monopoly, quality and regulation. *Bell Journal of Economics, 6*, 417–429.

Chapter 8
Factor Endowments and the Pattern of Commodity and Factor Trade

8.1 Introduction

In the traditional theory of international trade, it is customary to assume that the factors of production are prohibited from moving from country to country for some reason or another. This assumption of factor immobility has an important function, especially in the theory of comparative advantage. The standard Heckscher–Ohlin theory explains the pattern of commodity trade in terms of factor endowment proportions of different countries on the assumption that no factors of production are internationally mobile (for an excellent recapitulation and generalization of the doctrine, see Dixit and Woodland 1982). In reality, however, some factors are known to move across national borders, as exemplified by the international transfer of entrepreneurial resources and labor services (often through direct investment), as well as by international capital movements.

Furthermore, it is at times difficult or even misleading to explain the observed patterns of trade without reference to international factor mobility. For example, the standard Heckscher–Ohlin theorem is contradicted by the well-known observation by Leontief (1954) that the United States, apparently a capital-rich country, had a comparative advantage in labor-intensive commodities rather than in capital-intensive commodities. It is also at variance with the recent development of capital-intensive industries such as steel, chemical, or shipbuilding in some of the labor-abundant, newly industrializing countries (notably Korea and Taiwan). The failure of the standard theory to explain these facts may be attributable, among other things, to its basic assumption that national boundaries delimit the areas within which factors are mobile. In the world where capital is internationally mobile, the employment of capital in a country is not constrained by its endowment of capital (i.e., the amount of capital owned by its residents). Therefore, although a

---

This chapter is adapted from "Factor Endowments and the Pattern of Commodity and Factor Trade," *Keio Economic Studies*, Vol.26, No.1, 19–29, 1989.

© Springer Japan 2016

M. Ohyama, *Macroeconomics, Trade, and Social Welfare*, Advances in Japanese Business and Economics 14, DOI 10.1007/978-4-431-55807-1_8

capital-rich country may export capital and import capital-intensive commodities, a labor-abundant country may import capital and export capital-intensive commodities.

The purpose of this chapter is to extend the Heckscher–Ohlin theory to the situation in which some (but not all) factors of production are internationally mobile. In our view, the problem of comparative advantage under factor mobility has received less attention than it deserves in the related literature on international capital mobility. Jones and Ruffin (1975) and Ferguson (1978) provide interesting studies focusing on the pattern of commodity trade under international capital mobility. However, their analyses are confined to the familiar two-commodity, two-factor model of international trade in which capital mobility is a perfect substitute for commodity trade in the absence of technological differences. Thus, they deviate from the main theme of the Heckscher–Ohlin theory, which ascribes the positions of comparative advantage to differences in factor endowments.[1] More recently, Svensson (1984) and Ethier and Svensson (1986) attempted to generalize this theme directly, but their conclusion is rather weak in the sense that it requires a substantial reinterpretation of "trade pattern." In this chapter we also generalize the standard multi-commodity, multi-factor model to allow for international factor mobility and, in the wake of Dixit and Woodland (1982), investigate the relationship between factor endowments and the pattern of commodity and factor trade in an alternative manner.

The plan of the chapter is as follows. In Sect. 8.2, we introduce a two-country model of international trade in which some factors, as well as commodities, are internationally mobile. Assuming identical technologies with constant returns to scale and identical homothetic preferences for commodities, we elucidate the effects of small endowment changes in one of the countries on its excess supplies in the free trade international equilibrium. In Sect. 8.3, we scrutinize their implications for the dependence of trade patterns on factor endowments. The pattern of commodity trade is shown to be basically determined by differences in the endowment of internationally *immobile* factors, except for singular cases. Obviously, this observation is nothing but an extension of the Heckscher–Ohlin theorem to the present context. In contrast, the pattern of factor trade depends most clearly on differences in the endowment of internationally *mobile* factors and less clearly on those in the endowments of immobile factors. We also find that the structure of the balance of payments (the balance of commodity or factor trade) is unambiguously affected by the endowments of *mobile* factors. In Sect. 8.4, we sharpen some of these results in the context of a simple two-commodity, two-factor model of international trade.

[1] Hence, it is technological differences between countries that give rise to comparative advantage positions in their model.

8.2 A Model of Commodity and Factor Trade

In this section, we develop a general framework to investigate the relationship between factor endowments and trade patterns in the world where some factors are internationally mobile. For simplicity, suppose that the world is composed of two countries, home and foreign (or overseas). Each country is potentially able to produce n commodities using m internationally immobile factors and l internationally mobile factors under given technologies. Its endowment of every factor is given exogenously, and perfect competition is assumed to prevail in all markets.

The following basic notation is used to denote the variable of the home country.

$Y = (Y_1, \ldots, Y_n)$: supply vector of commodities.
$X = (X_1, \ldots, X_n)$: demand vector of commodities.
$N = (N_1, \ldots, N_M)$: endowment vector of immobile factors.
$K = (K_1, \ldots, K_l)$: endowment vector of mobile factors.
$V = (V_1, \ldots, V_l)$: input vector of mobile factors.
$p = (p_1, \ldots, p_n)$: price vector of commodities.
$w = (w_1, \ldots, w_m)$: price vector of immobile factors.
$r = (r_1, \ldots, r_l)$: price vector of mobile factors.
Z: aggregate disposable income.

We indicate the corresponding foreign variables by asterisks. The endowment of a factor in each country is defined here as the amount of the factor owned by its residents. Needless to say, it generally differs from the input (or employment) of the factor in the country if the factor is internationally mobile.

Let us assume that the prices of internationally immobile factors are always adjusted to clear the domestic markets of those factors in each country. We may then express them generally as functions of the prices of commodities and mobile factors, and of the endowments of immobile factors:

$$w = w(p,\ r,\ N), \tag{8.1}$$

$$w^* = w^*\left(p^*,\ r^*,\ N^*\right). \tag{8.2}$$

We may also write the supplies of commodities and the inputs of internationally mobile factors as functions of the same variables:

$$Y = Y(p, r, N), \tag{8.3}$$

$$V = V(p, r, N), \tag{8.4}$$

$$Y^* = Y^*\left(p^*, r^*, N^*\right), \tag{8.5}$$

$$V^* = V^*\left(p^*, r^*, N^*\right). \tag{8.6}$$

The consumers of each country are assumed to possess identical and homothetic preferences for commodities, which enables us to express their demands for commodities as functions of commodity prices and aggregate disposable income:

$$X = D(p, Z), \tag{8.7}$$
$$X^* = D^*(p^*, Z^*). \tag{8.8}$$

where, in the long-run equilibrium with zero profits,

$$Z = wN + rK,$$
$$Z^* = w^* N^* + r^* K^*.$$

In view of Eqs. (8.1) and (8.2), we may rewrite Eqs. (8.7) and (8.8) as

$$X = X(p, r, N, K), \tag{8.9}$$
$$X^* = X^*(p^*, r^*, n^*, K^*). \tag{8.10}$$

To ease notation, define the excess supply vectors by

$$E = Y - X = E(p, r, N, K),$$
$$F = K - V = F(p, r, N, K),$$
$$E^* = Y^* - X^* = E^*(p^*, r^*, n^*, K^*),$$
$$F^* = K^* - V^* = F^*(p^*, r^*, n^*, K^*).$$

By virtue of Eqs. (8.2, 8.3, 8.4, 8.5, 8.6), and Eqs. (8.9) and (8.10), the excess supplies of each country are functions of the prices of commodities and mobile factors and of factor endowments.

Suppose that initially the home and foreign countries have the same factor endowment proportions, or $N = \lambda N^*$ and $K = \lambda K^*$ (λ is a positive scalar). Following the tradition of the Heckscher–Ohlin theory of international trade, let us also assume constant returns to scale in production, identical technologies, and identical homothetic preferences across countries. Given the same commodity and factor prices, the size of the foreign economy would be exactly λ times that of the home economy. Hence, we may write

$$E^*(p, r, n^*, K^*) = \lambda E(p, r, N, K), \tag{8.11}$$
$$F^*(p, r, n^*, K^*) = \lambda F(p, r, N, K). \tag{8.12}$$

The same relationships also hold for the partial differentiation of excess supply functions with respect to prices. Thus,

$$E_p^* = \lambda E_p, \tag{8.13}$$

$$E_r^* = \lambda E_r, \tag{8.14}$$

$$V_p^* = \lambda V_p, \tag{8.15}$$

$$V_r^* = \lambda V_r, \tag{8.16}$$

where subscripts signify partial differentiations.

Under autarky, the equilibrium prices of the home country, $\overline{p}$ and $\overline{r}$, are determined by the conditions

$$E(\overline{p}, \overline{r}, N, K) = 0, \tag{8.17}$$

$$F(\overline{p}, \overline{r}, N, K) = 0, \tag{8.18}$$

and the equilibrium prices of the foreign country, $\overline{p}^*$ and $\overline{r}^*$, by the conditions

$$E^*\left(\overline{p}^*, \overline{r}^*, N^*, K^*\right) = 0, \tag{8.19}$$

$$F^*\left(\overline{p}^*, \overline{r}^*, N^*, K^*\right) = 0. \tag{8.20}$$

Under free commodity and factor trade, international equilibrium prices, p^f and r^f, are determined by the conditions

$$E\left(p^f, r^f, N, K\right) + E^*\left(p^f, r^f, N^*, K^*\right) = 0, \tag{8.21}$$

$$F\left(p^f, r^f, N, K\right) + F^*\left(p^f, r^f, N^*, K^*\right) = 0. \tag{8.22}$$

We assume that Eqs. (8.11) and (8.12) hold in the initial situation. The autarkic equilibrium of one country then implies that of another and therefore the international equilibrium of the two countries. With no international trade or factor movements actually taking place, the relative prices of commodities and factors are equalized internationally. Using a common numeraire, we have

$$\overline{p} = \overline{p}^* = p^f, \tag{8.23}$$

$$\overline{r} = \overline{r}^* = r^f. \tag{8.24}$$

in the initial situation.

Starting from this situation, we wish to consider the effects of changes in the factor endowments of the home country on the pattern of free trade in both commodities and factors. For this purpose, we differentiate totally the conditions for international equilibrium, Eqs. (8.21) and (8.22), to obtain[2]

$$\left(E_p + E_p^*\right)dp^f + \left(E_r + E_r^*\right)dr^f + E_N dN + E_K dK = 0,$$
$$\left(V_p + V_p^*\right)dp^f + \left(V_r + V_r^*\right)dr^f - dK + V_N dN = 0.$$

Making use of Eqs. (8.13), (8.14), (8.15), and (8.16), we have

$$(1+\lambda)\left(E_p dp^f + E_r dr^f\right) + E_N dN + E_K dK = 0, \tag{8.25}$$
$$(1+\lambda)\left(V_p dp^f + V_r dr^f\right) - dK + V_N dN = 0 \tag{8.26}$$

These equations implicitly define the changes in commodity and factor prices resulting from changes in the home country factor endowments. It is not necessary to derive their explicit solution for the present purpose.

Because there is no trade in the initial equilibrium, the excess supplies of the home country in the new international equilibrium must be equal to the changes in its excess supplies from their initial (zero) values. Taking account of Eqs. (8.25) and (8.26), we may express them as

$$\begin{aligned} dE &= E_p dp^f + E_r dr^f + E_N dN + E_K dK \\ &= [\lambda/(1+\lambda)](E_N dN + E_K dK), \end{aligned} \tag{8.27}$$

$$\begin{aligned} dF &= -V_p dp^f - V_r dr^f + dK - V_N dN \\ &= [\lambda/(1+\lambda)](dK - V_N dN). \end{aligned} \tag{8.28}$$

These are the fundamental equations relating the home country's external trade with its factor endowments.[3] They show that the sign pattern of the home country's excess supplies in the new equilibrium coincide with that of the changes in its excess supplies caused by changes in factor endowments at the initial commodity and factor prices. It should be noted that all excess supplies are scaled down equiproportionately as a result of the equilibrating price changes.

[2] We assume throughout the chapter that excess supply functions are differentiable with respect to all their arguments. If the number of commodities is greater than the number of internationally immobile factors (i.e., $n>m$), the supplies of commodities may not be uniquely determined for given prices. We exclude this "singular" case from our analysis arbitrarily. Jones and Ruffin (1975) and Ferguson (1978) discuss the "Ricardian" case in which $n = 2$ and $m = 1$.

[3] They extend the result of Dixit and Woodland (1982, p. 208) to the present context.

8.3 Factor Endowments and the Pattern of Trade

In the preceding section, we derived the expressions for the effects of endowment changes upon the home country's commodity and factor trade. We are now in the position to examine them more closely. It is natural to consider internationally mobile and immobile factors separately.

Let us begin by considering the relationship between the endowments of immobile factors and the pattern of commodity trade. Needless to say, it occupies a central position in the Heckscher–Ohlin theory of international trade. Setting $dK = 0$ in Eq. (8.27) and taking account of Eqs. (8.3), (8.4), and (8.9), we obtain

$$\begin{aligned} dE &= [\lambda/(1+\lambda)]E_N dN \\ &= \left[\frac{\lambda}{1+\lambda}\right](Y_N - D_Z w) + dN, \end{aligned} \tag{8.29}$$

which shows that the pattern of commodity trade in the new international equilibrium is indicated by the sign structure of $Y_N - D_Z w$. The (j, i) element of matrix $(Y_N - D_Z w)$ may be written as

$$\partial E_j/\partial N_i = \partial Y_j/\partial N_i - w_i D_j/Z \tag{8.30}$$

using the relationship, $\partial D_j/\partial Z = D_j/Z$, applicable when consumer preferences are homothetic. It is convenient to express this in terms of elasticities. Let us define the Rybcynski elasticity of commodity j with respect to the endowment of factor i by

$$\gamma_j i = (N_i/Y_j)(\partial Y_j/\partial N_i)$$

Also, define the share of factor i in national income as

$$\theta_i = w_i N_i/Z.$$

Recall that there is no trade in the initial equilibrium, so $D_j = Y_j$. Then, Eq. (8.30) becomes

$$\partial E_j/\partial N_i = (\gamma_j i - \theta_i)Y_j/N_i \tag{8.31}$$

We may say from this that commodity j will be exported when the endowment of immobile factor i is increased if the Rybczynski elasticity of commodity j exceeds the share of factor i in national income. This is a straightforward extension of the Heckscher–Ohlin theorem as recapitulated by Dixit and Norman (1980) to the world where some factors are internationally mobile.

It may be useful to consider the implications of Eq. (8.31) in the special case where the numbers of commodities and immobile factors are equal $(n = m)$ and where there is no joint production. If there is an ordering of commodities and factors such that the square matrix of Rybczynski elasticities, $[\gamma_j i]$, has diagonal elements all greater than unity and off-diagonal elements all negative, commodity i will be exported and all other commodities imported when the endowment of immobile factor i is increased. As we see in the next section, there is indeed such an ordering of commodities and factors in the case where $m = n = 2$, provided that factor intensity differs from commodity to commodity.

Proposition 8.1: Immobile Factors and Pattern of Trade *Suppose that the numbers of commodities and immobile factors are equal. An increase in the endowment of an immobile factor will lead to the export of the commodity that uses the factor relatively intensively and the import of the other commodity.*

Thus, the gist of the familiar Heckscher–Ohlin theorem is shown to remain valid as it relates the pattern of commodity trade with the endowments of *immobile* factors, regardless of the presence of any number of internationally mobile factors. The relationship between the pattern of trade and the endowments of immobile factors is not essentially affected by the introduction of mobile factors, even in the case where the number of commodities differs from that of immobile factors.[4]

Our next concern is to see how the pattern of factor trade is related to the endowments of immobile factors. Set $dK = 0$ in Eq. (8.28) to obtain

$$dF = -[\lambda/(1+\lambda)]V_N dN. \tag{8.32}$$

The pattern of factor movements is thus shown to coincide with the sign pattern of matrix $-V_N$. Very little is known of this matrix in the literature. Consider again the special case where the numbers of commodities and factors are equal $(n = m)$ and suppose that the matrix of Rybczynski elasticities has diagonal elements all greater than unity and off-diagonal elements all negative. We may then presume that an increase in the endowment of immobile factor i increases the output of commodity i and decreases that of all other commodities, thereby inducing the inflow of those mobile factors that are used "intensively" in the production of commodity i and the outflow of all other factors. We shall illustrate this point in the context of a simple 2×3 model in the next section.

Let us now turn to the effects of changes in the endowments of mobile factors on the pattern of commodity and factor trade. They are simpler and easier to work out than the effects of endowment changes of immobile factors. Setting $dN = 0$ in Eqs. (8.27) and (8.28) and making use of Eqs. (8.3), (8.7), and (8.9), we obtain

$$dE = -[\lambda/(1+\lambda)]D_z r dK, \tag{8.33}$$

[4] As noted before, the effects of endowment changes on the pattern of trade may become indeterminate if the number of commodities exceeds that of immobile factors. But we have the same problem in the standard model of international trade where no factors are internationally mobile.

$$dF = \left[\frac{\lambda}{1+\lambda}\right] dK. \tag{8.34}$$

The following conclusions are immediate from these equations.

Proposition 8.2: Mobile Factors in the Balance of Trade *An increase in the endowments of each mobile factor induces all commodities to be imported. On the other hand, an increase in the endowment of mobile factors results in their outflow but leaves the trade of all other mobile factors unaffected.*

In fact, it increases the national income and therefore the demands for all commodities (remember that preferences are homothetic) at the initial prices without affecting their supplies. Thus, it causes all commodities to be in excess demand at the initial prices and to be imported even after the prices have changed to reestablish international equilibrium. Second, an increase in the endowment of each mobile factor results in its outflow but leaves all other mobile factors unaffected. This result occurs because the input of each factor remains unaffected at the initial prices.

It should be noted here that an increase in the endowment of a mobile factor causes the balance of commodity trade to turn to a deficit and the balance of factor (service) trade to exhibit a surplus. From Eq. (8.37) and Eq. (8.38), we have

$$pdE + rdF = [\lambda/(1+\lambda)](1 - pD_I)rdK = 0.$$

This finding means that the deficit in the balance of commodity trade must be exactly matched by the surplus in the balance of factor trade to maintain the equilibrium of the current account.

8.4 Illustration by a 2 × 3 Model

To bring into sharper focus some of the points made in the previous analysis, we turn to a 2 × 3 model of commodity and factor trade in this section. Suppose that the home and foreign countries produce two commodities, labeled 1 and 2, by means of three factors labeled 1, 2, and k. Of the three factors of production, 1 and 2 are internationally immobile and k moves freely across the national border. Needless to say, this is a special case of the model described and analyzed in the previous two sections, and its structure has been investigated recently by such authors as Batra and Casas (1976), Ruffin (1981), Suzuki (1983), Jones and Easton (1983), and Hill and Mendes (1983).

In view of the symmetry of our world, it will suffice to consider only one of the two countries, and so we shall henceforth concentrate on the home country. Let w_1, w_2 denote the price of factors 1, 2, and k, and let p_1 and p_2 denote the prices of commodities 1 and 2, respectively. The competitive forces entail the zero profit conditions:

$$a_{11}w_1 + a_{12}w_2 + a_{k1}r = p_1, \tag{8.35}$$

$$a_{12}w_1 + a_{22}w_2 + a_{k2}r = p_2, \tag{8.36}$$

where a_{ij} is the input of factor i per unit output of commodity j $(i = 1, 2, k, j = 1, 2)$. Firms are assumed to operate under constant returns to scale and determine input coefficients, a_{ij}, so as to minimize the unit cost of production taking factor prices as given. Thus, a_{ij}'s are functions of w_1, w_1, and r, which may be written as

$$a_{ij} = b_{ij}(w_1, w_2, r) \ \ (i = 1, 2, k, j = 1, 2).$$

Given the prices of commodities and mobile factors p_1, p_2, and r, Eqs. (8.39), (8.40), and (8.41) are taken to determine the prices of immobile factors, w_1 and w_2, and the input coefficients, a_{ij}., which means that w_1, w_2 and a_{ij}'s are functions of p_1, p_2, and r, or

$$w_i = w_i(p_1, p_2, r), \ \ (i = 1, 2), \tag{8.37}$$

$$a_{ij} = a_{ij}(p_1, p_2, r) \ \ (i = 1, 2, j = 1, 2, k). \tag{8.38}$$

in the present model.[5]

Let N_1 and N_2 denote the endowments of immobile factors 1 and 2, and let Y_1 and Y_2 equal the outputs of commodities 1 and 2, respectively. Given prices, the outputs of commodities are adjusted to clear the markets for immobile factors. Hence, we have the full employment conditions:

$$a_{11}Y_1 + a_{12}Y_2 = N_1, \tag{8.39}$$

$$a_{21}Y_1 + a_{22}Y_2 = N_2. \tag{8.40}$$

Given the supplies of commodities, the input $V$of mobile factor, k, is given by

$$a_{k1}Y_1 + a_{k2}Y_2 = V. \tag{8.41}$$

Thus Y_1, Y_2, and V are functions of p_1, p_2, r, N_1, and N_2, or

$$Y_j = Y_j(p_1, p_2, r, N_1, N_2)\,(j = 1, 2), \tag{8.42}$$

$$V = V(p_1, p_2, r, N_1, N_2). \tag{8.43}$$

[5] It should be noted that the prices of immobile factors are generally dependent on their endowments, as shown in Eqs. (8.1) and (8.2). This dependence disappears in the present setup only because we have constant returns to scale in production *and* the numbers of commodities and immobile factors are equal.

Note that the general results obtained previously are directly applicable to the present model if we assume that the preferences for commodities are everywhere identical and homothetic.

Now let us use this model to consider the effects of changes in the endowments of immobile factors upon the pattern of commodity and factor trade. Suppose that immobile factor 1 is used relatively intensively in the production of commodity 1 and factor 2 in the production of commodity 2; that is,

$$a_{11}/a_{12} > a_{21}/a_{22} \tag{8.44}$$

for all factor prices. To interpret Eq. (8.29) or Eq. (8.32) in the present context, it is necessary to investigate the dependence of Y_1, Y_2, and V on N_1 and N_2 in Eqs. (8.48) and (8.49).

Assuming that all prices, and therefore all input coefficients, are given, differentiate Eqs. (8.42), (8.43), (8.44), and (8.45) to obtain

$$\lambda_{11}\widehat{Y}_1 + \lambda_{12}\widehat{Y}_2 = \widehat{N}_1, \tag{8.45}$$

$$\lambda_{21}\widehat{Y}_1 + \lambda_{22}\widehat{Y}_2 = \widehat{N}_2, \tag{8.46}$$

$$\lambda_{k1}\widehat{Y}_1 + \lambda_{k2}\widehat{Y}_2 = \widehat{V}. \tag{8.47}$$

where λ_{ij} denotes a fraction of factor i employed in the production of commodity j and circumflex ($\widehat{\ }$) indicates the rate of change of the variable. For instance, $\lambda_{11} = a_{11}Y_1/N_1$ and $\widehat{Y}_1 = dY_1/Y_1$. Solving them, we obtain

$$\widehat{Y}_1 = \frac{\lambda_{22}\widehat{N}_1 - \lambda_{12}\widehat{N}_2}{|\lambda|}, \tag{8.48}$$

$$\widehat{Y}_2 = -\frac{\lambda_{21}\widehat{N}_1 - \lambda_{11}\widehat{N}_2}{|\lambda|}, \tag{8.49}$$

$$\widehat{V} = \frac{|\lambda_2^k|\widehat{N}_1 + |\lambda_1^k|\widehat{N}_2}{|\lambda|}. \tag{8.50}$$

where

$$|\lambda| = \lambda_{11}\lambda_{22} - \lambda_{21}\lambda_{12},$$
$$|\lambda_1^k| = \lambda_{11}\lambda_{k2} - \lambda_{12}\lambda_{k1},$$
$$|\lambda_2^k| = \lambda_{22}\lambda_{k1} - \lambda_{21}\lambda_{k2}.$$

By definition we may write

$$|\lambda| = \lambda_{11} - \lambda_{21} = \lambda_{22} - \lambda_{12}.$$

By virtue of (8.44), this implies that $|\lambda|$ takes on a positive value smaller than unity.

Let us first consider Eqs. (8.49) and (8.50). It is easy to see from them that an increase in the endowment of an immobile factor brings about a more than proportionate increase in the output of the commodity that uses it intensively in production and a decrease in the output of the other commodity. Suppose as before that the foreign country has the same technologies, preferences, and factor proportions as the home country in the initial situation, which implies that there is no trade between the two countries. Equations (8.49) and (8.50), together with Eq. (8.31) in the preceding section, tell us that if, starting from this situation, the home country endowment of an immobile factor, say 1, increases, the home country will end up exporting commodity 1 and importing commodity 2. This result is in perfect consonance with the message of the traditional Heckscher–Ohlin theory of international trade. In fact, it extends the latter to the case in which there is a third, *and internationally mobile*, factor of production.

Turning to Eq. (8.46), we observe that the effect of an increase in the endowment of an immobile factor on the aggregate input of mobile factor k differs depending on whether the expanding sector uses factor k vis-a-vis the other immobile factor more intensively than the contracting sector. For instance, an increase in the endowment of factor 1 increases the input of factor k if and only if $|\lambda_2^k|>0$, or $\lambda_{k1}/\lambda_{21}>\lambda_{k2}/\lambda_{22}$. Note that as the endowment of factor 1 increases, the output of commodity 1 increases and that of commodity 2 decreases. Given the endowment of factor 2, the input of factor k increases if and only if more of factor k is used in combination with one unit of factor 2 in the production of commodity 1 than in the production of commodity 2. Similarly, an increase in the endowment of factor 2 increases the input of factor k if and only if $|\lambda_1^k|>0$, or $\lambda_{k2}/\lambda_{12}>\lambda_{k1}/\lambda_{11}$.

In view of Eq. (8.31) in the preceding section, we may infer from the foregoing analysis that an increase in the endowment of *any* immobile factor brings about an inflow of mobile factor k starting from the initial situation of no trade, if and only if

$$\lambda_{11}/\lambda_{12}>\lambda_{k1}/\lambda_{k2}>\lambda_{21}/\lambda_{22}$$

This condition means that factor k is the "middle factor" in the words of Jones and Easton (1983), occupying an intermediate position between the two "extreme" factors 1 and 2 in factor intensity ranking. If it fails to be satisfied, an increase in the endowment of an immobile factor may give rise to an outflow of factor k.

References

Batra, R. N., & Casas, F. R. (1976). A synthesis of the Heckscher–Ohlin and the neoclassical models of international trade. *Journal of International Economics, 6*, 21–38.

Dixit, A. K., & Norman, V. (1980). *Theory of international trade, a dual general equilibrium approach*. New York: Cambridge University Press.

Dixit, A., & Woodland, A. (1982). The relationship between factor endowments and commodity trade. *Journal of International Economics, 13*, 201–214.

Ethier, W. J., & Svensson, L. E. O. (1986). The theorems of international trade with factor mobility. *Journal of International Economics, 20*, 21–42.
Ferguson, D. G. (1978). International capital mobility and comparative advantage—The two-country, two-factor case. *Journal of International Economics, 8*, 373–396.
Hill, J. K., & Méndez, J. (1983). Factor mobility and the general equilibrium model of productions. *Journal of International Economics, 19*, 18–26.
Jones, R. W., & Easton, S. T. (1983). Factor intensities and factor substitution in general equilibrium. *Journal of International Economics, 19*, 65–99.
Jones, R. W., & Ruffin, R. (1975). Trade patterns with capital mobility. In M. Parkin & A. R. Nobay (Eds.), *Current economic problems: The proceedings of the Association of University Teachers of Economics* (pp. 307–332). Manchester: Cambridge University Press.
Leontief, W. W. (1954). Domestic production and foreign trade: The American capital position reexamined. *Economia Internazionale, 7*, 9–45.
Ruffin, R. (1981). Trade and factor movements with three factors and two goods. *Economics Letters, 7*, 177–182.
Suzuki, K. (1983). A synthesis of the Heckscher–Ohlin and the neoclassical models of international trade: A comment. *Journal of International Economics, 14*, 141–144.
Svensson, L. E. O. (1984). Factor trade and goods trade. *Journal of International Economics, 16*, 365–378.

Chapter 9
Partial Free Trade Agreements and Economic Welfare: Reconsidering GATT Article 24

Free trade agreements (FTA) have surged after the advent of the EU and the NAFTA in the 1990s. On the other hand, the World Trade Organization (WTO) was started in the mid-1990s to succeed and strengthen the General Agreement on Tariffs and Trade (GATT) as the organization to promote global free trade. For the time being, the FTA and the WTO, the seemingly inconsistent organizations, are serving as the twin engines of international trade. The important question is how they can be made compatible to each other and under what conditions. Bagwell and Staiger (2001) argued convincingly that the view of the WTO as a forum for expanding and securing market property rights serves to deal with global labor and environmental issues it faces. In this chapter, we shall also argue that the FTAs conformable with the same view of WTO are potentially beneficial to the welfare of the world.

As is well known, Article 24 of the GATT approves the formation of FTAs provided that (1) trade barriers against non-member countries do not rise on average; and (2) member countries eliminate all tariffs and other trade restrictions on 'substantially all' intra-regional exchanges of goods within a 'reasonable' length of time. Condition (1) is somewhat ambiguous and allows different interpretations. One possible, but unorthodox, interpretation is that member countries adjust their external tariffs so as to keep the volume of trade with non-member countries at the same level as before. Ohyama (1972) and Kemp and Wan (1976) demonstrated that the customs union that satisfies this condition increases the potential welfare of its members without affecting the rest of the world.[1] This result, known as the Kemp–Wan Theorem nowadays, brought about a turnaround in the traditional skepticism

This chapter is adapted from my original article, "Partial Free Trade Agreements and Economic. Welfare: Reconsidering GATT Article 24." Review of Development Economics 11, 621–628.

[1] Kemp (1964) provided the original idea and Vanek (1965) proposed a similar message without providing exact proofs. Ohyama (2007) extended this result, showing that the free trade area satisfying the same condition is also welfare improving.

© Springer Japan 2016

M. Ohyama, *Macroeconomics, Trade, and Social Welfare*, Advances in Japanese Business and Economics 14, DOI 10.1007/978-4-431-55807-1_9

about FTA entertained by trade theorists since the pioneering work of Viner (1950). Condition (2) is clear enough to exclude multiple interpretations, but its economic significance is not so clear. In view of the fact that there are many FTAs, real and potential, that fail to satisfy this condition fully, it seems worth reconsidering this condition from the aspect of welfare economics.

The primary objective of this chapter is to generalize the Kemp–Wan theorem to cover "partial and incomplete" FTAs that reduce intra-regional tariffs only on a limited set of industries. We shall show that they can be welfare improving if each member adjusts its tariffs against other member countries, as well as those against non-members, so as to honor the market access rights of all concerned parties. This generalization of the Kemp–Wan theorem seems to be relevant to the present world where there are many such FTAs. In fact, the WTO itself is nothing but a huge "partial and incomplete" FTA. Our result indicates that even "global" tariff reductions negotiated on the WTO rounds may not improve the economic welfare of the world as a whole unconditionally. Our result also suggests that condition (2) stipulated in Article 24 of the GATT for eligible FTAs is not only unrealistically stringent but also economically dubious.

9.1 Tariffs and Economic Welfare

Let us consider the economy of a single country (or a group of countries) engaging in external trade. The economy is assumed to be static in the sense that its technology, factor endowment and the preferences of its consumers are all given and fixed. There are a finite number of commodities produced and consumed in competitive markets.[2]

The model is general enough to accommodate all kinds of commodities: final consumption goods and services, intermediate goods, factor services, any of which may be traded or non-traded. Consider two distinct open economic situations, S' and S'' and their general equilibria under tariffs.[3] For simplicity, we assume that there are no domestic taxes or subsidies and abstract from domestic distortions arising from external economies and diseconomies. Let p' and p'' denote the domestic equilibrium price vectors and let x' and x'' denote the aggregate equilibrium consumption vectors in situation S' and S'' respectively. Then, one can show that if

$$p''x'' \geq p''x', \tag{9.1}$$

situation S'' is potentially preferable to S' from the point of view of the country (or the union of the countries) in the sense that some consumers can be made better

[2] The analysis below is also applicable to the models of imperfect competition under certain conditions. See Ohyama (1999).

[3] See Ohyama (1972) for the concept of economic situation and its general equilibria.

off with other consumers being kept as well off in situation S'' as in situation S'.[4] Note that if a commodity is a pure intermediate good, its consumption is identically zero in all situations. Suppose that the government imposes a tariff at ad valorem rate t' on the trade of commodity i in situation S''. Let q' and q'' be the international price vectors in S' and S'' and let T'' signify the diagonal matrix with the ith diagonal element t_i''. If t_i'' is positive, it represents an import tax or an export subsidy depending on whether commodity i is imported or exported. If t_i'' is negative, it represents an export tax or an import subsidy. In the absence of transportation costs, the arbitrage entails

$$p'' = q''\left(I + T''\right). \tag{9.2}$$

Let y' and y'' denote the equilibrium output vectors, a' and a'' the endowment vectors, e' and e'' the excess demand (or net import) vectors in situation S' and S''. By definition, we have

$$e' = x' - y' - a', \tag{9.3}$$

$$e'' = x'' - y'' - a''. \tag{9.4}$$

If a commodity is non-traded, its excess demand becomes identically zero in all situations. Let b' and b'' denote the net income transfers from the rest of the world in situation S' and S''. The balance of current account payments is assumed to be in equilibrium in both situations, implying

$$q'e' = b', \tag{9.5}$$

$$q''e'' = b''. \tag{9.6}$$

Assuming that $a' = a''$, we obtain, from Eqs. (9.2), (9.3), (9.4), (9.5), and (9.6),

$$p''x'' - p''x' = b'' - b' + \left(q' - q''\right)e' + q''T''\left(e'' - e'\right) = +p''\left(y'' - y'\right). \tag{9.7}$$

The assumption of profit maximization implies $p''y'' \geq p''y'$. In view of Eq. (9.7), we have the following.

Theorem 9.1: Welfare Comparison *Consider two distinct situations, S' and S'', with common initial endowment and production set. If*

[4] This point is well recognized in the literature on the evaluation of real income. See Ohyama (1972) for a detailed explanation and discussion of the subject.

$$\left(b'' - b'\right) + \left(q' - q''\right)e' + q''T''\left(e'' - e'\right) \geq 0, \tag{9.8}$$

situation S'' is potentially preferable to situation S'.

The first bracketed term on the left-hand side of condition (9.8) represents the difference in the net income transfer, the second term the difference in the terms of trade, and the third term the difference in the tariff revenue index calculated by using tariffs in situation S'' and trade volume in situation S'. For brevity, they may be termed the "income transfer" effect, the "terms of trade" effect, and the "tariff revenue" (or alternatively "trade volume") effect of transition from situation S' to S''. The first and the second effects are self-explanatory, but the third term may need some annotation. For instance, a positive tax on the import of a commodity implies that its domestic price exceeds the import price by the value of the tax. An increase in the volume of its import should increase the potential welfare of the country because its marginal domestic value signified by its domestic price is greater than its marginal cost measured by its import price. Similarly, if an import subsidy (or a negative tax) is given to the import of a commodity, a decrease of its import should be beneficial because its marginal domestic value signified by its domestic price is smaller than its marginal cost measured by its import price. Note also that condition (9.8) does not by itself ensure that S'' is *actually* preferable to S' unless income distribution realized in the former is judged to be not worse than income distribution realized in the latter.

9.2 The Kemp–Wan Theorem and Beyond

As already noted, the Kemp–Wan theorem (Kemp and Wan (1976)) helped to alleviate the strong skepticism against FTA and Article 24 of the GATT, which had prevailed among trade theorists under the influence of the pioneering work by Viner (1950). Let us begin by reconfirming the Kemp–Wan theorem using the theorem of welfare comparison derived in the preceding section.

Proposition 9.1: The Kemp–Wan Theorem *The customs union improves the potential economic welfare of member countries without adversely affecting the rest of the world if it adjusts its common external tariffs so as to keep its trade volumes of all commodities with non-member countries at the pre-union level.*

Proof We may regard the customs union as a federation of member countries in which all consumers face common commodity prices and apply the theorem of welfare comparison to the customs union as a whole. Let S' and S'', respectively, stand for the situation before and after the formation of the union. If the union adjusts its tariffs against the rest of the world so as to keep its external trade at the pre-union level, $e' = e''$ and $q' = q''$. Furthermore, we may set $b' = b''$ on the assumption that the union does not affect its receipt of net transfer from the rest of the world. Condition (9.8) is then satisfied with equality.[5]

Ohyama (2007) and Krishna and Panagaria (2002) independently extended the Kemp–Wan theorem to cover the free trade area in which each member country abolishes all tariffs against other members and adjusts its tariffs against non-member countries so as to keep its trades with them at the previous level. Kemp (2001, Chapter 10) also pointed out that the Kemp–Wan type customs unions are more beneficial from the world aspect than the free trade areas, which keep its trades of all commodities with non-member countries at the pre-union level. In fact, this conclusion easily follows from the proof of Proposition 9.1 if we let situation S'' stand for the Kemp–Wan type customs union and S' for the corresponding FTA.

In the real world, however, there are many FTAs that allow member countries to preserve intra-regional tariffs on sensitive commodities in violation of condition (2) required by Article 24 of the GATT. It is thus worthwhile to further generalize the Kemp–Wan theorem to cover such "partial free trade agreements" (PFTA).[6]

Proposition 9.2: PFTA *A PFTA improves the potential economic welfare of member countries without adversely affecting the rest of the world if each member country adjusts its tariffs so as to keep its trade volumes of all commodities with non-members at their previous levels, not to decrease its trade volumes of commodities with other member countries restricted by trade taxes and not to increase its trade volumes of commodities with other member countries promoted by trade subsidies.*

Proof Let S' stand for the situation before the formation of the PFTA and S'' for the situation after that. Let e_i be the i's total external trade vector of member country i, e_{im} be the vector of its trade with other member countries, and e_{in} be the vector of its trade with non-member countries. Furthermore, let e_{imf} be the vector of its tariff-free trade with other member countries and e_{imr} the vector of its tariff-ridden trade with member countries. By definition, we have $e_i = e_{imf} + e_{imr} + e_{\text{in}}$. Applying condition (9.8) to member country i,

$$b_i'' - b_i' + \left(q' - q''\right)e_i' + q''T''\left(e_i'' - e_i'\right) \geq 0. \tag{9.9}$$

[5] Ohyama (1972) provided the original proof of the theorem in the context of the present general equilibrium model.

[6] Kemp (2001, Chapter 11) argued that the Kemp–Wan theorem is extendable to what he termed "partial preferential trading associations," in which member countries fix the outputs of certain domestic industries at the pre-union levels by means of production subsidies (or direct control). This important extension is also implied by our theorem of welfare comparison, but his "partial preferential trading associations" are customs unions which abolish intra-union tariffs on all industries and differ from our "partial and incomplete" FTAs in which member countries retain tariffs on part of their domestic industries against other members.

By the property of the PFTA under consideration, $e''_{\text{in}} = e'_{\text{in}}$ and $e''_{imr} \geq$ (resp. $\leq$) e'_{imr} if $t''_{imr} \geq$ (resp. $\leq$) 0. Hence, inequality (9.10) obtains if

$$b''_i - b'_i + \left(q' - q''\right)e'_i \geq 0. \tag{9.10}$$

The net transfer, b_i, received by country i is the sum of the net transfer, b_{im}, from member countries and the net transfer, b_{in}, from non-member countries, or $b_i = b_{im} + b_{\text{in}}$. For simplicity, let us assume that $b'_{\text{in}} = b''_{\text{in}} = b'_{im} = 0$. We can then rewrite (9.10) as

$$b''_{im} + \left(q' - q''\right)e'_i \geq 0. \tag{9.11}$$

This inequality can be satisfied if the loss from the country i's terms of trade deterioration is compensated by net transfer from other member countries:

$$b''_{im} = \left(q'' - q'\right)e'_i. \tag{9.12}$$

To see that the scheme of intra-regional transfer that makes all member countries better off than before is feasible; sum Eq. (9.11) over all member countries to obtain

$$\sum b''_{im} = \left(q'' - q'\right)\sum\left(e'_{im} + e'_{\text{in}}\right) = 0. \tag{9.13}$$

Note that $\sum e'_{im} = 0$, because the imports from the member countries match the exports of member countries and $q'' \sum e'_{\text{in}} = q'' \sum e''_{\text{in}} = q' \sum e'_n = 0$ by the balance of payments condition and the property of the PFTA under consideration.

The economic intuition of the proof should be clear. The PFTA considered here does not affect commodity prices in the rest of the world, generating no terms of trade effects against the rest of the world. At the same time, each member country does not reduce the trade volumes of all goods protected by trade taxes, neither does it increase the trade volumes of all goods promoted by trade subsidies so that the volume of trade effects are nonnegative. Two caveats are in order. First, to achieve the conditions of this proposition, each member country must adjust tariffs (import and export taxes and subsidies) on all trades with non-member countries and all tariff-ridden trades with member countries. In other words, commodities are distinguished not only by physical nature but also by origin and destination, that is, by the country from which they are imported and that to which they are exported. In fact, a country needs the same number of tariffs (policy instruments) as the number of commodities the trade volumes (policy targets) of which it wants to control. Second, to make each member country better off after the formation of the PFTA, intra-regional income transfer must be carried out from the member countries who gained from intra-regional terms of trade improvement to those who suffered from intra-regional terms of trade deterioration.

Proposition 9.2 presupposes that the members of the PFTA abolish their tariffs completely on the agreed set of commodities. In fact, there is no need for such a restriction. Clearly, we can put forward a more general proposition applicable to "partial and incomplete" free trade agreements or arrangements of "preferential tariff reduction" (PTR) among a group of countries.

Proposition 9.3: PTR *Consider a group of countries that agree to reduce or abolish tariffs on the imports of some commodities from member countries preferentially. The PTR improves world potential welfare if each member country adjusts its tariffs so as to keep its trade volumes of all commodities with non-member countries at their previous levels, not to decrease its trade volumes of commodities with member countries restricted by trade taxes and, not to increase trade volumes with member countries promoted by trade subsidies.*

Proof Let S' and S'', respectively, stand for the situations before and after the PTR. Apply the lemma of welfare comparison to country i in the group and proceed as in the proof of Proposition 9.2.

As noted before, Article 24 of the GATT requires that FTAs remove all intra-regional tariffs within a reasonable length of period. It should be noted, however, that a further reduction of intra-regional tariffs in an "incomplete and partial" FTA may not be beneficial in general, given their tariffs against the rest of the world. For the rest of the world is likely to suffer from terms of trade deterioration as a result of the trade diversion effects of such a preferential tariff reduction. The FTA may also suffer as a whole through the adverse volume of trade effects. Proposition 9.3 provides a sufficient condition for avoiding such consequences.

All the foregoing propositions give sufficient conditions for various FTAs to be potentially beneficial to member countries without being harmful to non-member countries. They are, however, not necessary conditions for the desired property of FTAs. Moreover, they are rather stringent and even unrealistic in the sense that they require each participating country to adjust its tariffs so as to control all its trade volumes finely, involving the use of differential and discriminative tariffs on different commodities and different trading partners. Thus, it may be worthwhile to supplement Proposition 9.3 with a simpler and more realistic proposition obtained by the direct application of our theorem of welfare comparison.

Proposition 9.4: PTR *Consider a group of countries that agree to reduce or abolish tariffs on the imports of some commodities from member countries preferentially. The PTR improves the potential welfare of member countries if each member adjusts its tariffs so as to keep its terms of trade against countries outside the group as before and not to decrease the tariff revenue index calculated by using the post-PTR tariffs and pre-PTR trade volumes.*

Proof Let S' and S'', respectively, stand for the situations before and after the PTR. By hypothesis, condition (9.8) as applied to country i in the group reduces to

$$b_i'' - b_i' + \left(q' - q''\right)T''e_i' \geq 0. \tag{9.14}$$

As in the proof of Proposition 9.3, this condition can be satisfied if international income transfer in the group is appropriately carried out. In fact, the intra-regional terms of trade effects cancel out when each member country keeps its terms of trade against countries outside the group.

To satisfy the condition given in Proposition 9.4, each member country must adjust at least two distinct tariffs, those on trades with other members and those on trades with non-member countries, but its burden seems to be far lighter than that of satisfying the condition given in Proposition 9.3. Note that the PTR may adversely affect the terms of trade of some countries in the rest of the world, rendering them worse off in the absence of international income transfer among countries outside the group.

9.3 Concluding Remarks

In this chapter we have generalized the Kemp–Wan theorem to cover any form of preferential tariff reduction (Proposition 9.3), as well as partial free trade agreements (Proposition 9.2). The common requirement for welfare-improving FTAs is that they keep the volumes of all commodity trades with the rest of the world at the level before their formation. This requirement may be taken as an interpretation of the first condition of the GATT's Article 24 for approving FTAs that they should not raise trade barriers against non-member countries. This interpretation accords perfectly with the recent characterization of the GATT/WTO as a mechanism for securing market access property rights advocated by Bagwell and Staiger (2001). It may be technically difficult, however, for FTAs to achieve the requirement precisely. Proposition 9.4 is designed to give a simpler and perhaps manageable alternative requirement. The first condition of the GATT Article 24 is notoriously ambiguous and accommodates various other interpretations. It should be revised to require that they do not affect the volumes of trade with non-member counties or that they do not affect the terms of trade against the rest of the world and the tariff revenue index defined here.[7] These propositions also suggest the economic irrelevance of the second condition of Article 24 that the members of FTAs eliminate all tariffs and other trade restrictions on "substantially all" intra-regional exchanges of goods within a "reasonable" length of time. If the condition is to be abode by faithfully, it virtually rules out most of the promising FTAs under negotiation because every country has some politically strong industries clamoring for continued protection. From the point of view of economic welfare, however, the

[7] McMillan (1993) argued for the revision of Article 24 along the line of the Kemp–Wan theorem.

important requirement is that they do not reduce the imports of the commodities they continue to protect against other member countries.

References

Bagwell, K., & Staiger, R. W. (2001). The WTO as a mechanism for securing market access property rights: Implications for global labor and environmental issues. *Journal of Economic Perspectives, 15*, 69–88.

Kemp, M. C. (1964). *The pure theory of international trade*. Englewood Cliffs: Prentice-Hall.

Kemp, M. C. (2001). *International trade and national welfare*. London: Routledge.

Kemp, M. C., & Wan, H. Y., Jr. (1976). An elementary proposition concerning the formation of customs unions. *Journal of International Economics, 6*, 95–97.

Krishna, P., & Panagaria, A. (2002). On necessarily welfare enhancing free trade areas. *Journal of International Economics, 57*, 353–367.

McMillan, J. (1993). Does regional integration foster open trade? Economic theory and GATT's Article XXIV. In K. Anderson & R. Blackhurst (Eds.), *Regional integration and the global trading system*. New York: Harvester Wheatsheaf.

Ohyama, M. (1972). Trade and welfare in general equilibrium. *Keio Economic Studies, 9*, 37–73.

Ohyama, M. (1999). Market, trade and welfare in general equilibrium. *Japanese Economic Review, 50*, 1–24.

Ohyama, M. (2007). Partial free trade agreements and economic welfare: Reconsidering GATT Article 24. *Review of Development Economics, 11*, 621–628.

Vanek, J. (1965). *General equilibrium of international discrimination*. Cambridge: Harvard University Press.

Viner, J. (1950). *The customs union issue*. New York: Carnegie Endowment.

Chapter 10
Market, Trade, and Welfare in General Equilibrium

10.1 Introduction

The recent theoretical research in economics has paid much attention to imperfect competition and increasing returns to scale, uncovering new and useful findings about the market behavior of firms and their implications for economic welfare. More often than not, the analysis of these phenomena has been carried out within the framework of partial equilibrium models. This is a notable, and perhaps inevitable, turnabout from the dominance of general equilibrium analysis in the 1950s to 1970s. The traditional general equilibrium models à la Arrow and Debreu (1954) and McKenzie (1959) are appropriate for the proof of the existence of general equilibrium, but their generality restricts the comparative-static (or dynamic) analysis of practical economic problems even under the assumption of perfect competition. The same comment applies, a fortiori, to Negishi's (1961) ingenious extension of the Arrow–Debreu model to the case of monopolistic competition. Although partial equilibrium models are useful for the analysis of a single industry (or a set of closely related industries), they are inadequate in addressing its relationships with the rest of the economy, both through their negligence of income effects and because of their loose recognition of the inter-industry flow of resources. I need to develop tractable general equilibrium models incorporating imperfect competition and increasing returns at the expense of generality. The present chapter takes a small step forward in this direction.

For this purpose, it is natural to focus on the simple general equilibrium model with fixed endowments of factors used for the production of final consumption goods. The model has served as the workhorse for most of the developments in the

---

The original version of this chapter is taken from Ohyama (1999), which is a refined manuscript of the Presidential Address to the Japanese Economic Association held at Ritsumeikan University, Kusatsu, September 1998. It is adapted to refresh style and presentation.

© Springer Japan 2016

M. Ohyama, *Macroeconomics, Trade, and Social Welfare*, Advances in Japanese Business and Economics 14, DOI 10.1007/978-4-431-55807-1_10

pure theory of international trade and in other branches of applied economics.[1] Needless to say, the original model delineates the world on the assumption of perfect competition and constant returns to scale. There are already a number of attempts to generalize this model, taking into consideration elements of increasing returns and imperfect competition. To name only a few, mainly in the field of trade theory, with which I am more or less familiar, Negishi (1972, ch. 8), Melvin and Warne (1973), Dixit and Norman (1980), Markusen (1981), Brander and Krugman (1983), Helpman and Krugman (1985, ch. 5), and Ohyama (1991, 1993) examined the implications of either monopoly, duopoly, or oligopoly in the two-country, two-commodity models of international trade. On the other hand, Krugman (1979, 1980), Lancaster (1980), Dixit and Norman (1980), Helpman (1981), Woodland (1982), Laurence and Spiller (1983), Kikuchi (1996), and Ohyama (1997) analyzed the models of international trade under monopolistic competition.[2] Although these works are illuminating in their respective ways, they commonly had failed to consider the significance of antitrust (or merger) policy by the implicit assumption that collusion between firms either are perfect or are ruled out. As pointed out by Levinsohn (1996), this lack of interest in antitrust policy in the trade theory literature is both curious and deplorable. Moreover, their models are largely dependent upon special assumptions about the number of commodities and production factors or upon those about utility and production functions.[3]

In this chapter, we present a slightly more general model of an economy accommodating an arbitrary number of factors and commodities and allowing for possible collusion between firms. In so doing, we wish to design the model as an extension of the simple general equilibrium model embracing as special cases the Heckscher–Ohlin–Samuelson (HOS) model, as well as the Ricardian model, used and popularized in the theory of international trade. We also wish to make it tractable in the sense that we can analyze the implications of market structure (or competition policies) for potential economic welfare and international trade. With these purposes in mind, we shall follow Jones (1965) in formulating the long-run production equilibrium in which the profits of firms decline to predetermined levels (possibly zero) under free entry and all factors of production are fully employed. We shall express the market structure of the model economy by two sets of basic parameters: the degree of competition, and the markup ratio prevailing in each industry. The productivity of each industry and the general equilibrium of the model turn out to depend crucially on these parameters.

In the next section, we define the long-run equilibrium of an industry and elucidate its important properties. In Sect. 10.3, we formulate a general equilibrium model of many industries, each of which is supposed to be in the long-run industry

---

[1] In the words of Jones (1965, p. 557).

[2] Perhaps, I should also cite Jones (1968), Negishi (1969), Ethier (1982), and Kemp and Schiinberger (1991), who considered the implications of increasing returns as the result of external economies. Their models are, however, best interpreted as those of perfect competition.

[3] See Helpman (1984) for a survey, and Helpman and Krugman (1985) for a systematic exposition of alternative models of imperfect competition and international trade. Kemp (1995) contains a number of his contributions to the subject.

equilibrium. Given degrees of competition and markup ratios, the supply side of the model is shown to be isomorphic to the standard multi-factor and multi-commodity HOS model of production. In Sect. 10.4, we introduce the concept of the "production feasibility frontier" and demonstrate the robustness of traditional competitive equilibrium analysis in the presence of increasing returns and imperfect competition. Section 10.5 considers the welfare implications of market structure, or the welfare effects of antitrust (or merger) and entry policies in the framework of an isolated economy. We shall also characterize the combination of entry policies and production taxes that guarantees an efficient allocation of resources. Section 10.6 is concerned with the implications of market structure for international trade. Among other things, we shall clarify conditions under which the gains from trade under imperfect competition are greater than those under perfect competition as argued by many authors. Finally, we discuss the limitations of the present model in Sect. 10.7.

10.2 Firms in Industry Equilibrium

Let us first consider a single industry as a building block of the general equilibrium model that we will formulate later in the next section. Suppose that firms, potential or actual, can produce a homogeneous commodity with identical technology, using l distinct factors of production. The production function, common to all firms, is written as

$$Y = f(X_1, \ldots, X_l), \tag{10.1}$$

where Y denotes output and X_i, the input of factor i. As usual, it is twice continuously differentiable with positive first-order derivatives (i.e., positive marginal productivity of factors). Furthermore, it is assumed to be homogeneous in all factor inputs. The expansion path implied by the production function is a straight line from the origin. We depart here, however, from the standard neoclassical production function and allow for variable returns to scale. Typically, the implied average cost curve is assumed to be U shaped, but it may be downward sloping indefinitely over the relevant range owing to indivisible technology and limited managerial capacity. In contrast to the usual neoclassical firms with constant return-to-scale technologies, the firms here are clearly defined as solid entities with indivisible technology or limited managerial capacity.[4]

We allow for cartels (or mergers) of firms in the sense that a certain set of firms collude in their output decisions.[5] For simplicity, we assume that cartels are

[4] A firm is envisaged here as an indivisible unit of production in each industry dependent on the nature of technology and required managerial resources.

[5] Each cartel may be regarded as a large firm consisting of several indivisible units of production; see fn. 4.

symmetrical, that is, that they consist of an identical number of firms. Each cartel in the industry is assumed to determine its output so as to maximize its total profit, taking factor prices and other cartel outputs as given.

Let p^r denote the producer's *real* price of the commodity and w_i^r the real price of factor i (to be precisely defined later). The first-order conditions for profit maximization and Cournot–Nash equilibrium are as follows:

$$\gamma p^r f_i = w_i^r \ (i = 1, \ldots, l), \tag{10.2}$$

where f_i denotes the partial derivative of production function $f(X_1, \ldots, X_l)$, with respect to X_i, ω_i the *relative* price of factor i, vis-à-vis factor 1, and γ the degree of competition prevailing in the industry, defined by

$$\gamma = 1 - \mu\eta, \tag{10.3}$$

where μ is the rate of (industrial) concentration and η is the inverse of the perceived elasticity of demand for the industry's product. The second-order conditions for profit maximization are assumed to be satisfied. The term $\mu\eta$ is the so-called degree of monopoly. The rate of concentration is defined as the ratio of the number of firms, m, in the cartel to the total number of firms, n, in the industry.[6]

Note that the degree of competition, γ, or the degree of monopoly $\mu\eta$, is crucially important in the determination of the equilibrium output. We assume that all firms perceive a common subjective or objective demand function for their product consistent with the state of the market.[7] The perceived price elasticity of demand, η, may generally be a function of commodity prices or outputs of related commodities. For the major part of this chapter, however, we assume that the degree of competition is a parameter controlled by the government's antitrust (or merger) policy. It is perhaps natural to suppose that the permissible number of firms, m, in the cartel is dictated by the government and that $\mu\eta$ is determined in the long-run equilibrium of the industry to be defined next. The present assumption presupposes that the government controls $\mu\eta$ by adjusting m appropriately.[8] As will be seen, it is extremely useful as a simplifying and clarifying assumption. We depart from this assumption toward the end of the chapter.

The number of firms may vary over time by the entry or exit of firms. In what follows, we shall focus on the long-run equilibrium of the industry (industry equilibrium for short) in which the number of firms becomes stationary. The

---

[6] m is usually referred to as the coefficient of conjectural variations. Here it is construed as the number of firms that collude in their decision of output. See Seade (1980) for this interpretation.

[7] Firms must perceive a subjective demand function in some form or another when they behave as price-setters. See Negishi (1961) for use of subjective inverse demand functions in the proof of the existence of general equilibrium under monopolistic competition. See also Nikaido (1975) for a critique of this approach.

[8] Furthermore, it is implicitly assumed here that firms wish to collude as extensively as possible to maximize their short-run profits.

markup ratio of a firm is defined as the ratio of the market price of its product to unit cost. Traditionally, this is considered to be unity in the industry equilibrium, but it could actually be greater than unity if a certain minimum reward is reserved per unit of output for entrepreneurial efforts. Denoting the firm's markup ratio by ρ, we have

$$\rho = \frac{p^r Y}{\sum w_i{}^r X_i}. \tag{10.4}$$

Given γ, we can interpret an increase in ρ as an entry restriction designed to achieve a markup ratio higher than the prevailing ratio. An alternative and perhaps more natural policy instrument for entry restriction is obviously direct control of the total number of firms in the industry with a given number of firms in each cartel. In this chapter, we abstain from considering the effect of this instrument for the sake of conceptual clarity. From Eqs. (10.1), (10.2), and (10.4), we obtain

$$\frac{f_i}{f_1} = \frac{w_i}{w_1} = \omega_i,\ (i = 2, \ldots, l), \tag{10.5}$$

and

$$\beta \sum f_i X_i = f(X_1, \ldots, X_l), \tag{10.6}$$

with $\beta = \gamma\rho$ and $w_1 = 1$. We interpret β as a parameter measuring the intensity of the firm's behavioral constraint because γ is the degree of competition and ρ is the imposed markup ratio. In the industry equilibrium it also serves as a measure of the local economies of scale (see Helpman and Krugman 1985, p. 33).

Given β and ω_i, $(l + 1)$ equations in Eqs. (10.1), (10.5), and (10.6) may be taken to determine the $l + 1$ variables, Y and X_i. In other words, the equilibrium values of these variables may be considered as the functions of β and ω_i. Under the assumption of homogeneous production function, the equilibrium output is an increasing function of β but independent of ω_i. Thus, we can write[9]

$$Y = y(\beta),\ y' > 0. \tag{10.6}$$

It should be easy to see that equilibrium input of factor i is an increasing function of β and a decreasing function of ω_i; that is,

$$X_i = x_i(\beta, \omega_2, \ldots, \omega_l),\ x_{i\beta} > 0,\ x_{i\omega_i} < 0. \tag{10.7}$$

The firm's input coefficients are defined as

[9] See Appendix A of Ohyama (1999) for a proof.

Fig. 10.1 Industry equilibrium and average cost curve

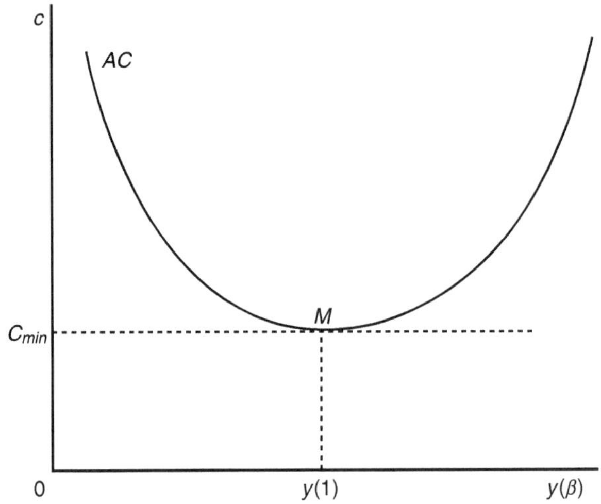

$$a_i = \frac{X_i}{f(X_1, X_2, \ldots, X_l)}$$

In view of Eq. (10.8), their equilibrium values are functions of β and ω_i. From (10.7) and (10.8), an increase in ω_i decreases a_i. It can be shown that an increase in β decreases (respectively increases) a_i if $\beta<1$ (respectively $\beta>1$).[10] Hence, we may write

$$a_i = a_i(\beta, \omega_2, \ldots, \omega_l),\ a_{i\beta} < 0\ (> 0)\,\text{if}\,\beta < 1\ (> 1),\ a_{i\omega_i} < 0. \tag{10.8}$$

The average cost is defined as

$$c = \sum \omega_i a_i.$$

In light of Eqs. (10.2), (10.5), and (10.7), we have

$$\sum \omega_i \frac{\partial a_i}{\partial \omega_k} = 0\,(i, k = 2, \ldots, l). \tag{10.9}$$

Because a_i is a decreasing (respectively increasing) function of β if $\beta<1$ (respectively $\beta>1$), c is also a decreasing (respectively increasing) function of β if $\beta<1$ (respectively $\beta>1$). Thus, we have

$$c = c(\beta, \omega_2, \ldots, \omega_l),\ c_\beta < 0\ (> 0)\,\text{if}\,\beta < 1\ (> 1),\ c_{\omega_i} = a_i. \tag{10.10}$$

Figure 10.1 illustrates the relationship between the average cost of the firm and β via function $y(\beta)$. The U-shaped average cost curve, AC, is drawn on the assumption

[10] See Appendix B of Ohyama (1999) for a proof.

that factor prices ω_i are fixed at predetermined levels. If $\beta = 1$, the firm operates at the bottom, M, of the curve and achieves the minimum average cost: this is the case of standard competitive industry equilibrium where the degree of monopoly is zero and the firm's profit declines to zero. If $\beta < 1$ (respectively $\beta > 1$), the firm operates at a point to the left (respectively right) of M with the average cost higher than the minimum level.

10.3 General Equilibrium

In the foregoing section we presented the basic concepts and relationships focusing on the behavior of firms in the long-run stationary state of a single industry. In this section we turn to the task of developing a simple general equilibrium model of an economy with many industries. Suppose that there are k industries using l common factors of production. In each industry firms are assumed to behave oligopolistically as described in the preceding section, taking the prices and outputs in the rest of the economy as given. As is seen next, the model turns out to be an extended version of the k -commodity, l -factor HOS model of production and trade in the form considered by Jones (1965). It coincides completely with the standard HOS model when all firms are price-takers and their markup ratios are reduced to unity in the industry equilibrium. It also embraces the Ricardian model of production and trade as a special case where there is only one factor of production.

To avoid complications, we assume that there exists at least one industry in which firms behave as price-takers. Let us indicate a variable pertaining to industry j by subscript j. Without further loss of generality, suppose that industry 1 is such an industry with $\gamma_1 = 1$. Let commodity 1, the product of this industry, serve as the numeraire of the economy. The market prices of other commodities and factors are all measured in terms of commodity 1.[11] Suppose that there exists a commonly accepted price level function,

$$p = p(p_1, \ldots, p_k),$$

where p_j is the market price of commodity j with $p_1 = 1$.[12] Let t_j be the ad valorem rate of production tax imposed on industry j, and define

$$\tau_j = \frac{1}{1 - t_j}.$$

[11] This assumption would be redundant if I could assume the existence of fiat money serving as a common accounting unit and define the price elasticity of demand appropriately. See Das (1982) for a similar argument.

[12] This assumption is ill founded when consumers are possessed of a common homothetic utility function.

The real producer's prices of commodity j and factor i used by firms in maximizing their profits are related to their respective market prices by

$$p_j^r = \frac{p_j}{\tau_j p(p_1, \ldots, p_k)} \; (j = 1, \ldots, k),$$

and

$$w_i{}^r = \frac{w_i}{p(p_1, \ldots, p_k)}, \; (i = 1, \ldots, l),$$

where w_i is the market price of factor i.

The general equilibrium of production is defined by three conditions. First, the industry equilibrium conditions are written

$$\tau_j \rho_j \sum a_{ij}(w_2, \ldots, w_l, \gamma_j \rho_j) w_i = p_j, \; (i = 1, \ldots, l) \tag{10.12}$$

Second, the factor market equilibrium conditions are written

$$\sum a_{ij}(, \gamma_j \rho_j) Z_j = L_i \; (i = 1, \ldots, l), \tag{10.13}$$

where L_i is the given endowment of factor i and Z_j is the total output of industry j. Third, the total output of industry j must be consistent with the equilibrium number and output of firms therein. This condition is given by

$$Z_j = n_j y_j(\gamma_j \rho_j)(j = 1, \ldots, k). \tag{10.14}$$

where n_j is the number of firms in industry j.

There are $2k + l$ independent equations in Eqs. (10.12), (10.13), and (10.14). This system of equations constitutes the production model of the economy. Suppose that γ_j, ρ_j, and τ_j are exogenously given in addition to L_i. We assume that γ_j can be controlled by the government, as well as ρ_j and τ_j. Although p_j are determined in the industry equilibrium, it is convenient to regard them as exogenous variables at this stage of analysis. Let us note two alternative interpretations of this model. The first one views it as the long-run equilibrium where ρ_j are given at predetermined levels (possibly unity). Then there are $2k + l$ unknowns, w_i, n_j, and Z_j. Disregarding the integer problem, we presume that the system of equations, Eqs. (10.12), (10.13), and (10.14), determines the equilibrium values of these $2k + l$ unknowns. Note that the number of firms in each industry is endogenously determined by the entry and exit of firms. The second interpretation is relevant to the short-run equilibrium where the number of firms is given in each industry. Take n_j as given instead of ρ_j. The system then determines the equilibrium values of ρ_j in addition to w_i and Z_j.

In what follows, we concentrate on the long-run equilibrium version of the model, assuming that ρ_j are given. The important special case is the standard long-run equilibrium under free entry where $\rho_j = 1$ for all j. Suppose that this is the case, and therefore $\beta_j = \gamma_j$. If in addition $\gamma_j = 1$ for all j, the system of Eqs. (10.12) and (10.13) becomes formally identical to the standard k-commodity, l-factor HOS model of a small country facing given commodity prices in the world market. There is a vast literature on the HOS model investigating the relationships between commodity and factor prices and those between factor endowments and commodity outputs.[13] Clearly, all the important theorems such as the Stolper–Samuelson and the Rybczynski theorems established in the context of the HOS model carry over to the present model provided that γ_j are fixed at given levels (not necessarily at unity) in addition to ρ_j.

The total supply, Z_j, of commodity j may be derived from the production system (Eqs. (10.12), (10.13), (10.14)] as

$$Z_j = S_j(p, \rho, \gamma, \tau, L)(j = 1, \ldots, k), \tag{10.15}$$

where p denotes the vector of commodity prices, $(p_1, \ldots, p_k)$, ρ the vector of markup ratios, $(\rho_1, \ldots, \rho_k)$ and so on. Clearly, $S_j(\cdot)$ are homogeneous of degree zero in p.

To determine the equilibrium commodity prices, we need to introduce the demand side of the economy. As usual, let us assume that the consumers are price-takers both in product and factor markets, and determining their demand for products so as to maximize utility subject to budget constraints. Suppose further that each consumer's shares in all income sources are predetermined. The total demand, C_j, for commodity j is then derived as a function of the same variables as in the total supply functions; ie,

$$C_j = D_j(p, \rho, \gamma, \tau, L)\,(j = 1, \ldots, k) \tag{10.16}$$

Needless to say, $D_j(\cdot)$ are also homogeneous of degree zero in p.[14]

In the case of a closed economy, the commodity equilibrium conditions,

$$S_j(\cdot) = D_j(\cdot)(j = 1, \ldots, k), \tag{10.17}$$

determine the equilibrium values of $k - 1$ relative commodity prices in view of Walras' law and the homogeneity of supply and demand functions. In the case of international economies, we must posit the production model described by Eqs. (10.12), (10.13), and (10.14) for each of the trading countries, and the commodity equilibrium conditions for the trading world as a whole. Once this is done, the model may be considered to determine the equilibrium world commodity prices and the corresponding equilibrium values of factor prices outputs and consumptions of commodities pertaining to each of the trading countries.

---

[13] See Chang (1979), Ethier (1984), and Takayama (1982) for discussions.

[14] The subjective demand function perceived by individual firms need not coincide with this "objective" demand function.

In passing, consider the aforementioned special case where pure competition prevails in all industries. In each industry, an individual firm operates at the minimum point of its average cost curve in the long-run equilibrium, and the total output of each industry is adjusted by the entry or exit of firms. Thus, an individual firm is able to determine their output behaving as price-takers, while the aggregate production function of each industry exhibits constant returns to scale. This structure of the present model is similar to that of the more general model considered by McKenzie (1959) to prove the existence of general equilibrium.[15] I believe that it dissolves Samuelson's paradox of indeterminacy under purist competition (see Samuelson 1947, pp. 78–80).

10.4 Robustness of Traditional Competitive Analysis

The general equilibrium production model described by Eqs. (10.12), (10.13), and (10.14) is formally identical to the standard k -commodity, l -factor competitive equilibrium model used for the theory of international trade except for the fact that it contains two parameters, γ_j and ρ_j, which characterize the market structure of the model economy. As already mentioned, this observation establishes that, given γ_j and ρ_j, all the positive results of traditional comparative-static analysis obtained in the simple competitive equilibrium model are applicable to the present model. It remains to be seen, however, whether the normative results of traditional comparative-static analysis are also valid in the present model.

The change in the potential economic welfare of a closed economy consequent upon a slight structural disturbance may be approximated by the resultant change in the value of the national product evaluated in terms of initial commodity prices (see Ohyama 1972). The analysis of Eqs. (10.12) and (10.13) entails

$$\sum p_j dZ_j = \sum w_j \sum \tau_j \rho_j dL_{ij} + \sum p_j Z_j \varepsilon_j \hat{\beta}_j, \tag{10.18}$$

where $L_{ij}\left(= n_j X_{ij}\right)$ is the total employment of factor i in industry j and ϵ_j is the elasticity of the average cost of commodity j, c_j, with respect to β_j defined by

$$\epsilon_j = -\frac{\beta_j}{c_j}\frac{\partial c_j}{\partial \beta_j},$$

[15] In the words of McKenzie, "it is not unreasonable to consider the constant returns model as the truly general competitive model, approximating to the situation with freedom of entry and firms which are considered to be small compared to their industries."

with $\widehat{\beta}_j$ indicating the relative infinitesimal change of variable β_j, or $d\beta_j/\beta_j$. Note that from Eq. (10.9) ϵ_j is positive (respectively negative) if $\beta_j<1$ (respectively $\beta_j>1$).[16] In the two-commodity case where i is given, Eq. (10.8) reduces to

$$\sum p_j \mathrm{d}Z_j = (\tau_2\rho_2 - \tau_1\rho_1)\sum w_i \mathrm{d}L_{i2} + \sum p_j Z_j \epsilon_j \widehat{\beta}_j. \tag{10.19}$$

The first term on the right-hand side of Eq. (10.18) or Eq. (10.19) represents the effect of inter-industry reallocation of factors on the national product evaluated at the initial prices, given degrees of competition and markup ratios. Note that it vanishes to zero when $\tau_1\rho_1 = \cdots = \tau_k\rho_k$. The second term on the right-hand side shows how a change in β_j affects the value of national output, given the inter-industry allocation of factors. In light of Eqs. (10.9) and (10.11), an increase in β_j raises the factor productivity of industry j and augments national output if and only if $\beta_j<1$, that is, if and only if it operates under decreasing costs in the long-run equilibrium.

For the purpose of considering welfare implications of exogenous disturbances, it is useful to introduce a geometric characterization of the long-run general equilibrium of the production model described in the preceding section. Given β_j and L_i, k equations in Eq. (10.13) define the combination of possible commodity outputs for all possible values of factor prices, ω_j. Let us refer to the locus of possible commodity outputs for a given set of β_j as a "production feasibility frontier." There are infinitely many production feasibility frontiers. The production frontier in the usual sense (or production possibility surface) is the production feasibility frontier that corresponds to the special case where $\beta_j = 1$ for all j. As is clear from Eq. (10.18) or (10.19), when $\tau_1\rho_1 = \cdots = \tau_k\rho_k$, the price ratio of any pair of commodities is equal to the marginal rate of transformation between them along the production feasibility frontier. The special case of this situation is the long-run tax-free general equilibrium in which profits decline to zero under free entry in all industries.

Figure 10.2 illustrates the geometric implication of Eq. (10.19) for the two-commodity, two-factor (two-by-two) case when $\beta_1 = 1$, $\beta_2<1$ and $\tau_1\rho_1 = \tau_2\rho_2 = 1$. The curve Tt is the production feasibility frontier, and the line Pp has the slope equal to the relative price of commodity 2 prevailing in the market. The general equilibrium of production is characterized by the equality of the marginal rate of transformation between commodities 1 and 2 to their relative prices even when firms behave oligopolistically in industry 2. Thus, it is isomorphic to the competitive equilibrium of production in every respect except for the fact that the economy's production feasibility frontier Tt is located below its production possibility curve TT because β_2 is less than unity.

The foregoing analysis clearly entails the following proposition.

[16] See Appendix C of Ohyama (1999) for the derivation of Eq. (11.18).

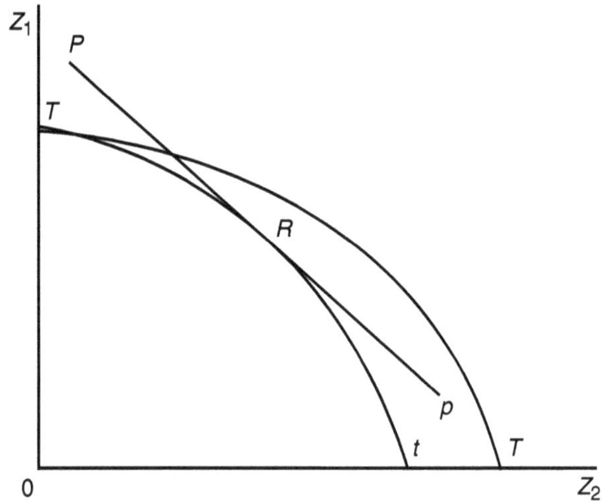

Fig. 10.2 Production feasibility frontier

Proposition 10.1: Robustness of Traditional Analysis *Suppose that* $\tau_1\rho_1 = \cdots = \tau_k\rho_k$ *and that* γ_j *are given. Then the traditional positive and normative results of competitive equilibrium analysis remain valid in the present model with* γ_j *possibly less than unity.*

Generally, a reallocation of factors from a low-markup industry to a high-markup industry augments the value of national output in the absence of production taxes. In other words, the price of the former relative to the latter tends to be smaller than the marginal cost of the former relative to the latter. Thus, it is the differences in the markup ratios of different industries that undermine the applicability of welfare propositions derived from traditional competitive analysis.

10.5 Market and Welfare

In the preceding section, we demonstrated the robustness of the traditional results of general equilibrium analysis. The traditional literature fails, however, to consider how market structure affects the general equilibrium of the model because of the underlying assumption that $\rho_j = 1$ and $\gamma_j = 1$ for all j. The degree of competition may be smaller than unity under imperfect competition, depending on the perceived price elasticity of demand for its product and the rate of industrial concentration. Moreover, the markup ratios may not reduce to unity even in the long run on account of the government's entry policies, or because of possible reservation of entrepreneurial resources under a minimum rate of profit per unit of output. The competition policies are generally defined as the set of measures designed to affect the market structure of an economy with a view to improving its economic welfare. Within the present framework, this consists of two distinct measures: antitrust policy and entry (restriction) policy. To be more precise, we interpret a change in γ_j as a change in antitrust (merger) policy and a change in ρ_j as a change in entry policy with respect to industry j. In this section we consider the effects of these policy measures on the welfare of a closed economy.

Using Eq. (10.18) (or Eq. (10.19)), we can deduce the welfare effects of alternative competition policies. Let us first consider the effects of the government's antitrust policy.

Proposition 10.2: Antitrust Policy *Let* $\tau_1\rho_1 = \cdots = \tau_k\rho_k$ *and* $\beta_h < 1$ *in the initial equilibrium. Then, an increase in the degree of competition in industry* $h(h \neq 1)$ *improves potential economic welfare.*

Proof Let $\widehat{\gamma}_j = 0$ for all $j \neq h$ and $\widehat{\rho}_j = 0$ for all j in Eq. (10.18) to obtain

$$\sum p_j \frac{\mathrm{d}Z_j}{\mathrm{d}\gamma_h} = \frac{\epsilon_h p_h Z_h}{\gamma_h} > 0,$$

because $\beta_h < 1$ and, therefore, $\epsilon_h > 0$.

In other words, the strengthening of antitrust policy in any industry operating under decreasing costs is unambiguously beneficial to the economy in the free entry equilibrium where $\tau_1\rho_1 = \cdots = \tau_k\rho_k$. This result is intuitively natural, because an increase in the degree of competition in any industry is ceteris paribus qualitatively identical to a Hicks-neutral technological progress in that industry. It is thus optimal for the government to achieve the maximum possible degree of competition, or the minimum possible degree of monopoly in each industry. Figure 10.3 illustrates, for the two-by-two case, how an increase in the degree of competition in industry 2 brings about an outward shift of the production feasibility frontier, thereby augmenting the representative consumer's utility.

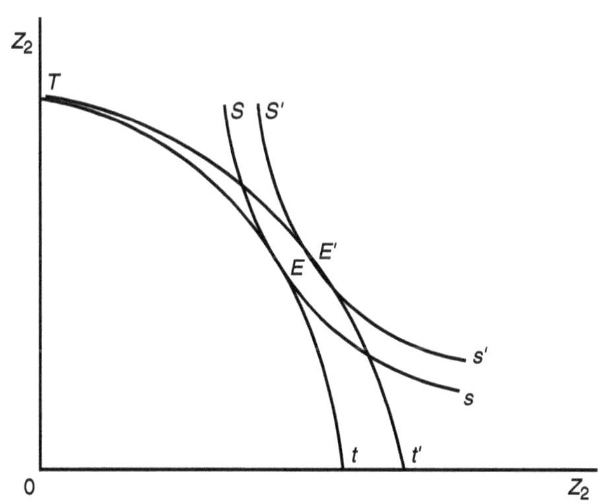

Fig. 10.3 The effect of antitrust policy

An increase in γ_h may be assumed to increase the total output of commodity h (see Appendix D). For simplicity, suppose that there are no production taxes (i.e., τ_j is unity) and that different markup ratios prevail in different industries in the initial equilibrium. In such a case, a reallocation of resources to an industry from industries with higher markup ratios tends to decrease real national product along a given production feasibility frontier. Therefore, if $\rho_h < \rho_j$ for all $j \neq h$, the conclusion may be reversed. Moreover, β_h could be greater than unity, violating the basic assumption of the thesis. If so, firms operate under increasing costs in industry h and a decrease in the degree of competition would improve economic welfare.

Next, let us consider the effects of the government entry restriction policy on the potential welfare of the model economy. Here, we consider the restriction of entry into an industry designed to achieve a given increase in its markup ratio. This definition of entry restriction implies that the government must regulate both the number of firms in the industry and the number of firms in each cartel in the industry. Thus, it differs from the usual definition of entry restriction requiring only the regulation of the number of firms in the industry. I believe that the present definition is useful in clarifying the distinction between antitrust policy and entry policy.

Proposition 10.3: Entry Policy *Let* $\tau_1\rho_1 = \cdots = \tau_k\rho_k$ *and let* $\beta_h < 1$ *in the initial equilibrium. An entry restriction designed to increase* ρ_k *slightly improves potential economic welfare.*

Proof Let $\widehat{\gamma}_j = 0$ for all j and $\widehat{\rho}_j = 0$ for all $j \neq h$ in Eq. (10.18) to obtain

$$\sum p_j \frac{dZ_j}{d\rho_h} = \frac{\epsilon_h p_h Z_h}{\rho_h}.$$

The conclusion then follows, because $\epsilon_h > 0$ for $\beta_h < 1$.

This result may be interpreted as a version of the well-known excess entry thesis in that it is socially beneficial to reduce the number of firms below the free-entry Cournot equilibrium level. As noted earlier, however, an increase in ρ_h, considered here is a result of restricting n_h and (m_j) simultaneously because γ_h is assumed to be given in the present setting. The usual excess entry thesis has been proved mostly in the context of partial equilibrium models.[17]

Caveats are, however, in order. First, if $\beta_h > 1$, a decrease in ρ_h will improve economic welfare (see Ohyama 1993). Given γ_h, the assumption of $\beta_h < 1$ implies

[17] For instance, see Mankiw and Whinston (1986) and Suzumura and Kiyono (1987) for partial equilibrium analyses. Konishi et al. (1990) provided a proof for the theorem in a simple general equilibrium model with the representative consumer possessing a quasi-linear utility function.

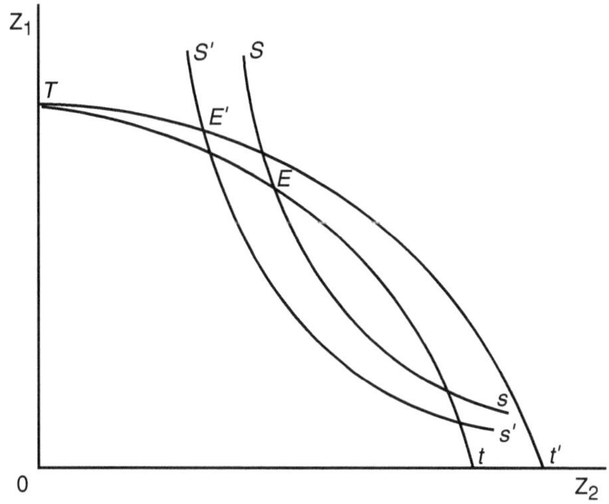

Fig. 10.4 The perverse effects of entry restriction

$$\rho_h < \frac{1}{\gamma_h}.$$

In words, the markup ratio of the industry cannot exceed the inverse of the degree of competition. Second, the crucial assumption here is that $\tau_1\rho_1 = \cdots = \tau_k\rho_k$ in the initial free-entry equilibrium. Given τ_j, the conclusion of Proposition 10.3 may not hold if the markup ratio in industry h beomes greater than the markup ratios in other industries. For the two-by-two case, Fig. 10.4 illustrates the possibility that the regulation of markup ratio in industry 2 may be harmful when $\tau_2\rho_2 > \tau_1\rho_1$. Last but not least, the restriction of entry may actually increase the rate of concentration and ends up by decreasing β_2. I have so far ruled out this possibility by assumption, for analytical simplicity. It seems to limit the relevance of the excess entry thesis rather severely.

An arbitrary targeting of markup ratio of any single industry may deteriorate potential economic welfare. Given the degrees of competition in industries, however, one can think of a combination of production taxes and markup ratios that ensures an efficient allocation of resources.

Proposition 10.4: Optimal Policy Mix *Suppose that γ_j are given. The government can achieve an efficient resource allocation by setting ρ_j and τ_j such that*

$$\tau_1\rho_1 = \cdots = \tau_k\rho_k,$$

and

$$\rho_j = \frac{1}{\gamma_j}.$$

Proof In view of Eq. (10.11), firms are operating at the lowest point of their average cost curve in all industries when $\beta_j = \gamma_j \rho_j$ for all j: this implies that the corresponding production *feasibility* frontier coincides with the production *possibility* frontier. Moreover, Eq. (10.18) entails that the marginal rate of transformation between any pair of commodities along the production possibility frontier is made equal to their relative market (consumer's) price by virtue of the assumption that $\tau_1 \rho_1 = \cdots = \tau_k \rho_k$.

This result means that appropriate application of production taxes and instruments of entry restriction leads to the first-best solution of resource allocation. Without loss of generality, suppose that industries are numbered in the order of their degree of competition, or $\gamma_1 = 1 > \gamma_2 > \cdots > \gamma_k$, and that the rate of production tax imposed on the industry with the smallest degree of competition is zero, or $\tau_k = 1$. Then, the first-best production taxes are characterized by

$$\tau_j = \frac{\gamma_j}{\gamma_k} \; (j = 1, \ldots, k),$$

which implies that

$$t_1 > t_2 > \cdots > t_k = 0.$$

To achieve an efficient allocation of resources, the government must tax industries at rates increasing in the order of the degree of competition.

10.6 Trade and Welfare

As pointed out here, all the basic HOS theorems carry over to the present model in the absence of production taxes (i.e., where $\tau_1 = \cdots = \tau_k = 1$), given the parameters γ_j and ρ_j determining the market structure of the economy. For instance, we can recapitulate the HOS proposition on the pattern of trade, that each country exports the product intensive in its abundant factor of production if the two countries are otherwise identical, as well as the factor price equalization theorem, that factor prices are equalized internationally through trade. Despite the much publicized new trade theory, all the comparative-statics results of the old trade theory are obviously valid within the framework of the present model with increasing returns and imperfect competition so long as the parameters of market structure are kept unchanged.[18] Both old and new trade theories are, however, largely silent on the role of international differences in market structure for comparative advantage and gains from trade. In this section, let us consider the implications of market structure for the pattern of trade and gains from trade.

Suppose that there are two countries, say the home country and the foreign country (or the rest of the world), initially identical in every respect in the sense that they are possessed of identical homothetic performances, identical production functions, and identical factor endowment proportions. Furthermore, suppose that they have identical market structures and that there are no production taxes. Then, there should be no trade between the two countries, even in the absence of trade impediments. Next, suppose that this initial international equilibrium is disturbed by changes in the market structure of the home country while the foreign country remains unchanged. We can predict the resulting pattern of international trade by examining their effects on the production pattern of the country at given commodity prices.

Let us first consider the effects of an increase in the degree of competition in industry h of the home country. As already noted, it is qualitatively identical to a Hicks-neutral technological progress in that industry if $\beta_h<1$. With this change in the market structure, the home country will generally produce relatively more of commodity h and less of other commodities than the foreign country when they realize the same commodity prices. Following the convention in trade theory, let us distinguish foreign variables from home variables by giving the former asterisks. For instance, let γ_j and γ_j^* denote, respectively, the home and foreign degree of competition in industry j. We can then state the following.

Proposition 10.5: Antitrust Policy and the Pattern of Trade *Suppose that there are no production taxes in both countries and that $\rho_j = \rho_j{}^*$ for all j, $\gamma_j = \gamma_j{}^*$ for $j \neq h$ and $\beta_h < 1$. Then, if*

$$\gamma_h > \gamma_h{}^*,$$

the home country exports commodity h and imports at least one of the other commodities in the free trade equilibrium.

Proof Because $\beta_h<1$ by assumption, $\epsilon_h>0$. Thus, an increase in γ_h increases the relative output of commodity h at given prices. (See Appendix D for the proof for the two-by-two case.)

Let us turn to the implications of entry restriction imposed on an industry for the pattern of trade. Entry restriction increases the output and productivity of individual firms in the industry when they are operating under decreasing costs. Therefore, its effect on the total output of the industry is generally ambiguous. It can be shown,

[18] Most of the novel results from new trade theory are obtained in short-run equilibrium models in which the number of firms is fixed in imperfectly competitive industries. For trade policy implications of new trade theory, see Krugman (1987), Helpman and Krugman (1989), and Chang and Katayama (1995).

however, that entry restriction imposed on industry h decreases its total output if the elasticity of its firm's average cost with respect to the scale of output, ϵ_h, is sufficiently small.[19] Note that this gives rise to the outward shift of the home country's production feasibility frontier via its favorable effects on the productivity of firms. Thus, the home country's entry restriction in industry h is likely to reduce the *relative* output of commodity h, thereby inducing her to import commodity h and export at least one of the other commodities.

A similar reasoning reveals the effects of market structure on the terms of trade and welfare of the two countries. Suppose that the two countries are initially in the free trade equilibrium. From the textbooks of standard trade theory, we know that technical progress in a country's export industry deteriorates its terms of trade and may result in immiserizing growth, and that technical progress in its import-competing industry improves its terms of trade and necessarily enhances its potential welfare. Recalling that an increase in the degree of competition in industry h is qualitatively equivalent to a Hicks-neutral technical progress if $\beta_h < 1$, we obtain the following proposition.

Proposition 10.6: Antitrust Policy and the Terms of Trade *Suppose that firms are operating under decreasing costs in industries of a country under free trade. Antitrust policy applied to the country's export industry worsens its terms of trade and may bring about a loss of welfare, whereas antitrust policy applied to the country's import-competing industry improves its terms of trade and necessarily increases its potential welfare.*

Clearly, antitrust policy, wherever applied, improves world potential welfare in the absence of distortions arising from production taxes and different markup ratios across industries. Suppose that the government seeks to maximize national welfare using only the instruments of antitrust policy without recourse to those of entry policy and production taxes. Barring the possibility of immiserizing growth, it will then strive to increase the degree of competition everywhere and as far as possible. Thus, there is no need for international coordination of national antitrust policies in this case. In contrast, the boundless restriction of entry into an industry is not warranted because it necessarily distorts resource allocation. As has been pointed out, an increase in the markup ratio of industry h decreases its output if ϵ_h is small. Suppose that this is the case: it will then bring about a rise in the relative price of commodity h. In other words, its terms of trade effect will be opposite to that of a stricter antitrust policy. Because of this terms-of-trade effect, the self-seeking government will restrict entry excessively for export industries and inadequately for import-competing industries, from the world point of view. In such a case, there is room for international coordination of national entry policies.[20]

---

[19] See Appendix D of Ohyama (1999) for the exact analysis of the two-by-two case.

[20] We discussed international coordination of entry policies in a different setting using a simple model of increasing returns and monopolistic competition: see Ohyama (1997).

It has been often argued that free trade provides an effective remedy for domestic monopoly because it introduces new competitive pressures from abroad. This argument is intuitively appealing and has been partly formalized (Dixit and Norman 1980, chap. 9; Helpman and Krugman 1985, chap. 5; Schweinberger 1996). On the other hand, skeptical views have been expressed since Graham (1923) about the gains from trade under increasing returns and imperfect competition (Negishi 1969; Markusen 1981; Ethier 1982; Markusen and Melvin 1984). It is, therefore, important to show how, and in what sense, imperfect competition and decreasing costs may strengthen the argument for free trade within the present general equilibrium framework. For this purpose, let us slightly modify the assumption that the degree of competition in each industry is controlled by the government. In some cases it is more plausible to assume that the number of *colluding* firms is controlled in each industry. The number of firms in the industry may not be freely controllable depending on the state of a firm's internal scale economies relative to the size of the market and the government's ability to enforce an appropriate antitrust policy; for instance, the domestic market for a product may be so small that it cannot accommodate more than one firm in autarky. In such a case, the rate of industrial concentration in the industry is unity in autarky but will be endogenously determined, together with the total number of firms in the world, under free trade.

Compare the home country's free trade equilibrium (situation F) with its autarkic equilibrium (situation A). Let superscript g denote a variable's equilibrium value in situation g $(g = F, A)$. We can then put forward the following proposition.

Proposition 10.7: Gains from Free Trade *Suppose that there are no production taxes. Let*

$$\rho_j^A = \rho_j^F, \ (j = 1, \ldots, k),$$

and

$$\beta_j^A, \beta_j^F \leq 1.$$

Then, free trade is preferable to autarky for the country if

$$\gamma_j^F \geq \gamma_j^A \text{ or } \mu_j^F \eta_j^F \leq \mu_j^A \eta_j^A, \ (j = 2, \ldots, k).$$

Furthermore, the greater the difference between the degrees of competition in the two situations, the greater are the gains from free trade.

Proof By assumptions, the marginal rate of transformation along a given production feasibility frontier between any pair of commodities is equal to their relative price, and Eq. (10.18) reduces to

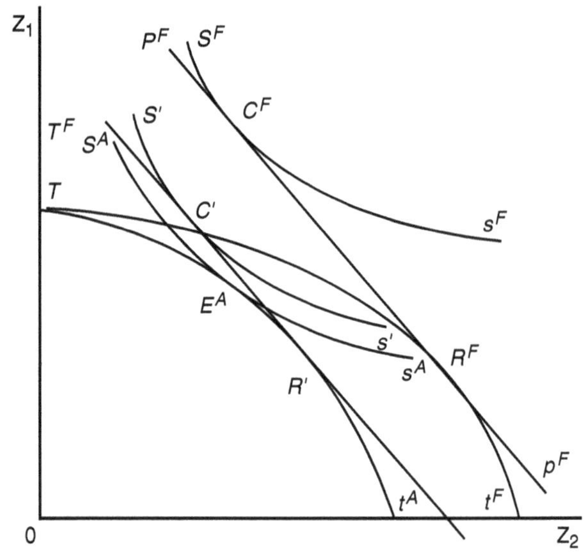

Fig 10.5 Gains from free trade

$$\sum p_j \mathrm{d}Z_j = \sum p_j Z_j \epsilon_j \widehat{\gamma}_j.$$

Note that $\epsilon_j \geq 0$ because $\beta_j \leq 1$. Hence, an increase in γ_j augments the productivity of industry j, leading to an increase in the national product at given prices; this means that the country's production feasibility frontier under free trade lies northeast of its production feasibility frontier under autarky. The greater the difference between the degrees of monopoly in the two situations in any industry, the larger is the distance between the production feasibility frontiers in the two situations.

For a small price-taking country, the assumptions of this proposition are necessarily satisfied. Generally, the government can ensure gains from trade by keeping the degree of competition in each industry at a level not lower than in autarky. Figure 10.5 illustrates the gains from free trade for the two-by-two case. The curve Tt^A is its production feasibility frontier under autarky. The tangency point E^A, with a social indifference curve, $S^A s^A$, indicates the autarkic equilibrium. With the advent of free trade, the production feasibility frontier will shift outward to Tt^F. Given the international relative price of the two commodities, which is equal to the slope of line $P^F p^F$, the equilibrium production point will move to R^F and the equilibrium consumption point to C^F with clear gains from trade. Were it not for the shift of the production feasibility frontier, the new production point would have been R' and the new consumption point C', and the gains from trade would have been smaller.

It is noteworthy that competition policy plays a role in realizing and even augmenting gains from trade. The welfare effects of any structural change depend crucially on the market structure of the economy, which in turn hinges on the government's competition policies. In fact, given the degree of competition and markup ratio in each industry, all the important welfare propositions obtained in the traditional literature concerning the terms-of-trade improvement, infant industry argument, customs unions issue, etc., carry over straightforwardly to the present model without any modification (Ohyama 1972).

10.7 Concluding Remarks

In this chapter, we have attempted to construct and advocate a tractable general equilibrium model incorporating elements of imperfect competition and increasing returns to scale. It can be regarded as an extension of the multi-commodity, multi-factor general equilibrium model familiar from the theory of international trade. We employed the model to explore the implications of two distinct measures of competition policy, that is, antitrust policy and entry restriction policy, for the long-run equilibrium and potential economic welfare of a country. W showed that the celebrated Heckscher–Ohlin theorems and other traditional comparative-static results in trade theory carry over to the present model under the given market structure. We demonstrated that antitrust policy (represented by an increase in the degree of competition) in an industry always improves the welfare of a country in the autarkic long-run equilibrium. In contrast, entry restriction policy (represented by an increase in the markup ratio) in an industry is beneficial to a country only if the markup ratio of the industry is sufficiently small. Furthermore, we considered the effects of these policies for the trade pattern and terms of trade of a country and clarified the conditions that ensure the gains from trade. We believe that the present model can be employed as a useful vehicle of analysis for various economic problems, but obviously it is restrictive in many ways. I now point out some limitations of the present model and possible extensions.

First, the present interpretation of the model approximates the situation in which firms' profits decline to predetermined levels (possibly zero) in all industries. As noted in Sects. 10.2 and 10.3, this situation represents the long-run equilibrium under free entry. Most of the unconventional and anomalous results attributed to increasing returns and imperfect competition arise in the short-run equilibrium of the model.[21] Therefore, it should be worthwhile to consider the short-run equilibrium, in which the number of firms is fixed and their markup ratio becomes variable, at least in some industries. We can easily reinterpret the basic model to carry out this task.[22]

Second, and related to the first point, note that the present model is applicable only to the economy in which firms are small compared with their industries. Suppose that the economies of scale in an industry are such that only one firm can survive with nonnegative profits. The adjustment of the total output in such an

[21] See Krugman (1987) for some examples.

[22] See Ohyama (1993) for an attempt to analyze the short-run equilibrium in the two-by-two case.

industry must be carried out by changing the output of the firm rather than the number of firms, each with a fixed output. Thus, it would be necessary to reinterpret the model so that the markup ratio (and consequently the output) of the firm, rather than the number of firms in the industry, becomes an endogenous variable of the model.

Third, some may feel uncomfortable assuming that the production functions of all firms are identical in each industry. As it stands, the model does not apply to the economy in which firms in some industries are possessed of different technologies. It is not difficult, however, to modify the model to accommodate firms with different technologies in the same industries. Suppose that there are two groups of firms, H and L, in an industry and that the production function of firms in group H is obtained by a Hicks-neutral technological progress of that of firms in group L. Clearly, these two groups of firms can coexist in the industry equilibrium if firms in group H achieve a higher degree of concentration than those in group L such that the average cost of the former is equal to that of the latter. The industry's total output is determined by demand conditions, but the composition of different firms in the industry becomes indeterminate.

Fourth, all commodities are assumed to be final goods and factor markets are assumed to be competitive. Needless to say, there are a number of pure and non-pure intermediate goods, and some factor markets (such as labor and land markets) are monopolized in the real world. The basic analysis of the paper would carry through, however, even if I alleviate these assumptions, so long as the buyers are assumed to be price-takers in all cases. Adding the assumption of monopsonic power would, however, complicate the analysis considerably.

Finally, the problem of product differentiation is not explicitly addressed in the present model. For simplicity, we made no mention of product differentiation anywhere in the foregoing discussion. One is able, however, to consider product differentiation even in the present model by grouping together several industries whose products are close substitutes for one another and regarding them as one large industry. In modeling international trade, one may assume that each country produces its own national products within such a large industry of the world. This trick would suffice to give rise to intra-industry trade between countries with a similar economic structure.

References

Arrow, K. J., & Debreu, G. (1954). Existence of an equilibrium for a competitive economy. *Econometrica, 22*, 256–290.

Brander, J., & Krugman, P. R. (1983). A reciprocal dumping model of international trade. *Journal of International Economics, 15*, 313–321.

Chang, W. W. (1979). Some theorems on trade and general equilibrium with many goods and factors. *Econometrica, 47*, 709–726.

Chang, W. W., Katayama, S. (eds) (1995). *Imperfect competition in international trade*. Boston: Kluwer Academic

Das, S. P. (1982). Economies of scale, imperfect competition, and the pattern of trade. *The Econometrics Journal, 92*, 684–693.
Dixit, A. K., & Norman, V. (1980). *Theory of international trade*. Cambridge: Cambridge University Press.
Ethier, W. J. (1982). Decreasing costs in international trade and Frank Graham's argument for protection. *Econometrica, 50*, 1243–1268.
Ethier, W. J. (1984). Higher dimensional issues in trade theory. In R. W. Jones & P. B. Kenen (Eds.), *Handbook of international economics* (Vol. 1). Amsterdam: North-Holland.
Graham, F. (1923). Some aspects of protection further considered. *The Quarterly Journal of Economics, 37*, 199–227.
Helpman, E. (1981). International trade in the presence of product differentiation, economies of scale and monopolistic competition. *Journal of International Economics, 11*, 305–340.
Helpman, E. (1984). Increasing returns, imperfect markets and trade theory. In R. W. Jones & P. B. Kennen (Eds.), *Handbook of international economics* (Vol. 1). Amsterdam: North-Holland.
Helpman, E., & Krugman, P. R. (1985). *Market structure and foreign trade*. Cambridge: MIT Press.
Helpman, E., & Krugman, P. R. (1989). *Trade policy and market structure*. Cambridge: MIT Press.
Jones, R. W. (1965). The structure of simple general equilibrium models. *The Journal of Political Economy, 73*, 557–572.
Jones, R. W. (1968). Variable returns to scale in general equilibrium theory. *International Economic Review, 9*, 261–272.
Kemp, M. C. (1995). *The gains from trade and gains from aid*. London/New York: Routledge.
Kemp, M. C., & Schweinberger, A. G. (1991). Variable returns to sale and non-uniqueness of equilibrium and the gains from international trade. *The Review of Economic Studies, 58*, 807–816.
Kikuchi, T. (1996). Increasing costs in product diversification and gains from trade. *The Japanese Economic Review, 47*, 384–395.
Konishi, H., Okuno-Fujiwara, M., & Suzumura, K. (1990). Oligopolistic competition and economic welfare: A general equilibrium analysis of entry regulation and tax-subsidy schemes. *Journal of Public Economics, 42*, 67–88.
Krugman, P. R. (1979). Increasing returns, monopolistic competition, and international trade. *Journal of International Economics, 9*, 469–479.
Krugman, P. R. (1980). Scale economies, product differentiation, and the pattern of trade. *The American Economic Review, 70*, 950–959.
Krugman, P. R. (1987). Is free trade passé? *The Journal of Economic Perspectives, 1*, 131–141.
Lancaster, K. (1980). Intra-industry trade under perfect monopolistic competition. *Journal of International Economics, 10*, 151–175.
Laurence, C., & Spiller, P. T. (1983). Product diversity, economies of scale, and international trade. *The Quarterly Journal of Economics, 98*, 63–83.
Levinsohn, J. (1996). Competition policy and international trade. In J. Bhagwati & R. Hudec (Eds.), *Fair trade and harmonization* (Vol. 1). Cambridge: Cambridge University Press.
Mankiw, N. G., & Michael, D. W. (1986). Free entry and social inefficiency. *The Rand Journal of Economics, 17*, 48–58.
Markusen, J. R. (1981). Trade and the gains from trade with imperfect competition. *Journal of Econometrics, 11*, 531–551.
Markusen, J. R., & Melvin, J. R. (1984). The gains-from-trade theorem with increasing returns to scale. In H. Kierzkowski (Ed.), *Monopolistic competition and international trade*. Oxford: Clarendon Press.
McKenzie, L. W. (1959). On the existence of general equilibrium for a competitive market. *Econometrica, 27*, 54–71.
Melvin, J. R., & Warne, R. D. (1973). Monopoly and the theory of international trade. *Journal of International Economics, 3*, 117–134.

Negishi, T. (1961). Monopolistic competition and general equilibrium. *The Review of Economic Studies, 28*, 196–201.
Negishi, T. (1969). Marshallian external economies and gains from trade between similar countries. *The Review of Economic Studies, 36*, 131–135.
Negishi, T. (1972). *General equilibrium theory and international trade*. Amsterdam: North-Holland.
Nikaido, H. (1975). *Monopolistic competition and effective demand*. Princeton: Princeton University Press.
Ohyama, M. (1972). Trade and welfare in general equilibrium. *Keio Economic Studies, 9*, 37–73.
Ohyama, M. (1991). Firm's behavior and international trade: A reinterpretation and extension of the Ricardo–Mill model. *Mita Journal of Economics, 83*, 214–228 (in Japanese).
Ohyama, M. (1993). Firms, entry and hysteresis in the Heckscher–Ohlin–Samuelson model of production and trade. In W. J. Ethier, E. Helpman, & P. N. Neary (Eds.), *Theory, policy and dynamics in international trade*. Cambridge: Cambridge University Press.
Ohyama, M. (1997). Monopolistic competition, increasing returns and international coordination of entry policy. *Pacific Economic Review, 2*, 197–209.
Ohyama, M. (1999). Market, trade and welfare in general equilibrium. *The Japanese Economic Review, 1*, 1–25.
Samuelson, P. A. (1947). *Foundations of economic analysis*. Cambridge: Harvard University Press.
Schweinberger, A. G. (1996). Procompetitive gains from trade and comparative advantage. *Journal of International Economics, 37*, 361–375.
Seade, J. K. (1980). On the effects of entry. *Econometrica, 48*, 479–489.
Suzumura, K., & Kazuharu, K. (1987). Entry barriers and economic welfare. *The Review of Economic Studies, 54*, 157–167.
Takayama, A. (1982). On theorems of general competitive equilibrium of production and trade: A survey of some recent developments in the theory of international trade. *Keio Economic Studies, 19*, 1–37.
Woodland, A. D. (1982). *International trade and resource allocation*. Amsterdam: North-Holland.

Part III
Welfare and Efficiency

Chapter 11
Welfare and Efficiency: Socioeconomic Controversies in Modern Times

11.1 Introduction

In recent years, we have witnessed a number of critics and commentators who argue that the pursuit of efficiency spoils the realization of social values such as security, health, environment, and fairness. Is it really true that the pursuit of efficiency impedes social values? What are the social values to begin with? Are they to be distinguished from the individual values in the narrow sense defined in economics? In this chapter, we intend to review the relevant concepts and elucidate the relationship between social values and efficiency.

In Sect. 2, we explain the analytical framework of the present chapter. We extend the concept of private values based on consumption of "isolated individuals" to social values included in the social consumption of "ordinary individuals" who attach importance to human relations. For simplicity, we introduce the concepts of social indifference curves and value frontiers and also occasionally employ the method of partial equilibrium surplus analysis.

In Sect. 3, we take up the recent arguments in mass media that the pursuit of efficiency prevents the realization of social values and critically examine the examples of alleged trade-offs between security and efficiency. We conclude here that failure of the social optimum is attributable not to the pursuit of efficiency but to market failure in a broad sense. In Sect. 4, we point out the possibility that the government measures to remedy market failures give rise to various problems in themselves. In Sect. 5, we reexamine the recent views popularized in mass media that the deregulation advanced by the government had caused an undesirable gap in income distribution to develop in Japan. We illustrate the illogic of this view by way of simple geometry and, in so doing, interpret the costs of poll tax vis-a-vis an

This chapter is based on the draft of my lecture given at Kumamoto Gakuen University in commemoration of the Department of International Economics on June 26, 2010. I appreciate Professor Moriki Hosoe for arrangement for the lecture and helpful discussion.

© Springer Japan 2016

M. Ohyama, *Macroeconomics, Trade, and Social Welfare*, Advances in Japanese Business and Economics 14, DOI 10.1007/978-4-431-55807-1_11

appropriate tax-cum-subsidy policy to raise a given government revenue. In Sect. 6, we conclude by reconsidering the policy scheme of "mixed economies" and make clear what should be done and what should not be done from the point of view of efficient resource allocation.

11.2 Analytical Framework

The production of any valuable thing requires scarce resources. It is, therefore, vitally necessary to use resources efficiently. The popular view that the pursuit of efficiency demolishes social values is diametrically against this fundamental axiom of economics. There are trade-offs between different values, but absolutely no trade-offs between value and efficiency. We develop the following analytical framework to illustrate this point.

11.2.1 Social and Individual Values

Values are the generic name of useful things for human beings. Individual values are the values of goods and services used for individual (private) enjoyment, and social values are the values of goods and services reserved for collective (public) usage such as security, health, environment, and fairness, as already mentioned.

11.2.2 Production Frontier and Value Standard

The individual and social values are both produced using scarce resources. Given available resources and technologies, we can define the production (or value) frontier, as a locus of maximal output of goods and services the economy can produce. Consider the output of the private goods and services used for the realization of individual values (rice, for example) and that for the realization of social values (multi-family housing). They must be located on the production frontier (also known as transformation curve) if they are to represent the efficient combination of products. Curve *Tt* in Fig. 11.1 is a simplest illustration of the production frontier.

Curve *Tt* shows numerous combinations of efficient outputs. The question of social choice is "What is the socially desirable point?" To answer this question, we need to introduce a social value standard. Generally speaking, however, it is difficult to rationalize the social value judgment or its basic standard. Perhaps, economists are not qualified to carry out such a task, as Robbins (1938) and Arrow (1951) argued convincingly and elaborated even axiomatically.

Fig. 11.1 The social optimum

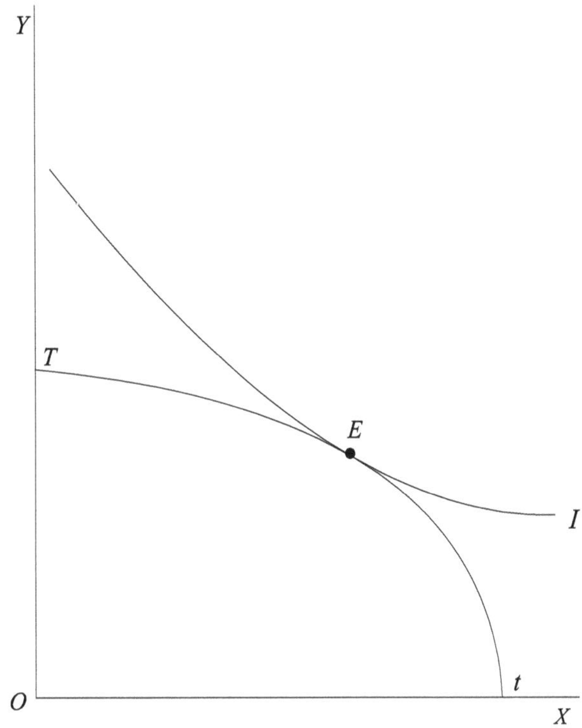

11.2.3 Social Optimum

Once a value standard is given, economists can pinpoint the efficient measure to realize the any specific policy target. To illustrate the role of economists, let us introduce the social indifference curves along with the consumer surplus. (See Marshall 1890; Samuelson 1956; Ohyama 1972 and Mas-Collelt et al. 1995 for the methods.)

Proposition 11.1: Social Optimum *The social optimum is shown as the intersection of production frontier and one of social indifference curves.*

The individual and social values on the production frontier are efficient by definition, and the intersection point achieves the highest of the indifference curves on the value frontier. If rice and multi-family housing are traded in perfectly competitive markets, and if there are no externalities, the social optimum is supposed to be realized at this intersection. (The fundamental theorem of welfare economics: cf. Mas-Collel et al. 1995.) In reality, however, the social optimum may not be realized because of monopolistic markets and external economies existing in the economy.

11.3 Security and Efficiency

"Deregulation without sanctuary" was the slogan advocated by the popular Koizumi Cabinet (2001–2006) for structural deregulation in Japan. In its last years, however, a series of scandalous events, which threatened security in various industries such as food, buildings, and transportation, was reported in the mass media. There were many commentators who accused "structural deregulation" for excessive competition bringing about damage to security. Let us begin by reviewing reports and comments in mass media on the *crisis* of security for those days.

11.3.1 Arguments in Mass Media

Example 1 Congested train schedules: the excessive competition between private and national railways in the Kansai District was the main cause of train accidents and the efficiency propaganda by the Koizumi cabinet was responsible for the negligence of security on the part of the railway companies.

Example 2 The deregulation of the public inspection system led to deficiencies in the structure and design of buildings. Security is the most important property of housing, which should never be sacrificed by profit motives stimulated by efficiency propaganda.

Example 3 Indication of food ingredients and duration were abused around 2006–2007 as exemplified by the well-known brands such as Nippon Milk Community, Fujiya-Peko, Meathope, and Akafuku. Short-run pursuit of efficiency apparently resulted in the shameless deeds that destroyed the public trust in food security.

11.4 Discussion

The foregoing quotations are the sample of comments reported in mass media such as newspapers and journals. The common feature of these comments is the presumption that the pursuit of efficiency (or least costs) damages the social values underlying security and peace of mind. They state that there are trade-offs between social value and efficiency. The trade-offs exist, however, between private value and efficiency, but *not* between social value and efficiency.

11.4.1 The Impossibility of Absolute Security

In 1999, ISO (the International Standard Organization) declared the impossibility of absolute security. It means that security must be measured in terms of the degree of "speed," or the degree of "preciseness," to be specified case by case relative to the basic standard. All interested parties are thus obligated to report honest information about the degree of security and the relative cost of removing the relevant insecurity.

11.4.2 Collective Housing and Security

Here, let us consider the deficient inspection system of anti-earthquake architecture design. Given the size of a collective housing (public good), the choice of the representative consumer between the degree of its security and the consumption of rice (the private good, or Marshallian "money") is the point at issue. In Fig. 11.2, we depict the trade-offs between security and rice along the value frontier *Tt* and social indifference curves *I*. The tangency point *E* of *Tt* and *I* shows the socially optimal degree of housing security. In practice, however, point *E* may not be realized because of the deficiency of the inspection system, or the deception of housing

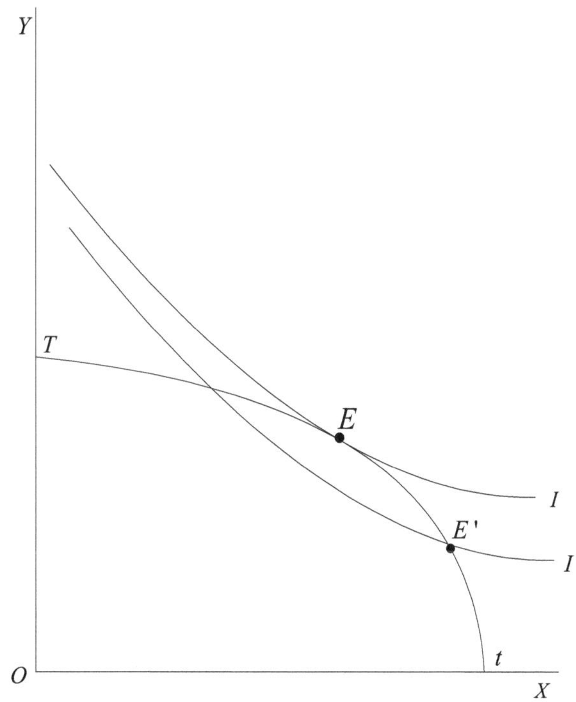

Fig. 11.2 Optimal security and fraud

companies. As a result, the socially suboptimal point E' may materialize. Note that this does not imply the existence of trade-offs between housing security and consumption; it only reveals that the selfish pursuit of profit motives by housing companies brings about social losses.

The emergence of suboptimal equilibria in the foregoing examples stems from asymmetrical information among private agents. It is found not only in the transactions of collective housing but also in those of second-hand cars and unsold food products in supermarkets. The "adverse selection" is the name of the game. These market failures are not the outcome of efficiency pursuit and market fundamentalism. In terms of economic theory, they are the phenomena that take place from such problems as monopoly, externalities, and wage–price rigidities.

Proposition 11.2: Market Failures as the Cause of Suboptimal Equilibria The possible countermeasures include antitrust policy, fiscal policy, direct control of transactions, tax-cum-subsidies, aggregate demand control, and creation of a transactions market, depending upon the case in question...

11.5 Government Failure and Suboptimal Equilibria

In face of market failures, the government is generally recommended by economists to regulate and/or promote the economic activities of private agents and to create national enterprises producing public goods. These government policies, however, often backfire, and worsen the trouble originally designed to remedy. First, it may misuse the policy instrument for lack of information about the social needs for the public goods it intends to provide, or environmental pollutions it wants to improve, for example. Second, even when the government has correct information, it may fail to carry out the correct countermeasures, impeded by inefficient institutional arrangements; for instance, the wasteful use of tax money by soft budget constraint, and the improper working style of government officials (notorious "amakudari," as it is called in Japan).

11.5.1 Soft Budget Constraint

The budget constraint of an agent is said to be soft when it is adjustable for some reason, allowing the agent to expand its expenditure beyond the initially planned target. The government is occasionally entitled to collect taxes so that it can adjust the amount of expenditure by adjusting the amount of revenue when the budget is supposed to be soft. Kornai (1986) closed up this concept as one of the most serious evils of the old socialist planned economy. To be concrete, suppose that the government plans to expend a certain amount of money and entrust a national enterprise to provide a power plant. In such a case, we often observe the following.

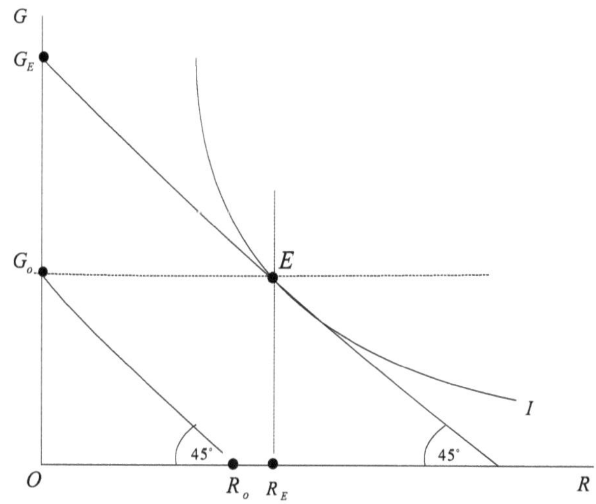

Fig. 11.3 Soft budget constraint

Proposition 11.3: Soft Budget Constraint *The cost of a public good expands a little more than expected, often leading to an enormous delay in initially promised delivery.*

Figure 11.3 illustrates the soft budget problem of this project as a simple game theoretical equilibrium between the government planning agency and the national enterprise. The equilibrium under soft budget constraint is shown at point E. The planning agency starts by announcing the budget (target) G_0 (= R_0), and the national enterprise renegotiates the contract to achieve its highest indifference curve I to settle down to the equilibrium budget (target) G_E (= R_E). The soft budget clearly misleads the allocation of scarce resources by misrepresenting the revelation of true social preference.[1] To overcome the soft budget problem, it would be necessary to deprive the national enterprise of its monopoly power and privatize it under strict watchdog commission.

11.5.2 "Amakudari" Practice

Government regulations are usually followed by private companies under the dictation and overseeing of the government's administration. In Japan, there is the well-known convention of "amakudari" (descent from heaven) practice, which allows the administration's officials to move to high-paying posts at the companies

[1] Given the budget (target) G_0 (= R_0), the socially optimal equilibrium must be located somewhere on the value frontier $G_O R_O$. The misallocation of resources arises from the swindle of the social indifference curve by that of the national enterprise.

after retirement. This practice has long been criticized as distorting the government regulations but somehow still remains active in various forms.

Before proceeding, we should distinguish two types of government regulations. Discriminatory regulation regulates the activities of economic agents by their characteristics and nondiscriminatory regulations regulates them uniformly irrespective of their characteristics. For instance, restrictions of newcomers to an industry are discriminatory because they typically regulate entrants and incumbents differently according to their initial status. On the other hand, corporation taxes and consumption taxes are nondiscriminatory if they are levied on all agents uniformly. Making use of a simple game-theoretical analysis, we can derive the following propositions regarding the outcome of this convention.

Proposition 11.4: Discriminatory Regulations *Under the convention of "amakudari," discriminatory regulations tend to be imposed too much beyond the socially optimal level.*

Consider the game between the administration to regulate and the organization of private companies to be regulated (the business organization for short). Their payoffs are supposed to depend on the level of regulation R, as well as the number of officials to be hired after retirement N. The administration's payoff function,

$$U = u(R, N), \tag{11.1}$$

is supposed to be increasing in N, nonincreasing for $R \leq R_B$, and decreasing for $R > R_B$. The greater the number of amakudari persons, the happier the administration is, but as for the level of regulation, there is the optimal level, R_B, for the administration, and the closer the level of regulation to R_B, the greater its satisfaction becomes. For simplicity, we may assume that R_B is also the socially optimal level of the regulation. The payoff function of the business organization,

$$V = v(R, N), \tag{11.2}$$

can be characterized differently depending on the nature of regulation. In case of discriminatory regulation, the stricter the regulation, the greater the satisfaction of the business organization would be. But in case of nondiscriminatory regulation, the business organization would support lower levels of regulation; therefore, $v_R < o$ in the former case, and $v_R < o$ in the latter case. As for the number of amakudari officials, all companies would like to accept them only up to a certain point $B_R > 0$. Thus, $V = v(R, N)$ may be assumed to be increasing in N for $N \leq N_B$ and decreasing in N for $N > N_B$.

What would be the outcome of the game between the administration and the business organization? Point C in Fig. 11.4 shows the Nash equilibrium of the game in case of discriminatory regulation. Curve II and curve JJ passing through E are the indifference curve of the administration and that of the business organization, respectively. At this point, the socially optimal level of regulation is realized by assumption, but it is *not* a Pareto optimum for the two players. If they cooperate,

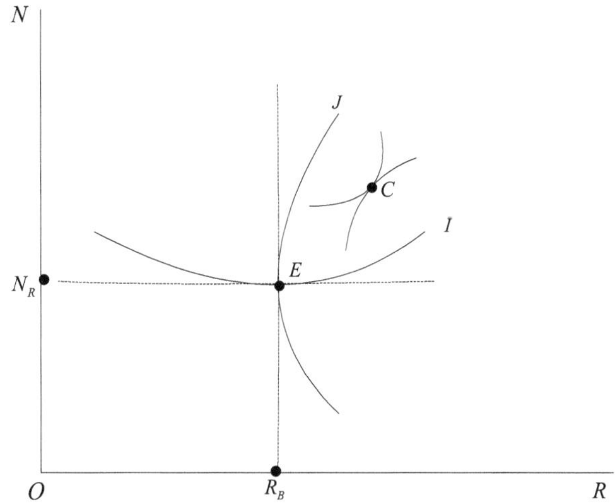

Fig. 11.4 Discriminatory regulation

they will become better off at point C, a Pareto optimum between the two. Note that the number of amakudari is greater and the level of regulation higher at C than at the socially optimal level E. In the present setting, however, the companies willing to enter the industry are not allowed to participate in this game. If they are allowed to participate, the level of discriminatory regulation may be alleviated. Consider the possibility that the association of foreign companies join the game as a third player.

In contrast, Fig. 11.2 compares the Nash equilibrium with the cooperative equilibrium between the administration and the business organization in case of nondiscriminatory regulations. At the cooperative equilibrium C between the two players, the level of the regulation turns out to be lower than at the socially optimal level to be achieved at the Nash equilibrium E. This point implies nondiscriminatory regulations generally leads to the outcome with lower regulations than the socially optimal level.

Proposition 11.5: Nondiscriminatory Regulations *Under the convention of "amakudari," nondiscriminatory regulations tend to be imposed too little, or below the socially optimal level.*

There are some instances in Japan that suggest the existence of cooperation between the government administration and the association of business companies leading to seemingly less strict regulation than the socially desirable standard in the industries such as agriculture, steel, petroleum, or medical supplies.

In view of this exercise, it is advisable to abolish the convention of amakudari totally in favor of better representation of social welfare in various industries. In addition to the administration and the business association, policy makers may also have an important role in the determination of the government regulations. In Japan, there are many dietmen working for regulated industries collaborating with the administration (the so-called zoku-giin). The present model seems to be especially relevant to such a situation.

11.6 Equity and Efficiency

The trade-off between equity and efficiency is often taken for granted, not only in mass media but also in textbooks of economics. Comments given in these seem to contain, however, confusions and misunderstandings.

11.6.1 Commentary in Textbooks

Example 1 New economy and inequalities (Stiglitz and Walsh, *Economics*, 4th edition): One of the factors in the recent development of inequalities in the US is the rise in the wage of computer-related workers. The rise in the efficiency of production resulting from the spread of computers has brought about the increase in inequalities.

Example 2 A trade-off between fairness and efficiency (Mankiw, *Economics I*, Chap. 12): Efficiency and fairness, the major two goals of the government tax system, are often incompatible.

Example 3 A trade-off between equity and efficiency (Krugman and Wells, *Microeconomics*, Chap. 13): There is normally a trade-off between equity and efficiency. The tax system can be made more efficient only by making it less fair, and vice versa.

11.7 Discussion

Notwithstanding the positions taken by Mankiw, and by Krugman and Wells, we believe that the real problem is not the trade-off between equity and efficiency, but the trade-off between equity and other values, namely, the consumption goods foregone to realize equity as its alternative cost. As for the commentary by Stiglitz and Walsh on the causes of recent increase in inequalities, it does not mean the necessity of efficiency loss to maintain equity; it only suggests the desirability of appropriate tax reforms to remedy the increased inequalities.

Suppose that the initial income of individual 1 is greater than that of individual 2 (Fig. 11.5). The government has an egalitarian social indifference curves and wants to redistribute income from individual 1 to individual 2. If it is able to accomplish this by way of lump-sum transfer without cost, it will achieve the socially optimal distribution B at the contact point of indifference curve Ss and the $-45°$ line.

It is, however, generally impossible to practice income redistribution without incurring some costs. Let us ignore here administrative costs for simplicity, but take account of incentive costs of income transfer. The government is supposed to tax

Fig. 11.5 Nondiscriminatory regulation

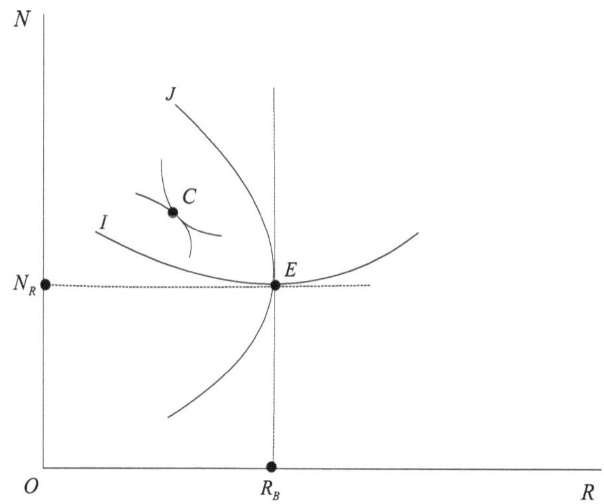

individual 1 and subsidize individual 2 by an equal amount. As the amount of tax on individual 1 increases and subsidy to individual 2 decreases equally, the work incentive of individuals will be adversely affected, thereby bringing down the value frontier of income redistribution from the −45° line under infeasible lump-sum transfer to *Tt* below. The socially optimal distribution will be accomplished at *C*, or the intersection of *Tt* and one of the government indifference curves.

Proposition 11.6: Lump-Sum Transfer and Income Redistribution *In the absence of lump-sum transfer, the government would be able to achieve equity by introducing an appropriate reform of the transfer system.*

The suggested reform of tax system taking account of work incentives generates the value frontier *Tt* and achieves the socially optimal distribution at point *C*. In the transition from the hypothetical lump-sum transfer to the present tax-cum-subsidy, the consumption of goods (rice) available as the society as a whole may seem to decrease more than under lump-sum transfer: there are no trade-offs between equity and efficiency. Compare points *A*, *B*, and *C* in Fig. 11.6. *A* is the outcome to be achieved under poll tax, *B* is the outcome under imaginary lump-sum tax, and *C* is the outcome under the suggested reform. Clearly, *A* is feasible but inferior to *C*, and *B* is not feasible.

11.7.1 Poll Tax: The End of the Thatcher Age

In March 1990, the poll tax introduced by Margaret Thatcher was widely unpopular. She resigned as Prime Minister of England and Leader of the Conservative Party in November 1990. The poll tax was how it all started, but why was it so unpopular?

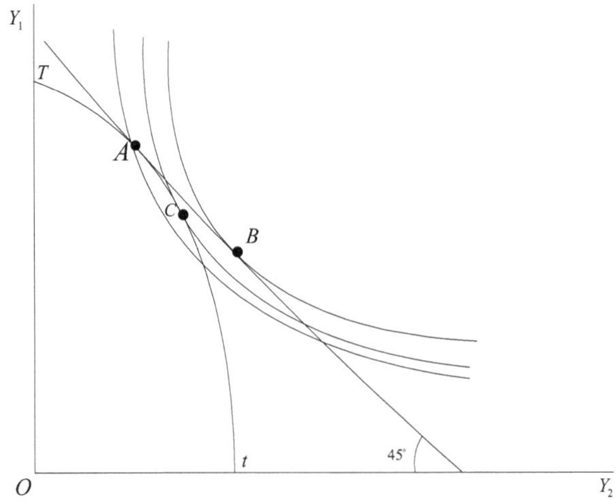

Fig. 11.6 Lump-sum transfer and poll tax

A partial answer is provided by Fig. 11.6, which compares the case in which poll tax is employed to secure the necessary government revenue (point A) with the case in which an additional measure of income transfer is introduced to rectify vertical unfairness caused by the poll tax (point C).[2]

11.8 Concluding Remarks

1. It is necessary to use scarce resources to provide goods and services embodying social values such as security and equity. Economists studies efficient utilization of resources for this purpose, as well as for the purpose of producing economic values, or ordinary private goods and services. Usually, we can provide social values with less than 100 % security and less than 100 % equity. There exist trade-offs between social and individual values. The role of economists is to investigate the production (value) frontier of social and individual values.
2. On the other hand, economists are not in the position to evaluate social and economic values. It is simply beyond their capacity. The evaluation of these values must be done either by the decision of a dictatorial leader or by voting based on democratic discussion. Those commentators who admit the existence of trade-offs between value and efficiency and denounce the pursuit of efficiency at the expense of value are virtually approving the wasteful use of resources. Economists should never be a party to such an attempt.

[2] The common view is that there are trade-offs between fairness (or equity) and efficiency. See Examples 2 and 3 above, or Mankiw (1998), Krugman and Wells (2006). We do not share this view.

3. This chapter is designed as a simple theory of economic policy for mixed economies in which households, business corporations, government organizations, and NPOs coexist. Relying on the concept of Marshall's externalities and Tinbergen's theory of economic policy, see Tinbergen (1952). It considers not only the inconsistencies of marginal rate of substitution in consumption and production (market failures) but also the shrinkage of the production frontier because of organizational inconsistencies (government failures), to strike out the countermeasures case by case. Under soft budget constraint, the self-seeking motivation of government enterprises leads to overuse of scarce resources in the production of public goods. Under the convention of "amakudari," the collaboration of the administration and the association of private companies leads to a stronger, or a weaker, level of government regulations than the socially optimal level. Both conventions work to increase the costs of government regulations, thereby shifting the value frontier inward. Deficiencies in taxation and social security systems for income redistribution would also lead to similar inefficiencies. To overcome the government failures, a number of countermeasures are suggested, including the abolition of inefficient organizations, the prohibition of the "amakudari" convention, and the reform of taxation and social security systems. In addition to government failures, market failures are also responsible for shrinkage of the value frontier. Private enterprises suffer from X-inefficiencies because of weak governance, and shortage of effective demand may arise from weak economic forecasts and expectations bringing about involuntary unemployment. As we discussed in Chap. 1, the government expenditure for public goods can be an effective measure to decrease unemployment and increase social welfare. Private-public partnership (PPP) may also help in this connection.

References

Arrow, K. J. (1951). *Social choice and individual values*. New Haven: Yale University Press.

Kornai, J. (1986). The soft budget constraint. *Kyklos, 39*(1), 3–30.

Krugman, P. H., & Wells, R. (2006). *Macroeconomics*. New York: Worth.

Mankiw, N. G. (1998). *Principles of economics*. Boston: South-Western Cengage Learning.

Marshall, A. (1890). *Principles of economics*. London: Macmillan.

Mas-Collel, A., Whinston, M. D., & Green, J. R. (1995). *Microeconomic theory*. Oxford: Oxford University Press.

Ohyama, M. (1972). Trade and welfare in general equilibrium. *Keio Economic Studies, 9*, 37–73.

Robbins, L. (1938). Interpersonal comparison of utility: A comment. *The Economic Journal, 48*, 692–712.

Samuelson, P. A. (1956). Social indifference curves. *The Quarterly Journal of Economics, 70*, 1–22.

Stiglitz JE (2005) *Economics*. Norton, New York

Tinbergen, J. (1952). *On the theory of economic policy*. Amsterdam: North-Holland.

Chapter 12
A Theoretical Framework of Mixed Systems

12.1 Introduction

The fundamental theorems of welfare economics prove under stringent conditions that the free market mechanism leads to the efficient allocation of economic resources. It is highly regarded as a theoretical underpinning of the "invisible hand" (Adam Smith), but generally inapplicable to the real economies in modern societies where externalities abound that cannot be addressed by the market mechanism. First, social needs for public goods are increasing in the face of rapid industrialization and urbanization. They call for construction and maintenance of stronger industrial infrastructure and further improvement of environmental and educational facilities. Second, governments are often required to employ taxes and subsidies to alleviate pollution, congestion, and depletion of natural resources stemming from Marshallian externalities interacted among a large number of citizens. The purpose of this chapter is to provide a comprehensive theoretical framework for mixed economies facing the problems of externalities and public goods.

In Sect. 12.2, we develop a model of mixed economies considering the distinction of private and public goods as well as the concept of various externalities. In Sect. 12.3, we define the general equilibrium of mixed economies and derive a common formula for the socially optimal tax-cum-subsidy policy on the assumption that the government is able to redistribute income among citizens through lump-sum tax and subsidies. In Sect. 12.4, we employ this formula to discuss some important problems of mixed economies such as the congestion of public goods, peak-load pricing, environmental pollution and depletion of natural resources, and elucidate their common structure.

© Springer Japan 2016

M. Ohyama, *Macroeconomics, Trade, and Social Welfare*, Advances in Japanese Business and Economics 14, DOI 10.1007/978-4-431-55807-1_12

12.2 The Basic Structure of Mixed Economies

12.2.1 Private Goods and Public Goods

Private goods are used by individual agents (households and firms) exclusively. In contrast, public goods are used by a large number of agents nonexclusively. Goods are generally distinguished and defined physically, timely and spatially. For instance, a 2015 model car available in Tokyo this month is a different good from a 2015 model car available in Osaka in the same month.

A service from a public good used by a large number of agents may also be enjoyed individually and exclusively and exchanged as a private good. For instance, airports, bypasses, parks, and harbors are open to many agents, and considered to be public goods, but their services are actually used more or less exclusively depending on their timing and location. In this instance, we must distinguish the availability of public goods and their actual usability. The actual use of these public goods tends to be congested, and fees are often charged for their services. In contrast, their availability does not cause congestion in themselves and thus they can be provided free of charge.

The people often enjoy the availability of many public goods, even that of the so-called pure public goods such as police, firehouses, and national defense. If they know that these public goods are available, they may feel safer and happier than in their absence even if they do not actually use their services. The need for the availability of these public goods in this sense is named optional demand (Weisbrod 1964), or probabilistic individual preference (Zeckhauser 1969). If we include the availability of public goods as services from them, the range of public goods becomes much wider than normally understood.

Profit-making facilities such as railroads, schools, hotels, housing complexes, and athletic stadiums may be regarded as public goods-generating services in this sense.

12.2.2 Notations

We assume that there are N private goods $(1,\ldots,N)$ and M public goods $(1,\ldots,M)$. They are used by H households $(1,\ldots,H)$ and produced by K firms (1,. . .,K). These households and firms are assumed to behave competitively as price-takers in the market. The government is assumed to redistribute incomes among households through lump-sum taxes and subsidies and control the demand and supply of goods and services through excise tax and subsidies. It is also assumed to purchase public goods in the market and provide them directly to the public, that is, households and firms. To describe the model, we use the following notations.

x_i^{h+}: quantity of private good i demanded by household h

x_i^{h-}: quantity of private good i supplied by household h
x_i^h: excess demand of private good by household h $(= x_i^h = x_i^{h+} + x_i^{h-})$
y_i^{k+}: quantity of private good i supplied by firm k
y_i^{k-}: quantity of private good i demanded by firm k
y_i^k: excess supply of private good i by firm k $(y_i^k = y_i^{k+} + y_i^{k-})$
$\widetilde{p}_i$: supply price of private good i
$\overline{p}_i$: demand price of private good i
p_i: market price of private good i
z_j^k: quantity of public good j supplied by the government
q_j: supply price of public good j
τ_i: specific consumption tax of private good i
θ_i: specific sales tax of private good i
σ_j:government price (subsidy) of public good j
t^h: transfer payment received by household h

Following convention, we assume that x_i^{h+}, y_i^{k+}, and z_j^k are nonnegative, and x_i^{h-} and y_i^{k-} are nonpositive. We denote the aggregate quantity by deleting the upper script from the notation of individual quantities. For instance,

$$x_i^+ = \sum_h x_i^{h+},\ x_i = \sum_h x_i^h,\ z_j = \sum_k z_j^k.$$

On the other hand, we denote the vector of each variable by gothic letter deleting the lower script from the notation of individual quantities. For instance,

$$\mathbf{x^{h+}} = \left(x_1^{h+}, \ldots, x_N^{h+}\right),\ \mathbf{x} = (x_1, \ldots, x_N),\ \mathbf{z} = (z_1, \ldots, z_M),$$
$$\mathbf{p} = (p_1, \ldots, p_N),\ \mathbf{q} = (q_1, \ldots, q_M),\ \boldsymbol{\tau} = (\tau_1, \ldots, \tau_N),$$

12.2.3 Households and Externalities

The utility u^h of household h is supposed to depend not only on its consumption $\mathbf{x^h}$ of private goods and the supply $\mathbf{z}$ of public goods but also on the aggregate consumption of private goods $\mathbf{x}^+ - \mathbf{y}^-$ and on the aggregate supply $\mathbf{y}^+ - \mathbf{x}^-$ of consumption goods. Thus, we may write the utility function of household h as

$$u^h = u^h\left(x^h, \mathbf{a}, \mathbf{b}, \mathbf{z}\right) \tag{12.1}$$

Where

$$\mathbf{a} = \mathbf{x}^+ - \mathbf{y}^-, \tag{12.2}$$

and

$$\mathbf{b} = \mathbf{y}^+ - \mathbf{x}^-. \tag{12.3}$$

Element i of vector $\mathbf{a}, \mathbf{b}$ are defined by $a_i = x_i{}^+ - y_i{}^-, b_i = y_i{}^+ - x_i{}^-$, respectively; this means that the utility of each household may be affected by all possible externalities from the consumption of all households and the production of all firms.

The aggregate demand and supply of private goods are supposed to affect the utility of individual households directly through their impacts on the environments in a broad sense. For example, an increase in the aggregate demand for gasoline may aggravate air pollution and add to global warming, thereby lowering the utility of every household. Similarly, an increase in the supply of public goods may affect the utility of individual household either positively or negatively. As already pointed out, the use of many public goods incurs congestion and may decrease the utility of the average household for this particular reason. A typical example is the congestion of expressways or airports by the additional entry of automobiles and airplanes.

Suppose that utility function $u^h(\mathbf{x^h}, \mathbf{a}, \mathbf{b}, \mathbf{z})$ is strictly quasi-concave in $\mathbf{x^h}$. The marginal utility of a private good is nonnegative, that is,

$$\frac{\partial u^h}{\partial x_i{}^h} \geq 0.$$

The marginal utility of the aggregate demand and aggregate supply is nonnegative if they exert beneficial external impacts and nonpositive if they exert harmful external impacts.

Household h determines its consumption so as to maximize utility function u^h $(x^h, \mathbf{a}, \mathbf{b}, \mathbf{z})$, subject to budget constraint

$$\overline{p}x^{h+} + \widetilde{p}x^{h+} = t^h \tag{12.4}$$

taking market prices of private goods $\mathbf{p}$ and the aggregate variables $\mathbf{a}, \mathbf{b}, \mathbf{z}$ as given. The first-order condition for utility maximization is

$$\frac{\partial u^h}{\partial x_1{}^h} \Big/ \frac{\partial u^h}{x_i{}^h} = \frac{\widetilde{p}_i}{\overline{p}_1}$$

$$\text{for } x_i{}^h > 0 \qquad (i = 2, \ldots, N) \tag{12.5}$$

and

$$\frac{\partial u^h}{\partial x_i{}^h} \Big/ \frac{\partial u^h}{x_1{}^h} = \frac{\widetilde{p}_1}{\overline{p}_i}$$

$$\text{for } x_1{}^h > 0 \qquad (i = 2, \ldots, N). \tag{12.6}$$

Without loss of generality, we set $x_i{}^{h+} = x_i{}^h, x_i{}^{h-} = 0$ for $x_i{}^h \geq 0$ and $x_i{}^{h-} = x_i{}^h$, $x_i{}^{h+} = 0$.

12.2.4 Firms and Externalities

Let us turn to the production side of mixed economies. Their input–output structure also depends on the aggregate demand and supply of private goods $\mathbf{a}, \mathbf{b}$ as well as the supply of public good $\mathbf{z}$. Thus, the production structure of firm k may be written as

$$g^k\left(\mathbf{y^k}, \mathbf{z^k}, \mathbf{a}, \mathbf{b}, \mathbf{z}\right) = 0. \tag{12.7}$$

This summation amounts to what is called the transformation function. It shows implicitly how the firm's input–output is affected by all kinds of externalities from the aggregate behavior of private goods and the supply of public goods.

The aggregate demand and supply of some private goods gives rise to air, soil, and water pollution, depletion of natural resources, noise, vibration, and bad smells, all of which deteriorate the productivity of industries such as agriculture, mining, fishery, food, or machinery. On the other hand, the supply of public goods or the so-called social overhead capital such as roads, bays, railways, dams, bridges, and shore protection works is indispensable to many industries in improving their productivity. The services of social overhead capitals are more or less subject to exclusion principle and often traded as private goods in the market. Their aggregate demand and supply may adversely affect the productivity of many firms through congestion and pollution. The transformation function $g^k(\mathbf{y^k}, \mathbf{z^k}, \mathbf{a}, \mathbf{b}, \mathbf{z})$ is strictly quasi-concave in $(\mathbf{y^k}, \mathbf{z^k})$, and the partial derivatives with respect to $(\mathbf{y^k}, \mathbf{z^k})$ are nonnegative:

$$\frac{\partial g^k}{\partial y_i{}^k} \geq 0 \ (i = 1, \ldots, M),$$

$$\frac{\partial g^k}{\partial z_j{}^k} \geq 0 \ (j = 1, \ldots, M).$$

Given the constraint of transformation function (12.7), firm k determines its production so as to maximize its profit function:

$$\pi^k = \widetilde{p}y^{k+} + \overline{p}y^{k-} + qz^k.$$

For simplicity, let us suppose that firm k has a positive demand for private good ${y_1}^k < 0$. We then have the first-order condition for profit maximization:

$$\frac{\partial g^k}{\partial {g^k}_i} \bigg/ \frac{\partial g^k}{\partial {g^k}_1} = \frac{\widetilde{p}_i}{\overline{p}_k}$$
$$(i = 1, \ldots, N) \tag{12.8}$$

For ${y_i}^k > 0$, and

$$\frac{\partial g^k}{\partial {g^k}_i} \bigg/ \frac{\partial g^k}{\partial {g^k}_1} = \frac{\overline{p}_i}{\widetilde{p}_k}$$
$$(i = 1, \ldots, N). \tag{12.9}$$

For ${y_i}^k < 0$.

Without loss of generality, we set $y^{k+} = {y_i}^k, {y_i}^{k-} = 0$ for ${y_i}^k \geq 0$ and ${y_i}^{k-} = {y^k}_i$, ${y_i}^{k+} = 0$ for ${y_i}^k < 0$.

12.3 General Equilibrium and Social Optimum

12.3.1 The General Equilibrium of Mixed Economies

The general equilibrium of an economy is the state of affairs that satisfies three conditions: (1) the utility maximization of all households; (2) the profit maximization of all firms; and (3) the equilibrium of demand and supply of all goods. We have already explained the first two conditions. The third condition means

$$a_i = b_i \ \ (i = 1, \ldots, N). \tag{12.10}$$

The supply price and market price of each good are related as

$$\overline{p}_i = p_i + \tau_i \ \ (i = 1, \ldots, N), \tag{12.11}$$
$$\widetilde{p}_i = p_i - \theta_i \ \ (i = 1, \ldots, N). \tag{12.12}$$
$$q_j = \sigma_j \ \ (i = 1, \ldots, N) \tag{12.13}$$

We take good 1 as the numeraire and set its price equal to 1. Summing the budget constraint (12.4) over all households, $(h = 1, \ldots, H)$, we have

$$\overline{p}\mathbf{x}^{+} + \widetilde{p}\mathbf{x}^{-} = \sum_{h}^{H} t^{h}, \tag{12.14}$$

where

$$\sum_{h}^{H} t^{h} = \tilde{\mathbf{p}}\mathbf{y}^{+} + \overline{\mathbf{p}}\mathbf{y}^{-} + \boldsymbol{\tau} a + \boldsymbol{\theta}\mathbf{b}. \tag{12.15}$$

The sum of the transfer the households receive from the government, $\sum_{h}^{H} t^{h}$, equals the sum of the firms' profits of $\widetilde{\mathbf{p}}\mathbf{y}^{+} + \overline{\mathbf{p}}\mathbf{y}^{-} + \mathbf{pz}$, and the government's net receipt of the tax-subsidy system, $\boldsymbol{\tau}\mathbf{a} + \boldsymbol{\theta}\mathbf{b} - \boldsymbol{\sigma}\mathbf{z}$. From Eqs. (12.2), (12.3), and (12.11)–(12.15), we obtain

$$\mathbf{pa} = \mathbf{pb}. \tag{12.16}$$

This is nothing but the Walras' law which says that the values of excess market demand of private goods must sum to zero. Thus, one of the N equations in Eq. (12.10) is not independent of the rest of equations. Given all taxes and subsidies, $N - 1$ independent equations in Eq. (12.10) determine $N - 1$ equilibrium values of market prices, $p_2, \ldots, p_N$

12.3.2 Optimal Income Distribution

We have so far discussed the basic role of the government, but what is the standard of the government policy? Let us introduce at this point the Bergson–Samuelson individualistic social welfare function as such a standard. It is written,

$$w = u\left[u^{1}\left(\mathbf{x}^{1}, \mathbf{a}, \mathbf{b}, \mathbf{z}\right), \ldots, u^{H}\left(x^{H}\left(\mathbf{x}^{\mathbf{H}}, \mathbf{a}, \mathbf{b}, \mathbf{z}\right)\right]. \tag{12.17}$$

The government is assumed to determine policy variables, τ_i, θ_i, σ_j, so as to maximize social welfare function (12.17) achieved in general equilibrium through market mechanism. In what follows, we shall consider the properties of tax and subsidy policy scheme in the socially optimal general equilibrium.

For the time being, let us consider the problem of adjusting the net transfer receipt of households, t^{h}, to optimize income distribution among households, given p_i, τ_i, θ_i, and σ_j. The households are here assumed to maximize their utility subject to budget constraint, and firms to maximize their profit subject to the transformation frontier. The household budget constraint (Eq. (12.4)) implies

$$\sum_i^N \overline{p}_i \frac{\partial x_i^{h+}}{\partial t^h} + \sum_i^N \widetilde{p}_i \frac{\partial x_i^{h-}}{\partial t^h} = 1 \quad (h = 1, \ldots, H).$$

Taking notice of the conditions of utility maximization, Eqs. (12.5) and (12.6), we can write the conditions of optimal income distribution as

$$\begin{aligned} \frac{1}{\overline{p}_1{}^h} \frac{\partial w}{\partial u^h} \frac{\partial u^h}{\partial x_1{}^h} &= \lambda + \sum_i^N \left(\alpha_i - {}^i\lambda\tau_i\right) \frac{\partial a_i}{\partial t^h} \\ &+ \sum_i^N (\beta_i - \lambda\theta_i) \frac{\partial b_i}{\partial t^h} - \sum_j^M \gamma_j \frac{\partial z_j}{\partial t^h} - \lambda \left(\sum_i^N \widetilde{p}_i \frac{\partial y_i{}^+}{\partial t^h} + \sum_i^N \overline{p}_i \frac{\partial y_i{}^-}{\partial t^h} \right) \\ &(i = 1, \ldots, H) \end{aligned} \tag{12.18}$$

Here, λ is the Lagrangian multiplier and α_i, β_i, and γ_j signify the externalities affecting households. They are defined, respectively, as

$$\alpha_i = -\sum_h^H \frac{\partial w}{\partial u^h} \frac{\partial u^h}{\partial a_i} \quad (i = 1, \ldots, N), \tag{12.19}$$

$$\beta_i = -\sum_h^H \frac{\partial w}{\partial u^h} \frac{\partial u^h}{\partial b_i} \quad (i = 1, \ldots, N), \tag{12.20}$$

$$\gamma_j = \sum_h^H \frac{\partial w}{\partial u^h} \frac{\partial u^h}{\partial z_j} {}^j \quad (j = 1, \ldots, M). \tag{12.21}$$

Taking account of the firms' profit maximization, we can further rewrite Eq. (12.18). Differentiating the transformation function (Eq. (12.7)) and summing the results over all firms using the conditions Eqs. (12.9, 12.10 and 12.11), we obtain

$$\sum_i^N \overline{p}_i dy_i{}^+ + \sum_i^N \overline{p}_i dy_i{}^- = -\sum_i^N \alpha_i' da_i - \sum_i^N \beta_i' db_i - \sum_j^M \left(\sigma^j - \gamma_j'\right) dz_j \tag{12.22}$$

The newly introduced variables, α_i', β_i', and σ_j' represent the externalities affecting firms. They are defined as

$$\alpha_i' = \sum_k^K \overline{p}_{ki} \frac{\partial g^k}{\partial a_i} \bigg/ \frac{\partial g^k}{\partial y_{ki}} \quad (i = 1, \ldots, N), \tag{12.23}$$

$$\beta_i^{'} = \sum_k^K \widetilde{p}_{ki} \frac{\partial g^k}{\partial b_i} \Bigg/ \frac{\partial g^k}{\partial y_{ki}{}^k} \quad (i = 1, \ldots, N), \tag{12.24}$$

$$\gamma_j^{'} = -\sum_k^K \overline{p}_{k1} \frac{\partial g^k}{\partial z_j} \Bigg/ \frac{\partial g^k}{\partial y_{k1}{}^k} \quad (j = 1, \ldots, M). \tag{12.25}$$

Using these, we can rearrange Eq. (12.18) as

$$\begin{aligned} \frac{1}{\overline{p}_1{}^h} \frac{\partial w}{\partial u^h} \frac{\partial u^h}{\partial x_1{}^h} &= \lambda + \sum_i^N \left(\alpha_i +^i \lambda \alpha_i^{'} - \lambda \tau_i \right) \frac{\partial a_i}{\partial t^h} \\ &+ \sum_i^N \left(\beta_i + \lambda \beta_i^{'} - \lambda \theta_i \right) \frac{\partial b_i}{\partial t^h} - \sum_j^M \left(\lambda \sigma_j - \gamma_j - \lambda \gamma^{'} \right) \frac{\partial z_j}{\partial t^h} \quad (h = 1, \ldots, H) \end{aligned} \tag{12.26}$$

Without loss of generality, set $\lambda = 1$ and write

$$\tau_i = \alpha_i + \alpha_i^{'}, \ (i = 1, \ldots, N), \tag{12.27}$$

$$\theta_i = \beta_i + \beta_i^{'}, \ (i = 1, \ldots, N), \tag{12.28}$$

$$\sigma_j = \gamma_j + \gamma_j^{'}. \ (i = 1, \ldots, M). \tag{12.29}$$

We can then simplify (12.18) to

$$\frac{1}{\widetilde{p}_{hi}} \frac{\partial w}{\partial u^h} \frac{\partial u^h}{\partial x_{hi}{}^h} = 1 \ (h = 1, \ldots, H). \tag{12.30}$$

This means that the social marginal utility of good $h1$ produced by all firms is equal to its supply price, which is the well-known condition for the optimal income distribution in the absence of externalities.

12.3.3 Optimal Tax-Subsidy Policy

On the premise that the socially optimal income distribution is fulfilled, let us now proceed to the problem of achieving the maximization of the social welfare through the adjustment of taxes and subsidies, τ_i, θ_i, and σ_j. Totally differentiating the social welfare function shown in Eq. (12.17), we obtain

$$dW = \sum_h^H \frac{1}{\widetilde{p}_{h1}} \frac{\partial w}{\partial u^h} \frac{\partial u^h}{\partial x_{hi}{}^h} \left(\sum_i^N \overline{p}_i dx_i{}^{h+} + \sum_i^H \widetilde{p}_i dx_i{}^{h-} \right) - \sum_i^N \alpha_i da_i \\ - \sum_i^N \beta_i db_i + \sum \gamma_j dz_j \tag{12.31}$$

Where all the demand and supply are determined to maintain the general equilibrium. It can be shown that the conditions (12.27, 12.28 and 12.29) are necessary for the maximization of the social welfare. In fact, (12.27, 12.28 and 12.29) imply (12.30), so that

$$\sum_h^H \frac{1}{\widetilde{p}_{h1}} \frac{\partial w}{\partial u^h} \frac{\partial u^h}{\partial x_{hi}{}^h} \left(\sum_i^N \overline{p}_i dx_i{}^{h+} + \sum_i^H \widetilde{p}_i dx_i{}^{h-} \right) \\ = \sum_i^N \overline{p}_i dx_i{}^{h+} + \sum_i^N \widetilde{p}_i dx_i{}^{h-}. \tag{12.32}$$

From Eqs. (12.14) and (12.16), on the other hand, we have

$$\sum_i^N p_i \left(dx_i{}^+ - dy_i{}^- \right) = \sum_i^N p_i \left(dy_i{}^+ - dx_i{}^- \right).$$

In view of (12.11, 12.12 and 12.13) and (12.22),

$$\sum_i^N p_i dx_i{}^+ + \sum_i^N p_i dx_i{}^- = \sum_i^N \left(\tau_i - \alpha_i^{'} \right) da_i \\ + \sum_i^N \left(\theta_i - \beta_i^{'} \right) db_i - \sum_j^M \left(\sigma_j - \gamma_j^{'} \right) dz_j. \tag{12.33}$$

Substituting Eqs. (12.32) and (12.33) into (12.31), we can derive

$$dw = \sum_i^N \left(\tau_i - \alpha_i - {}^i\alpha_i^{'} \right) da_i + \sum_i^N \left(\theta_i - \beta - \beta^{'} \right) db_i - \sum_j^M \left(\sigma_j - \gamma_j \right. \\ \left. - \gamma_j^{'} \right) dz_j. \tag{12.34}$$

Given Eqs. (12.27, 12.28 and 12.29), the infinitesimal changes of equilibrium variables consequent upon the adjustment of policy variables, τ_i, and σ_i satisfy $dw = 0$, showing that the social welfare function attains the local maximum. Conversely, the necessary conditions for the local maximization of the social welfare function are the realization of (12.27, 12.28 and 12.29) for all infinitesimal changes of policy variables. We have established the following.

Proposition 12.1: The General Formula for Optimal Tax-Subsidy Policy *Under the present setup, the socially optimal consumption tax* τ_i, *sales tax* θ_i, *and the government purchase price of the public good* σ_i *must satisfy the formulae of* Eq. (12.27), Eq. (12.28), *and* Eq. (12.29), *respectively.*

If an increase of the aggregate demand (supply) causes the aggravation of pollution or congestion, α_i, α_i', (β_i, and β_i') must assume positive values respectively, as is clear from the definitions of Eqs. (12.19), (12.21), (12.23), and (12.24). In such cases, the optimal consumption tax τ_i (sales tax θ_i) became positive, and the suppression of the aggregate demand (aggregate supply) is justified. On the other hand, if an increase in the aggregate supply of public good brings about net social benefit, $\gamma_j + \gamma_j'$ must be positive, as seen from Eqs. (12.21) and (12.23). The optimal subsidy σ_j becomes positive, and the government provision of public good is rationalized.

A variety of external economies have been discussed in partial or general equilibrium models. We can interpret and analyze them in the present theoretical framework. The foregoing proposition covers almost all market failures related to externalities formulating the structure of socially optimal tax-subsidy policy uniformly in a comprehensive fashion. It may seem, however, too general to be applied to concrete problems. Let us specify the present setup more concretely and explain its relevance to various cases of externalities in the sequel.

12.4 Applications to Specific Problems

12.4.1 *Pure Public Goods*

As is well known, Samuelson (1954, 1955) discussed the conditions for the optimal provision of the pure public good that does not incur congestion and is free from externalities of any kind. Needless to say, this is a special case of the present model, with $\alpha_i = \alpha_i' = \beta_i = \beta_i' = \gamma_j = 0$.Combined with Eq. (12.21) and Eq. (12.29), it implies

$$\sigma_j = \sum_h^H \frac{\partial w}{\partial u^h}\frac{\partial u^h}{\partial z_j} \quad (j = 1, \ldots, M) \tag{12.35}$$

From Eqs. (12.27, 12.28, 12.29 and12.30), Eq. (12.35) may also be written

$$\sigma_j = \sum_h^H \frac{\partial u^h}{\partial z_j} \Big/ \frac{\partial u^h}{\partial x_1{}^h} \quad (j = 1, \ldots, M) \tag{12.36}$$

Proposition 12.2: Lindahl Equilibrium *Individual households share the cost of the public good according to their demand price (see Lindahl 1919).*

If public good v exerts externalities to producers, Eq. (12.36) must be modified to

$$\sigma_j = \sum_h^H \frac{\partial u^h}{\partial z_j} \Big/ \frac{\partial u^h}{\partial x_1{}^h} - \sum_k^K \frac{\partial g^k}{\partial z_v} \Big/ \frac{\partial g^k}{\partial y_1{}^k}. \tag{12.36'}$$

When public good v exerts externalities that increase (or decreases) firms' productivity, the government purchase price of the public good must accordingly be increased (or decreased).

12.4.2 Congestible Public Good

The present setup is particularly suitable for the analysis of public goods, the service of which incur congestion such as parks, expressways, and harbor facilities. The problem of congestion was discussed by Pigou (1920) and Knight (1924) in classic papers, and more recent contributions Uzawa (1974), Oakland (1972), and Sandmo (1973) attracted attention as attempts to extend the Samuelsonian concepts of pure public goods.

The services of congestible public goods are often traded as are ordinary private goods in the market. In such cases, it is socially desirable to impose congestion taxes on the buyers those services to alleviate accompanying congestion. Consider a congestible public good, a park for example. Let an admission ticket for the park be a public good v, which is also tradable as a private good v. Ignoring the possibility that the congestion of the park may affect the production of firms, the optimal congestion tax on the entry to the park may be written as

$$\tau_v = -\sum_h^H \frac{\partial w}{\partial u^h} \frac{\partial u^h}{\partial a_v}. \tag{12.37}$$

This point is elucidated by many researchers, and especially stressed by Uzawa (1974)), but there seem to be still scant literature that considers the relationship between congestion tax and production subsidy. Let us specify the household utility function (12.1) as

$$u^h = u^h\left(\mathbf{x^h}, \pi_v(a_v, z_v), \ldots\right). \quad (h = 1, \ldots, H) \tag{12.1'}$$

Here, π_v is a measure of congestion (congestion function, so to speak) of public good v. For simplicity, the household utility is assumed to be affected by the supply of the public good z_v and its aggregate demand a_v only through congestion function π_v. The congestion tax on the use of public good v is then written as

$$\tau_v = -\sum_h^H \frac{\partial w}{\partial u^h}\frac{\partial u^h}{\partial \pi_v}\frac{\partial \pi_v}{\partial a_v}. \qquad (12.37')$$

From Eq. (12.29) and (12.29), the government purchase price (subsidy) of public good v becomes

$$\sigma_v = \sum_h^H \frac{\partial w}{\partial u^h}\frac{\partial u^h}{\partial \pi_v}\frac{\partial \pi_v}{\partial z_v}. \qquad (12.38)$$

As is clear from Eq. (12.37′) and Eq. (12.38), the relationship between τ_v and σ_v is determined only by the structure of congestion function π_v.

$$\frac{\tau_v}{\sigma_v} = -\frac{\partial \pi_v}{\partial a_v} \Big/ \frac{\partial \pi_v}{\partial z_v}. \qquad (12.40)$$

Proposition 12.3: Optimal Congestion Tax *The optimal congestion tax is related to the government purchase price (subsidy) of the public good by* Eq. (12.40).

Let us further simplify matters by assuming that the degree of congestion is a linear function of the degree of usage, or

$$\pi_v = \gamma(a_v/z_v) + s \ \ (\gamma, s > 0). \qquad (12.41)$$

For the public good such as a park, this specification seems to beacceptable. Combined with Eq. (12.40), this yields

$$\frac{\tau_v a_v}{\sigma_v z_v} = -\frac{\eta_a}{\eta_z}. \qquad (12.42)$$

where η_a and η_z stand for the elasticity of the congestion function π_v with respect to a_v and z_v, respectively.

Corollary: Mohring Rule: Financing Congestible Public Good *In this case, the desirable subsidy for public good is less than the revenue from the congestion tax if* $\eta_a \geq -\eta_z > 0$.

See Strotz (1965), Mohring-Boyed (1971), and Oakland (1972) for similar analyses in the context of simpler setups than the present one.

Note that the foregoing result depends on the specification of the household utility function (12.1′) and needs to be modified if households enjoy only the availability of public good v (but not its actual use), or if they trade diverse services stemming from it as private goods. One should also consider the possibility that the congestion incurred by the use of public good v may affect the productivity of firms.

12.4.3 Peak Load Pricing

There are some public goods that continue to exist for many periods of time but become congested only for some of them. Expressways, parks, power plants, telephone offices, and gas stations are typical examples of such public goods. As Steiner (1957) and Williamson (1966) argued, it is necessary to introduce peak load pricing for the services of such facilities.

In the present model, all goods are distinguished not only physically and spatially but also timely. Suppose that public good v (a power plant, say) can be used from period 1 through period T. Let z_v signify its size, and a_{vt} the aggregate demand for its service in period t, and suppose that the household utility function has the same specific structure considered in the preceding section, or it is affected only through the congestion function

$$\pi_v(a_v, z_v) = [\pi_v(a_{v1}, z_v), \ldots, \pi_v(a_{vT}, z_v)].$$

Ignoring the externalities on production, the optimal congestion tax in period t follows from Eqs. (12.21) and (12.29) as

$$\tau_{vt} = -\sum_h^H \frac{\partial w}{\partial u^h} \frac{\partial u^h}{\partial \pi_v} \frac{\partial \pi_v}{\partial a_{vt}}. \tag{12.43}$$

The peak load of public good v is defined as $\bar{\pi}_{vt}{}^h = \min_h \bar{\pi}_{vt}{}^h$ $(h = 1, \ldots, H)$where $\pi_v \leq \bar{\pi}_v{}^h$ implies $\tau_{vt} = 0$ and $\pi_v > \bar{\pi}_v{}^h$ implies $\tau_{vt} > 0$. Alternatively put, this follows.

Proposition 12.4: Peak Load Pricing *The congestion tax must be imposed only in the periods in which congestion exceeds its peak load.*

On the other hand, the government purchase price (subsidy) of public good v is given by

$$\sigma_v = \sum_h^H \frac{\partial w}{\partial u^h} \sum_t^T \frac{\partial u^h}{\partial \pi_v} \frac{\partial \pi_v}{\partial z_v}. \tag{12.44}$$

In light of Eqs. (12.42) and (12.43), we obtain

$$\sum_{t}^{T} \tau_v a_{vt} - \sigma_v z_v = -\sum_{h}^{H} \frac{\partial w}{\partial u^h} \sum_{t}^{H} \frac{\partial u^h}{\partial \pi_v} \pi_v (\eta_a + \eta_z). \tag{12.45}$$

We may conclude as in the preceding section.

Proposition 12.5: Financing Peak Load Pricing *The revenue from the congestion tax is sufficient to finance the subsidy for public good v if* $\eta_a \geq -\eta_z > 0$.

The present exercise extends the partial equilibrium analysis of peak load pricing by Steiner, Williamson, etc.

12.4.4 Pollution

Mohring-Boyed (1971) argued that pollution has a characteristic very similar to congestion. Formally, it may be regarded as a category of congestion. The concept of congestion is usually defined in relation to *man-made* public goods (road, railways, parks, etc.), as the phenomenon that an increase in the aggregate demand for them deteriorates their benefit to individual users. In comparison, pollution is ordinarily defined in relationship to *natural* public goods (air, water, soil, etc.) as the phenomena that are contaminated by an increase in the aggregate demand.

Incidentally, natural public goods are generally *not* recyclable, in contrast to man-made public goods. Their endowments are exogenously fixed, but it is often possible to alleviate the harm of pollution by increasing the use of man-made public goods. Suppose that the aggregate supply of private good μ (a high-polymer compound, say) contaminates water in a lake and proves to be harmful to the households in the vicinity. Suppose also that the construction of public good μ (a water purification plant) serves to reduce the contamination. For simplicity, suppose also that the aggregate supply of private good does not affect households whatsoever. Using Eqs. (12.22), (12.26), and (12.30), we obtain the formula of optimal subsidy for public good μ:

$$\theta_\mu = -\sum_{k}^{K} \bar{p}^k \frac{\partial g^k}{\partial b_\mu} \Big/ \frac{\partial g^k}{\partial y_{k1}{}^k}. \tag{12.49}$$

Proposition 12.6: Pollution Tax *If the relevant externalities work to improve (deteriorate) the productivity of firms,* $\partial g^k/\partial b_\mu < 0 (> 0)$*, and therefore,* $\theta_\mu < 0 (> 0)$.

This finding agrees with Marshall's recommendation that the government should provide a uniform subsidy (tax) for the aggregate supply of the private good that generate external economies (diseconomies) to firms inside the industry.

12.4.5 Decreasing Cost

Decreasing cost (or increasing returns) in the production of a firm arises from its fixed input v (private good) such as fixed material and fixed equipment. Therefore, they can be dissolved and its profit maximization can be made compatible with its competitive behavior if they are appropriately internalized, that is, if the government regards its fixed inputs as a sort of public good and shares its cost. Suppose that firm k is intrinsically subject to decreasing returns to scale in its production, but because of the government subsidy for its input being internalized as public good v is enabled to operate competitively. The subsidy is computed from Eqs. (12.9), (12.27), and (12.31), for $y_i{}^k > 0$,

$$\sigma_v = -\overline{p}_{k1}\frac{\partial g^k}{\partial z_v} / \frac{\partial g^k}{\partial y_{k1}{}^k} = -\overline{p}_i \frac{\partial g^k}{\partial z_v}\frac{\partial g^k}{\partial y_i{}^k}. \quad (12.50)$$

Proposition 12.7: Internalizing Firms Fixed Input *The government should provide subsidy equal to imputed price of this input as shown in* Eq. (12.50).

12.4.6 Individual Externalities

We have so far presumed that all goods are defined on the basis of their physical, spatial, and timely distinction. At this point, let as proceed a step forward by considering distinction of users. For instance, gasoline for cars of the same physical quality, to be used in the same period and same place, is a same good by our previous definition, but it can be further distinguished by asking who uses it. In other words, gasoline demanded by different individuals may be regarded as different goods.

Proposition 12.8: Internalizing Individual Externalities *Individual households must be levied different purchase (consumption) taxes according to condition* (12.29).

12.4.7 Representative Agents

Last, we must take up an important special case of representative agents considered in many theoretical studies on economic policy. See Samuelson (1956) and Mas-Collel et al. (1995) for instance. Let

$u^h = u$, $x_i{}^h = x_i$ for all h, $g^k = g$, $y_i{}^k = y_i$ for all k, and $t^h = 0$ for all h. Here, we only take up the case of pure public goods discussed in Sect. 4.1. By assumption, Eqs. (12.35) and (12.36) reduce to

$$\sigma_j = \sum_h^H \frac{\partial u^h}{\partial z_j} \Bigg/ _{\frac{\partial u}{\partial x_1{}^h}} = \frac{\overline{p}_j}{\widetilde{p}^h{}_1}. \quad (j = 1, \ldots, M) \tag{12.37}$$

Proposition 12.9: Representative Agents Pay the Same Individual Demand Price *The representative agents behave competitively in the market where the government levies them the same appropriate tax to let them face the same individual demand price. The aggregate payment for the public good is M× the individual payment. The government is in the position to dictate the number and quality of pubic goods and the representative agents take them as given.*

References

Knight, F. H. (1924). Some fallacies in the interpretation of social cost. *The Quarterly Journal of Economics, 38*, 582–606.

Lindahl, E. (1967). Just taxation: a positive solution. In R. A. Musgrave & A. T. Peacock (Eds.), *Classics in the theory of public finance* (pp. 168–187). London: Macmillan.

Marshall, A. (1890) *Principles of economics* (8th ed., 1920). London: Macmillan.

Mas-Collel, A., Whinston, M. D., & Green, J. R. (1995). *Microeconomic theory*. Oxford: Oxford University Press.

Mohring, H., & Boyed, J. H. (1971). Analyzing "externalities," "direct interaction" vs. "asset utilization" frameworks. *Economica, 38*, 347–361.

Mohring, H., & Harwitz, M. (1962). *Highway benefits: An analytical framework*. Evanston: North Western University Press.

Oakland, W. H. (1969). Joint goods. *Economica, 36*, 253–268.

Oakland, W. H. (1972). Congestion, public goods and welfare. *Journal of Public Economics, 1*, 339–357.

Pigou, A.C. (1920). *The economics of welfare* (4th ed., 1932). London: Macmillan.

Samuelson, P. A. (1954). The pure theory of public expenditure. *Review of Economics and Statistics, 36*, 387–389.

Samuelson, P. A. (1956). Social indifference curves. *The Quarterly Journal of Economics, 70*, 1–22.

Samuelson, P. A. (1969). The pure theory of public expenditure and taxation. In J. Margolis & H. Guitton (Eds.), *Public economics* (pp. 98–123). New York: St. Martin's Press.

Sandmo, A. (1973). Public goods and the technology of consumption. *The Review of Economic Studies, 40*, 517–528.

Steiner, P. O. (1957). Peak loads and efficient pricing. *The Quarterly Journal of Economics, 71*(4), 585–610.

Strotz, R. H. (1965). Urban transportation parables. In J. Margolis (Ed.), *The public economy of urban communities* (pp. 127–169). Washington, DC: Resources for the Future.

Uzawa, H. (1974). Sur la theorie du capital cllecvtif social. *Cahier du Econometrie et economique*.

Weisbrod, B. A. (1964). Collective consumption services of individual consumption goods. *The Quarterly Journal of Economics, 78*, 471–477.

Williamson, O. E. (1966). Peak load pricing and optimal capacity. *The American Economic Review, 56*, 810–827.

Zeckhauser, R. J. (1969). Resource allocation with probabilistic individual preferences. *The American Economic Review, 59*, 546–552.

Name Index

© Springer Japan 2016

M. Ohyama, *Macroeconomics, Trade, and Social Welfare*, Advances in Japanese Business and Economics 14, DOI 10.1007/978-4-431-55807-1

Subject Index

© Springer Japan 2016

M. Ohyama, *Macroeconomics, Trade, and Social Welfare*, Advances in Japanese Business and Economics 14, DOI 10.1007/978-4-431-55807-1

MIX
Papier aus verantwortungsvollen Quellen
Paper from responsible sources
FSC® C105338

FSC
www.fsc.org

If you have any concerns about our products,
you can contact us on
ProductSafety@springernature.com

In case Publisher is established outside the EU,
the EU authorized representative is:
Springer Nature Customer Service Center GmbH
Europaplatz 3, 69115 Heidelberg, Germany

Printed by Libri Plureos GmbH
in Hamburg, Germany